T0324536

God the peacemaker

Titles in this series:

NEW STUDIES IN BIBLICAL THEOLOGY 25

Series editor: D. A. Carson

God the peacemaker

HOW ATONEMENT BRINGS SHALOM

Graham A. Cole

APOLLOS

INTERVARSITY PRESS
DOWNERS GROVE, ILLINOIS 60515

APOLLOS
An imprint of Inter-Varsity Press, England
Norton Street
Nottingham NG7 3HR, England
Website: www.ivpbooks.com
Email: ivp@ivpbooks.com

InterVarsity Press, USA
P.O. Box 1400
Downers Grove, IL 60515-1426, USA
World Wide Web: www.ivpress.com
Email: email@ivpress.com

©Graham A. Cole 2009

Graham A. Cole has asserted his/her right under the Copyright, Designs and Patents Act, 1988, to be identified as Author of this work.

All rights reserved. No part of this publication may be reproduced, stored in a retrieval system or transmitted in any form or by any means, electronic, mechanical, photocopying, recording or otherwise, without the prior permission of the publisher or the Copyright Licensing Agency.

InterVarsity Press®, USA, is the book-publishing division of InterVarsity Christian Fellowship/USA® <www.intervarsity.org> and a member movement of the International Fellowship of Evangelical Students.

Inter-Varsity Press, England, is closely linked with the Universities and Colleges Christian Fellowship, a student movement connecting Christian Unions throughout Great Britain, and a member movement of the International Fellowship of Evangelical Students. Website: www.uccf.org.uk

All Scripture quotations, unless otherwise indicated, are taken from the Holy Bible, New International Version®. NIV®. Copyright © 1973, 1978, 1984 by International Bible Society. First published in Great Britain in 1979. Used by permission of Hodder and Stoughton Ltd., a division of Hodder Headline Ltd. All rights reserved. "NIV" is a registered trademark of International Bible Society. UK trademark number 1448790.

Scripture quotations marked NRSV are taken from the New Revised Standard Version of the Bible, Anglicized edition, copyright © 1989, 1995 by the Division of Christian Education of the National Council of the Churches of Christ in the USA. Used by permission. All rights reserved.

Scripture quotations marked ESV are from The Holy Bible, English Standard Version, published by HarperCollins Publishers © 2001 by Crossway Bibles, a division of Good News Publishers. Used by permission. All rights reserved.

First published 2009.

USA ISBN 978-0-8308-2626-1
UK ISBN 978-1-84474-396-4

 green press INITIATIVE

InterVarsity Press is committed to protecting the environment and to the responsible use of natural resources. As a member of Green Press Initiative we use recycled paper whenever possible. To learn more about the Green Press Initiative, visit <www.greenpressinitiative.org>.

British Library Cataloguing in Publication Data

A catalogue record for this book is available from the British Library.

Library of Congress Cataloging-in-Publication Data

Cole, Graham A. (Graham Arthur), 1949-
  God the peacemaker: how atonement brings Shalom / Graham A. Cole.
    p. cm.—(New studies in biblical theology ; 25)
  Includes bibliographical references and index.
  ISBN 978-0-8308-2626-1 (pbk.: USA : alk paper)
  1. Reconciliation—Religious aspects—Christianity. 2. Atonement.
  3. Peace—Religious aspects—Christianity. I. Title.
  BT738.27.C65 2009
  234'.5—dc22

                                                                        2009017675

P 24 23 22 21 20 19 18 17 16 15 14 13 12 11 10 9 8 7 6 5 4 3 2 1

Y 29 28 27 26 25 24 23 22 21 20 19 18 17 16 15 14 13 12 11 10 09

Set in Monotype Times New Roman
Typeset in Great Britain by Servis Filmsetting Ltd, Stockport, Cheshire

This work is dedicated to my mother, Elizabeth Cole, who taught me to revere the name of Jesus; to my mother-in-law, Megan Clark, who has shown me what such reverence looks like in life; and to my father-in-law, Livingstone Clark, whose preaching of the cross brought me to Christ.

Contents

Series preface

New Studies in Biblical Theology is a series of monographs that address key issues in the discipline of biblical theology. Contributions to the series focus on one or more of three areas: (1) the nature and status of biblical theology, including its relations with other disciplines (e.g. historical theology, exegesis, systematic theology, historical criticism, narrative theology); (2) the articulation and exposition of the structure of thought of a particular biblical writer or corpus; and (3) the delineation of a biblical theme across all or part of the biblical corpora.

Above all, these monographs are creative attempts to help thinking Christians understand their Bibles better. The series aims simultaneously to instruct and to edify, to interact with the current literature, and to point the way ahead. In God's universe, mind and heart should not be divorced: in this series we shall try not to separate what God has joined together. While the notes interact with the best of scholarly literature, the text is uncluttered with untransliterated Greek and Hebrew, and tries to avoid too much technical jargon. The volumes are written within the framework of confessional evangelicalism, but there is always an attempt at thoughtful engagement with the sweep of the relevant literature.

Few if any themes are more central to the Bible than atonement. The evidence depends on more than Paul's asseveration to the Corinthians, 'For I resolved to know nothing while I was with you except Jesus Christ and him crucified' (1 Cor. 2:2). The sacrificial systems of tabernacle and temple, the significance of Passover and Day of Atonement, the dramatic way in which all four canonical Gospels climax in the cross and resurrection (some wag has said they are all passion narratives with extended introductions), the nuanced arguments of Hebrews, the fact that the Apocalypse depicts the triumph (of all things!) of a slaughtered Lamb, all combine to provide powerful support for the centrality of the theme explored in this volume.

Even to begin to do justice to this theme one must attempt at least five things: (1) The way the theme of sacrifice and atonement develops in the Bible's storyline must be laid out. (2) Equally, the way this theme is intertwined with related themes (the holiness of God, the nature of sin, what salvation consists of, the promise of what is to come, and much more) must be delineated, along with (3) more probing reflection on a selection of crucial passages. These first three items belong rather tightly to biblical theology. Of course, (4) how these themes have been handled in the history of the church's theology must not be ignored. (5) Equally, if the volume is to speak to our generation, it must engage some of the more important current discussion.

Dr Graham Cole is well qualified to address all five of these dimensions. My hope and prayer is that this volume will become a 'standard' contribution in the field, informing and enriching its readers as to what God achieved by sending his dear Son to the cross on our behalf. Eternity itself will not exhaust our wonder at these truths. This book, I am sure, will establish many in the right direction.

D. A. Carson
Trinity Evangelical Divinity School

Author's preface

There is nothing like having to write a book to concentrate the mind on a subject. And what a subject it is – the atonement! I soon found that the more I explored the subject the more I saw the need to place the story of the atonement (the work of Christ on the cross in traditional terms) within the larger context of the triune God's grand purpose to restore a broken creation to his glory. And what a glorious purpose I have found that to be. I am indebted to many for this work. Particular thanks are due to colleagues D. A. Carson and P. T. O'Brien, and to doctoral students Josh Gregersen, Owen Strachan, Jim Franks, Jeremy Treat and Scott Harrower. I am especially grateful to Adam Johnson – another doctoral student – who read through much of the manuscript in draft, and made many helpful criticisms and comments. Thanks are also due to numerous students who presented papers, debated and discussed atonement issues past and present in doctoral seminars I have conducted on the subject over the years at Trinity Evangelical Divinity School. I am very appreciative too of the Board of Regents of Trinity for granting a sabbatical to pursue this project. My beloved wife, Jules, was wonderfully supportive as ever. The translation used throughout is the New International Version unless otherwise specified. Any errors remain my own.

Graham A. Cole

Abbreviations

1QH	*Thanksgiving Psalms/Hymns* (Dead Sea Scrolls)
1QS	*Rule of the Community* (Dead Sea Scrolls)
ANE	ancient Near East(ern)
Ant.	*Jewish Antiquities* (Josephus)
ATR	*Anglican Theological Review*
BBCNT	Bible Background Commentary: New Testament (EIRC)
BBCOT	Bible Background Commentary: Old Testament (EIRC)
BDT	*Beacon Dictionary of Theology*, ed. R. Taylor, Kansas City: Beacon Hill, 1983
c.	circa
CCC	Catechism of the Catholic Church (1994)
CD	*Damascus Document* (Dead Sea Scrolls)
CD	K. Barth, *Church Dogmatics*, ed. G. W. Bromiley and T. F. Torrance, 4 vols., Edinburgh: T. & T. Clark, 1936–77
ChrCent	*Christian Century*
CJC	*Canadian Journal of Criminology*
CJCC	*The Comprehensive John Calvin Collection*, Rio, Wisc.: Ages Software, 2002, CD-ROM version
CNTUOT	Commentary on the New Testament Use of the Old Testament
DBI	*Dictionary of Biblical Imagery* (EIRC)
DFTIB	*Dictionary of the Theological Interpretation of Scripture*, ed. K. J. Vanhoozer, London: SPCK; Grand Rapids: Baker Academic, 2005
Di	*Dialog*
Dial.	*Dialogue with Trypho* (Justin Martyr)
DJG	*Dictionary of Jesus and the Gospels* (EIRC)
DLNTD	*Dictionary of the Later New Testament and its Development* (EIRC)

DPHL	*Dictionary of Paul and His Letters* (EIRC)
EBC	Expositor's Bible Commentary, 1997, CD-ROM version
EDT	*Evangelical Dictionary of Theology*, ed. W. A. Elwell, Grand Rapids: Baker, 1994
EIRC	Essential IVP Reference Collection, Leicester: IVP, 2001, CD-ROM version
EJT	*European Journal of Theology*
Enc	*Encounter*
ERT	*Evangelical Review of Theology*
ESV	English Standard Version Bible
ETR	*Etudes théologiques et religieuses*
ExpTim	*Expository Times*
Gr.	Greek
HBT	*Horizons in Biblical Theology*
Hebr.	Hebrew
HSB	HarperCollins Study Bible New Revised Standard Version with the Apocryphal/Deuterocanonical Books, W. A. Meeks, New York: HarperSanFrancisco, 1993
HSOB	*Hard Sayings of the Bible* (EIRC)
IJP	*International Journal of Philosophy*
IJST	*International Journal of Systematic Theology*
Int	*Interpretation*
ITQ	*Irish Theological Quarterly*
JSB	The Jewish Study Bible, ed. A. Berlin, M. Z. Brettler and M. Fishbane, New York: Oxford University Press, 2003
lit.	literally
LXX	Septuagint
mg.	margin
MS(S)	manuscript(s)
NA	*New Advent: Featuring The Catholic Encyclopedia*, 2nd ed., Pennsauken, N. J.: Disc Makers, 2007, CD-ROM version
NBCRev	New Bible Commentary Revised (EIRC)
NBD	*New Bible Dictionary* (EIRC)
NDBT	*New Dictionary of Biblical Theology* (EIRC)
NDCA	*New Dictionary of Christian Apologetics*, ed. C. Campbell-Jack and G. J. McGrath, Leicester: IVP; Downers Grove: IVP, 2006

NDT	*New Dictionary of Theology* (EIRC)
NIB	*The New Interpreter's Bible*, ed. L. E. Keck, 12 vols., Nashville: Abingdon, 1993–2002, CD-ROM version
NIBC	New International Biblical Commentary, 2002, CD-ROM version
NIDNTT	*New International Dictionary of New Testament Theology*, ed. C. Brown, 3 vols., Grand Rapids: Zondervan, 2006, CD-ROM version
NIDOTTE	*The New International Dictionary of Old Testament Theology and Exegesis*, ed. W. A. VanGemeren, 5 vols., Grand Rapids: Zondervan, 1996, CD-ROM version
NIV	New International Version Bible
NIVACNT	NIV Application Commentary, New Testament, 1996, CD-ROM version
NRSV	New Revised Standard Version Bible
OBC	Oxford Bible Commentary
OCCT	*The Oxford Companion to Christian Thought*, ed. A. Hastings, A. Mason and H. Pyper, Oxford: Oxford University Press, 2000
OT	Old Testament
Per	*Perspectives*
pl.	plural
RelS	*Religious Studies*
RSV	Revised Standard Version Bible
RTR	*Reformed Theological Review*
SBET	*Scottish Bulletin of Evangelical Theology*
SBJT	*Southern Baptist Journal of Theology*
SJT	*Scottish Journal of Theology*
STRev	*Sewanee Theological Review*
ThTo	*Theology Today*
TOSB	The Orthodox Study Bible, New Testament and Psalms: Discovering Orthodox Christianity in the Pages of the New Testament
tr.	translation
TynB	*Tyndale Bulletin*
WBC	Word Biblical Commentary, 2004, CD-ROM version
WW	*Word and World*

Introduction

We live in a troubled world. As I write, there are reports of a devastating cyclone in Myanmar, an earthquake in China, fighting in the Sudan and Iraq, shooting death after shooting death on the south side of Chicago. The list could go on and on. The waste of human life is enormous. Some of these troubles and calamities involve nature without any help from us. A volcanic eruption is an example. But other troubles are caused by human beings. Some of us behave appallingly. The holocaust comes to mind. Yet Christians believe in a good God who as the Creator has never lost interest in his world. The key evidence and the chief symbol of that divine commitment is the cross of Christ. This God, revealed in the canon of Scripture, has a project. Novelist Frederick Buechner sums up the project in these terms: 'God creates the world, the world gets lost; God seeks to restore the world to the glory for which he created it.'[1] Central to the divine strategy is Christ, his coming and his cross. The troubles and calamities will end.[2]

The cross is scandalous, however, and has been from the start. Paul wrote to the Corinthians that to the Jews of his day the crucified Christ was a stumbling block and to the Greeks (non-Jews) foolishness (1 Cor. 1:23). In fact, the earliest extant depiction of the cross in Christian art comes from the sixth century. By then Christianity was the religion of empire, at least in the East. However,

---

[1] Buechner 1992: 44.
[2] The problem of evil is immense and beyond the scope of this study to address at any length. Scripture is non-postulational in character (the biblical writers do not float theories about the essence of things) and therefore shows little interest in explaining evil. The problem of evil has two dimensions. First, the *arrival-of-evil* problem has to do with how there can be evil in a creation which is the work of a good, wise, all-knowing and all-powerful deity. And secondly, the *survival-of-evil* problem has to do with what the good, wise all-knowing and all-powerful deity is going to do about it. Scripture is much more interested in the latter than the former and thus eschatology is a key part of the divine response to the biblical cry 'How long, O LORD?' (Ps. 13:1).

there are earlier depictions, by pagan critics, that illustrate Paul's point. The earliest is scratched on plaster and is dated circa AD 200. It is found in the Paedagogium on the Palatine Hill and may have been scratched by a servant in the imperial household. A man with an ass's head is on a cross and is being worshipped by one Alexamenos. The graffito reads, 'Alexamenos worships [his] God.'[3] How such a violent event can bring peace to creation is one of the questions this study will need to address.

A traditional theological code word to describe the core of the divine response to evil is 'atonement'.[4] The word has an interesting history in English-speaking theology and in fact is as James Beilby and Paul R. Eddy suggest 'one of the few theological terms that is "wholly and indigenously English"'.[5] William Tyndale (1494–1536) used it to translate Leviticus 23:28 (the Day of Atonement) and 2 Corinthians 5:18–19:

> Neverthelesse all thinges are of god which hath reconciled vs vnto him sylfe by Iesus Christ and hath geven vnto vs the office *to preach the atonement*. For god was in Christ and made agrement bitwene the worlde and hym sylfe and imputed not their synnes vnto them: and hath committed to vs *the preachynge of the atonment*. (My emphases)

In 1611 the Authorized Version replaced 'atonement' with 'reconciliation'.[6] Christ and his cross bring peace.

Paul in a big-picture passage written to the Colossians shows how the concepts of the cross and peace are intimately connected. He wrote this of Christ in some of the highest Christology found in the New Testament:

> For God was pleased to have all his fullness [*plērōma*] dwell in him, and through him to reconcile to himself all things, whether things on earth or things in heaven, by making peace

---

[3] For the substance of this paragraph I am indebted to 'Alexamenos *Graffito*', accessed 17 Dec. 2007.

[4] Markham (2008: 2) argues provocatively that '*Christian doctrine is the Christian response to the problem of evil*' (original emphasis).

[5] Beilby and Eddy (2006: 9) are quoting in part R. S. Paul.

[6] For this history I am indebted to Sykes (1997: 2–3). English spelling in the early sixteenth century was not standardized, and so in Tyndale's translation he spells 'atonement' in two slightly different ways. Before Tyndale's time Wycliffe, in the fourteenth century, had used 'onement' as a verb to signify to unite.

[*eirēnopoiēsas*] through his blood, shed on the cross. Once you were alienated from God and were enemies in your minds because of your evil behaviour. But now he has reconciled you by Christ's physical body through death to present you holy in his sight, without blemish and free from accusation – if you continue in your faith, established and firm, not moved from the hope held out in the gospel. This is the gospel that you heard and that has been proclaimed to every creature under heaven, and of which I, Paul, have become a servant. (Col. 1:19–23)

Clearly, Paul's gospel is no narrow affair. His theological vision is cosmic in scope 'to reconcile to himself all things'.[7] The cross touches the individual, the church and the wider creation. The cross makes peace.[8]

Peace in Scripture is not to be reduced to a mere absence of strife, nor to a psychological state of mind. According to S. E. Porter:

The concept of peace in the Bible is different in many ways from modern ideas of peace. Peace as the absence of strife, war or bloodshed, so often sought by humanity at any cost, is far removed from the focus of the biblical teaching. The biblical concept of peace is one in which God's authority and power over his created order are seen to dominate his relations with his world, including both the material and the human spheres.[9]

An Old Testament word that captures this idea is shalom. And the New Testament use of the term 'peace' (*eirēnē*) is an example of a Greek word used with rich Old Testament resonances. As T. J. Geddert notes, 'The Greek term *eirēnē* in classical Greek literature means little more than absence of war. In the NT, however, it incorporates the breadth of meaning conveyed by the Hebrew *šālôm*.'[10]

---

[7] Whether there is a centre to Pauline theology, and if so what that centre may be, is itself a matter of much debate. Martin (2001) boldly suggests, 'These far-ranging and distinctive ideas – covering cosmic, personal, societal and ethnic areas of our human story – are nevertheless part of a pattern, whose picture fills the tapestry. The various strands are closely textured and intricately woven together. Yet they are not aimlessly put into a frame. There is an emerging design and a coherent picture. And the most adequate and meaningful title for the result is, we submit, "reconciliation".'

[8] The reconciliation it brings is not automatic for the individual. Paul writes, 'if you continue in your faith' (Col. 1:23).

[9] Porter 2001a.

[10] Geddert 2001.

Nicholas Wolterstorff adds to the picture, 'To dwell in shalom is to *enjoy* living before God, to *enjoy* living in one's physical surroundings, to *enjoy* living with one's fellows, to *enjoy* life with oneself' (original emphases).[11] As we shall see in subsequent chapters, the great enemy of shalom is sin (angelic and human).

The title of this book, 'God the Peacemaker: How Atonement Brings Shalom', attempts to capture this important biblical perspective on what God intends for his broken creation.[12]

The big picture

From a literary point of view, the canon of Scripture presents a divine comedy. Literary scholar Leland Ryken defines a comedy as 'a work of literature in which the plot structure is U-shaped, with the action beginning in prosperity, descending into potentially tragic events, and ending happily'.[13] The *Dictionary of Biblical Imagery* amplifies his point in relation to the Bible per se:

> The overall plot of the Bible is a U-shaped comic plot. The action begins with a perfect world inhabited by perfect people. It descends into the misery of fallen history and ends with a new world of total happiness and the conquest of evil. The book of Revelation is the story of the happy ending par excellence, as a conquering hero defeats evil, marries a bride and lives happily ever after in a palace glittering with jewels.[14]

From Genesis to Revelation we see the U-shaped structure working itself out: from the harmony of Genesis 1 – 2 through the disharmony of Genesis 3 – Revelation 20 to harmony again and albeit of a higher

---

[11] Wolterstorff 1983: 70. Since so many writers employ 'shalom' rather than transliterate the Hebrew, I shall do the same for the rest of this study, unless the transliterated form appears in a quotation.
[12] Others have seen the value of peacemaking as an organizing idea. E.g. Swartley (in Jersak and Hardin 2007: 12) in his foreword suggests, 'To many quests here [in the book] to understand atonement, I commend *peacemaking* as an over-arching trope' (original emphasis). Clearly, I myself have drawn inspiration from Col. 1 and Paul's use of the idea of peace and its relation to the cross of Christ. Of course, other angles of vision are possible. Hence Boersma (2004: 261) in a most stimulating work on the atonement can employ the idea of the various faces of hospitality – divine, cruciform and public – as his organizing principle without neglecting the peace motif.
[13] Ryken 1980: 359.
[14] Ryken, Wilhoit and Longman 2001c.

kind in Revelation 21 – 22. Theologian Stephen Sykes also explores the doctrine of the atonement from a literary perspective, complementing both Ryken's and the *Dictionary of Biblical Imagery*'s analyses: 'In Christian narrative, God's world is the *setting*, the *theme* is the rescue of the fallen world and of humankind; the *plots* are the biblical narratives, from creation, election, to incarnation, crucifixion, resurrection and ascension; the *resolution* is the last judgment, heaven and hell' (original emphases).[15] Crucial to the resolution is the cross of Christ.[16]

The importance of the cross

The importance of the cross can be seen in the two key practices of Christian corporate life: baptism and the Lord's Supper. Miroslav Volf concurs:

> A good way to make the same point about the centrality of self-donation [the cross] would be to look at the two fundamental rituals of the church as described in the New Testament: baptism, which marks the beginning of the Christian life and therefore determines the whole of it; and the Lord's Supper, whose reiterated celebration enacts ritually what lies at the very heart of the Christian life.[17]

In these practices – as old as Christianity itself – it is the Good Friday and Easter Sunday stories that are accented. For Paul, baptism symbolically enacts our dying and rising with Christ (Rom. 6:1–7) and the Lord's Supper preaches 'the Lord's death until he comes' (1 Cor. 11:26). The *Book of Common Prayer* captures the Pauline note in its prayer of consecration in its Holy Communion service:

> All glory to you our heavenly Father, for in your tender mercy you gave your only Son Jesus Christ to suffer death on the cross for our redemption; who made there, by his one

[15] Sykes 1997: 14.

[16] In the light of the comedic structure of the canon, Vanhoozer's (2005) theodrama approach could more accurately be described in literary terms as a theocomedy approach. However, if the idea of theocomedy were adopted rigorously, then eschatology would need to feature more formally and materially in his stimulatingly rich book beyond pp. 357–359.

[17] Volf 1996: 24.

oblation of himself once offered, a full, perfect, and sufficient sacrifice, oblation and satisfaction for the sins of the whole world; and instituted, and in his holy gospel commanded us to continue, a perpetual memory of his precious death until his coming again.[18]

Important to observe is the fact that the centre of gravity in these practices is not the Christmas story but the Good Friday and Easter Sunday ones. Put another way, the incarnation is not central; the cross is. James Denney puts the point forcefully: 'Not Bethlehem, but Calvary, is the focus of revelation, and any construction of Christianity which ignores or denies this distorts Christianity by putting it out of focus.'[19]

A useful distinction

The story of the cross and the one who died upon it will be at the heart of this study, but not the whole of this study. As R. W. Yarbrough suggests:

'Atonement' may be defined as God's work on sinners' behalf to reconcile them to himself. It is the divine activity that confronts and resolves the problem of human sin so that people may enjoy full fellowship with God both now and in the age to come. *While in one sense the meaning of atonement is as broad and diverse as all of God's saving work throughout time and eternity, in another it is as particular and restricted as the crucifixion of Jesus.* For in the final analysis Scripture presents his sacrificial death as the central component of God's reconciling mercy. This explains why Revelation 22:3, for example, shows not only God but also the Lamb – slain to atone for sin – occupying the throne of heaven in the age to come.[20]

Narrowly conceived this study would simply focus on the cross. However, following Yarbrough's insight, this work needs to set the

---

[18] This form of words is taken from *A Prayer Book for Australia* (1999: 112), which in its First Order of Holy Communion puts the classic Book of Common Prayer service of 1662 into contemporary English.

[19] Denney 1973: 179.

[20] Yarbrough 2001; my emphasis. Beilby and Eddy (2006: 9) argue similarly, 'Broadly speaking *atonement* . . . refers to a reconciled state of "at-one-ness" between parties that were formerly alienated in some manner' (original emphasis).

cross in a much broader framework. This broader perspective reckons with God's grand plan to restore the created order, and places the story of Jesus, his cross and empty tomb within it.[21] Thus this work takes the broad approach but hopefully not in a way that masks 'the cruciality of the cross'.[22] As a way forward, when this study speaks of God's 'atoning project' or 'atoning work' it has the broader perspective in mind.[23] But when it refers to 'the atonement' per se, it is the cross of Christ in view.

In terms of the broader understanding of the divine atoning project, the grand goal of the divine comedy is nothing less than to secure God's people in God's place under God's reign living God's way enjoying God's shalom in God's loving and holy presence as both family and worshippers, to God's glory.

Some crucial questions

What then are the questions that animate this study?

- What, if anything, is there in God's character that requires atonement?
- Is God's love in conflict with his wrath?
- Is wrath an attribute of God, and, if so, what kind?
- What is so wrong with the human situation that it requires atonement?
- How do God's dealings with Old Testament Israel feature in the story of atonement?
- Is the cross of Christ the whole story of atonement?
- What place has the life of Christ and not just the death of Christ in the story of atonement?
- How important are the resurrection and the exaltation of Christ to the story of atonement?
- What are some of the controversial issues attending the atonement (e.g. violence and the cross, the cross as divine child abuse and so forth)? How might they be addressed?

---

[21] An example of the narrow approach – as I am using it, this is not a pejorative term – is the discussion in Boyd and Eddy 2002 (ch. 8, 'The Atonement Debate', deals with the death of Christ as understood by three of the historic interpretations of atonement). In contrast McKnight (2007) takes a broad approach.

[22] I am indebted to Forsyth (1909) for the phrase.

[23] One could also characterize the divine project broadly as God's at-one-ing, peacemaking or reconciliation project.

- How central, if at all, is penal substitution to a theology of atonement?
- Did Christ bear the sins of the world without exception or without distinction?
- How is the atoning work of Christ to be embraced by us for our benefit?
- Is the gospel good news for those who do not welcome God's shalom?
- What flows from the atoning work of Christ at the individual, corporate and cosmic levels?
- Can shalom-making sum up adequately the divine intention in the atoning work of Christ?
- How then are we to live individually and as God's people in the light of God's atoning project centred as it is on Christ?
- What is the divine motivation informing the atoning project?
- What is the divine intention driving the atoning project?
- How does atonement bring shalom?

Assumptions

Having set up the key questions addressed in this study, what is assumed in doing so? This study assumes a high view of Scripture as God's Word written. Scripture in my view is the product of an asymmetrical double-agency. Scripture is God-breathed (*theopneustos*). Even so, the concursive outworking of such inspiration does not mask the individuality of the biblical writers. Given divine inspiration predicated on a doctrine of God who not only acts (creation, providence, redemption and judgment) but also speaks (revelation), and, given this view of divine inspiration, one should expect a unity to Scripture in the midst of its diversity. Leland Ryken expresses it well:

> Although biblical literature is a collection of diverse works, it must also be regarded as possessing a high degree of unity. There is unity of national authorship, with only two books in the whole Bible (Luke and Acts) not having been written by [Israelites and] Jews. There is unity of subject matter, consisting most broadly of God's ways with people and the relationship of people to God and fellow humans. There is a unity of world view and general theological outlook from book to book. There is unity of purpose underlying all

26

biblical literature – the purpose of revealing God to people so that they might know how to order their lives.[24]

He develops this last important point:

> There is, finally, a unity of literature texture based on allusion. Various biblical writers allude to earlier works in the same canon, or to the same historical events, or to the same religious beliefs and experiences, or to the same cultural context. The resulting unity of reference is immediately evident when one consults a modern Bible containing cross references in the marginal notes. No other anthology of literature possesses the unified texture of allusions that biblical literature displays.[25]

Scripture is thus the touchstone, that which tests the quality of any theological proposal.

Touchstone is an interesting metaphor for Scripture's theological function in the life of God's people. A touchstone is a piece of quartz that can be used to test, for example, whether a piece of ore is really gold or merely fool's gold. Scripture as the Word of God is the norming norm (*norma normans*). If a putative doctrinal proposal is textless – that is to say, it lacks biblical support – then it may be held as a speculative possibility but not as a candidate for a non-negotiable conviction expressing the Faith. Of course, other authorities such as tradition, reason and experience are operative in Christian theology and life. But these lesser authorities are ruled norms (*norma normata*). In any conflict between authorities the appeal to Scripture is paramount since it is the touchstone and rules the others. In my own tradition, Article 21 of *The Articles of Religion* of the Church of England of 1562 expresses the point well: 'General Councils . . . may err, and sometimes have erred, even in things pertaining to God. Wherefore things ordained by them as necessary to salvation have neither strength nor authority, unless it may be declared that they be taken out of Holy Scripture.'[26] Similarly,

---

[24] Ryken 1980: 15.
[25] Ibid. 15–16.
[26] Reproduced in Grudem 1994: 1175. The nineteenth-century Christian leader Bishop J. C. Ryle captures the theological use of the metaphor in his sermon on the fallibility of ministers: 'Let us receive nothing, believe nothing, follow nothing, which is not in the Bible, nor can be proved by the Bible. Let our rule of faith, our touchstone of all teaching, be the written Word of God' (Ryle, accessed 30 July 2008).

reason (our ability to mount and demolish arguments) may err, especially if it is at the service of a world view that is inimical to biblical supernaturalism. And experience may mislead. It may, for example, be wrongly described theologically even if authentically of God. Some of the tongues-speaking that I have heard appears to be in this category. Those who practise it seem to benefit devotionally by it.

Another caveat is in order. Not all has been revealed. There are secret things that belong to the Lord, as Moses declared on the plains of Moab (Deut. 29:29). This should also remind the theologian that mystery or incomprehensibility attends the actions of God. Truth has been revealed, but not exhaustively so. An epistemic humility applies to any doctrinal construction or exploration of Scripture, including the present work. The theologian needs to distinguish carefully what proposals ought to be considered as non-negotiable convictions, what as opinion and what as speculation. In other words, some notion of dogmatic rank needs to be at work explicitly or implicitly.

Approach

This work is part of a series entitled *New Studies in Biblical Theology*, which raises the question 'How does the present study fit into the philosophy of the series as set out in the preface to it?' This study attempts the delineation of a biblical theme, which is summed up in the subtitle, 'How Atonement Brings Shalom'. The biblical theology dimension can be seen in the way the study broadly speaking follows the Bible's own plotline from the story of creation to the fall to redemption to the consummation, and not merely in the adducing of biblical texts as evidence for the assertions made – although such evidence is of paramount importance.[27] Appearances not withstanding, the fact that the first chapter treats the doctrine of God is in keeping with the approach. How so? We begin the substantive discussion where the canon begins; namely, with God (Gen. 1:1). I have attempted to keep technical discussion to the footnotes as much as I could in order to leave the text as uncluttered as possible.

---

[27] Rosner (2001) provides an excellent description of biblical theology: 'What is biblical theology? To sum up, *biblical theology may be defined as theological interpretation of Scripture in and for the church. It proceeds with historical and literary sensitivity and seeks to analyse and synthesize the Bible's teaching about God and his relations to the world on its own terms, maintaining sight of the Bible's overarching narrative and Christocentric focus*' (original emphasis).

What is the value of biblical theology for our task? Biblical theology helps the reader to know what the accents of Scripture are when canonically considered. Its work is descriptive in the main. Systematic theology asks the prescriptive or normative questions of what is to be both believed and lived in the light of the Scriptural testimony and does so informed by biblical theology and with sensitivity to the history of discussion (historical theology) and contemporary application (practical theology). Put another way, at the heart of this work is the theological interpretation of Scripture.[28] In this theological interpretation of Scripture, both the narratival and didactic portions of the biblical testimony have their place. With due apologies to Immanuel Kant – narrative without the didactic is blind, the didactic without the narratival is empty. This is not a new insight. In 1846 John Williamson Nevin put it this way:

> All turns on the stand-point of the interpreter, and the comprehensive catholicity of his view. He must be consciously within the horizon, and underneath the broad canopy, of the new supernatural creation, he is called to contemplate; and then each part of it must be studied and expounded, in full view of its relations to every other part, and to the glorious structure in which all are comprehended as a whole. This is the true conception of biblical theology. Only under this form, can bible proof, as it is called, in favour of or against any doctrine, be entitled to the least respect.[29]

Put another way, Nevin teaches us that the whole (the canon) and the parts (the various pericopes) need to be in constant dialogue.

The plan of the book

The first three chapters of this work deal with the human plight. J. Rodman Williams is right to argue, 'The basic problem to which atonement is related is twofold: *who God is* and *what man has become*.'[30] Thus the first chapter examines who God is in nature. Understanding the shape of the canonical story, and why the need

---

[28] For more discussion of the approach I favour see my article, Cole 2005a: 259–263.
[29] Nevin 2000: 230.
[30] J. R. Williams 1996: 354.

for Christ's life and death, is predicated on grasping that the righteous God is both love and light, or, to use P. T. Forsyth's pregnant expression, 'holy love'.[31] Holy love is not indifferent to sin. The second chapter examines the paradoxical nature of humankind outside Eden or 'what man has become'. Taking a cue from Pascal it examines how we are both the glory and the 'garbage' of the universe. Some grasp of the multifaceted problematic created by human sin is a prerequisite for understanding the depths of the divine response. This problematic is explored in chapter 3.

The next three chapters focus on the divine provision for humanity in the light of the human plight. The fourth chapter looks at the foundations of the divine provision in God's own loving nature, the *protoevangelium* (first gospel) of Genesis 3:15, and the call of Abraham, as well as its foreshadowings in the experience of Israel. The fifth chapter considers the atoning faithfulness of Christ exhibited in the righteous life he lived *coram Deo* (before God) as the faithful Son. The sixth chapter next looks at his atoning death on the cross, or the atonement per se, and some of the questions it raises. Sacrifice, victory, satisfaction and substitution will be key terms here.[32] This chapter also focuses on how Christ's faithful life and righteous death are both vindicated and validated by his resurrection from the dead and his subsequent enthronement at the right hand of the Father. Without that vindication it can be said of Christianity (to quote from W. B. Yeats's magnificent poem *The Second Coming*), 'Things fall apart; the centre cannot hold.'

Chapter 7 considers the 'peace dividend' – to use Rowan Williams's helpful phrase. In particular, it explores how the peace/shalom that comes through the cross works itself out at the personal, corporate and cosmic levels.[33] Chapter 8 asks the 'So what?' question. How then are we to live if these things are really so? Chapter 9 discusses the grand purpose behind it all and offers a theory as to why the divine desire for glory is not celestial narcissism. Chapter 10

---

[31] 'Holy love' (the conjunction of 'holy' and 'love' to form 'holy love') is found in many theologians' (besides Forsyth's) discussions of God's character. I am attracted to it because the conjunction reminds me not to sentimentalize God's love. For a history of the use of the expression 'holy love' in British, European and American theology see McCurdy 1999: 239–265.

[32] I am very much aware that for some the very mention of 'substitution', let alone 'penal substitution' (a view embraced in this work), is abhorrent. However, I hope that there is profit to be had for those of contrary opinions to my own in reading this work.

[33] R. Williams 2007: 81.

concludes the study proper by reviewing the journey. Furthermore, this final chapter addresses the question raised by the title of the study; namely, how God the peacemaker brings shalom through atonement in both the broad and narrow senses of the term. An appendix deals with a range of controversial aspects of the cross, including the centrality of penal substitution, the morality of penal substitution, whether moral influence and exemplarist theories are really atonement theories, whether there is healing in the atonement, the Holy Saturday debate and evaluating a new family of theories commonly known as non-violent theories of atonement. An extensive bibliography rounds out the study.

How to read this book

Three reading strategies commend themselves. One is to read from beginning to end: the traditional approach. Chapters 1–9 actually follow in the main the biblical storyline. Chapter 1, for example, begins where the Bible does with God, and chapter 9 examines the divine desire (glory). In other words, the familiar contours of the biblical story are in view: creation, fall, redemption and consummation. Another way to engage this work is to use the questions listed previously as a guide and ask, as you read, to what extent and how successfully they are being addressed. The final way is to start with the appendix to get a grasp of some of the current issues under vigorous discussion concerning the atonement before reading the main argument.

A caution

This study is an exercise in theology drawing upon the disciplines of biblical theology and systematic theology with an awareness of the history of theological discussion (historical theology) and an eye on contemporary Christian life with its challenges (practical theology). As such, there is much conceptual map work, which brings with it its own fascination. However, it must not be forgotten that the reality is of the God who was in Christ reconciling the world to himself (2 Cor. 5:18–19). Thus a caveat is in order and I know of no other writer who has put it as forcefully as J. S. Whale. He writes:

> We have to get somehow from *mandata Dei* [the commandments of God] to *Deus mandans* [the commanding God] if our

study of Christian doctrine is to mean anything vital. We want a living synthesis where those very facts, which the intellect dissects and coldly examines, are given back to us with the wholeness which belongs to life . . . Instead off putting off our shoes from our feet because the place whereon we stand is holy ground, we are taking nice photographs of the burning Bush, from suitable angles: we are chatting about theories of Atonement with our feet on the mantelpiece, instead of kneeling down before the wounds of Christ.[34]

Cool reflection ultimately needs to give way to worship. Again Whale is helpful: 'The need is obvious. Is it met anywhere? The answer is that it is met in the worship of the Church, where the Christian religion is given to us in all its living meaning.'[35] Whale, writing last century, would be amazed to find these days that for many worship has shrunk to singing love songs to Jesus without reference to the cross.

---

[34] Whale 1957: 146. The account of William Haslam's conversion provides a classic example. In 1851 in his Cornwall church during the course of his sermon on the atonement he froze. He saw the personal import of what he was preaching. He knelt down, as it were, mid sermon before the wounds of Christ. Parishioners streamed out of the service declaring, 'The Parson is converted! The Parson is converted! Hallelujah!' And converted he was. I am grateful to Dr Richard Turnbull, Principal of Wycliffe Hall in Oxford, for drawing my attention to this account. For more on Haslam's journey in his own words see C. Wright 2005: 49–60.

[35] Whale 1957: 146.

Chapter One

The righteous God of holy love

We start where Scripture does – with God. And the God revealed in Scripture is the righteous God of holy love. However, I live in a largely profane society, so understanding holiness does not come easily to me. I do not see temples on street corners and animals being led to sacrifice. I do not see thousands washing themselves in the Chicago River to become pure. (Given that river's history such would be an act of faith beyond compare!) Yet without an understanding of divine holiness the God of biblical presentation is problematical (to say the least) for many moderns in his acts of judgment. Moreover, the cross of Christ seems immoral as the linchpin of the divine plan of salvation. How could God be in Christ reconciling the world to himself in such a violent event? Likewise, the idea of divine righteousness does not immediately resonate with modern sensibilities. As R. T. France observes, 'Of all the uninviting words of an old fashioned religious jargon, "righteousness" is one of the worst. If it means anything at all to the average man, it expresses a stuffy legalism, prim and unattractive, or at best it is a Victorian synonym for good deeds.'[1] In fact, if I hear the term 'righteous' used in secular contexts, more often than not it has to do with describing someone pejoratively as 'self-righteous'. That is to say, conceited in their own sense of personal goodness in contrast to others.

The idea of a loving God comes more easily. This is not a new phenomenon. Lactantius (c. 250–325) dealt with it in the early church period. In his *On the Anger of God* he writes:

> But now we will argue against those who, falling from the second step, entertain wrong sentiments respecting the Supreme God. For some say that He neither does a kindness to any one, nor becomes angry, but in security and quietness enjoys the advantages of His own immortality. *Others, indeed,*

[1] France 1970: 92. This is not France's personal view, as we shall see.

33

take away anger, but leave to God kindness; for they think that a nature excelling in the greatest virtue, while it ought not to be malevolent, ought also to be benevolent. Thus all the philosophers are agreed on the subject of anger, but are at variance respecting kindness. [2]

Lactantius sweepingly asserts that the philosophers of the day would never ascribe anger to God. However, there were some prepared to predicate kindness of God. More recently, Catherine the Great of the eighteenth century supposedly said, 'Ah, God is good; he's bound to forgive us; that's his job.'[3] Not a hint of judgment here.

The sentimentalizing of God gives comfort to many, especially in the face of death. Such a God is sure to welcome us, or our loved ones, into the divine presence. This God is good for one's self-image. Such a mono-attributed God may be a darling to some of the affluent who live in a stable social order. But to the persecuted, to those who live on the underside of the exercise of power in a society, to those who know what injustice is, this God is no comfort at all. African-American theologian, Rufus Burrow, Jr., rightly decries 'the tendency to speak of God's attributes in monopolar terms. That is, to claim that God is only one thing, e.g., love, and nothing else.'[4] He argues powerfully for the recovery of the fully orbed biblical presentation of the God who is both love and light:

My claim is that the idea of divine love needs the truth in divine wrath as much as the latter needs the tenderness and care of God's compassion. As polar opposites we cannot know the fuller meaning of either without the other. A God who only loves but is not affected by violations of the divine image of God in persons and therefore will not condemn such violations may be deemed too soft and sentimental to respond realistically to much of the excruciating unearned suffering that Afrikan [*sic.*] Americans and other persons of color are forced to endure nearly every moment of their lives. And yet

[2] Lactantius 2007; my emphasis. Lactantius is attacking Stoics and Epicureans in particular, and according to McGuckin (2004: 202–203), 'His antipagan apologia was the most sustained, and reasoned, of all the early Latin writers (with the possible exception of Tertullian).'

[3] Quoted in Carson 2000: 66.

[4] Burrow 1998: 384. Some theologians have privileged holiness as the key divine attribute (e.g. W. G. T. Shedd); still others, justice (e.g. A. H. Strong). See the discussion in Bloesch 1995: 139–145.

a God who is essentially wrath and anger would not be worth the time of day, and most assuredly would not be worthy of worship.[5]

Burrow rightly points out the problem with reductionism of the left (a God only of love) and reductionism of the right (a God only of wrath).

In biblical terms, we are created to be worshippers. Yahweh created an entire people with that great end in mind:

> the people I formed for myself
> that they may proclaim my praise.
>
> (Isa. 43:21)

According to Jesus, the Father is seeking worshippers who do so in spirit and in truth (John 4:23). The eternal gospel of the book of Revelation is 'Worship him who made the heavens, the earth, the sea and the springs of water' (Rev. 14:7). There is no higher pursuit than the worship of the living God. Indeed, we become like the God or gods we adore and serve for good or ill. All hangs upon the nature of the God or gods we follow. How then we construe God's character is of utmost importance. If we serve the living God of biblical revelation, then we shall image him. If we follow idols, we shall image them. A. W. Tozer saw this clearly:

> What comes into our minds when we think about God is the most important thing about us . . . The history of mankind will probably show that no people has ever risen above its religion, and man's spiritual history will positively demonstrate that no religion has ever been greater than its idea of God . . . Always the most revealing thing about the Church is her idea of God, just as her most significant message is what she says about Him or leaves unsaid, for her silence is often more eloquent than her speech. She can never escape the self-disclosure of her witness concerning God.[6]

Tozer stood on solid exegetical ground for his view. The psalmist says of the worship of idols in Psalm 115:8:

---

[5] Burrow 1998: 397–398.
[6] Tozer 1965: 9.

> Those who make them will be like them,
> and so will all who trust in them.
>
> (Ps. 115:8)

And in the New Testament, if by the Spirit we contemplate (*katoptrizō*, 'looking at as in a mirror') Christ we shall be transformed into his likeness from one degree of glory to the next (2 Cor. 3:18).[7] In his argument for the necessity for atonement, Anselm famously says to Boso, 'You have not yet considered what a heavy weight sin is.'[8] To which may be added, 'You have not yet considered who God is as scripturally revealed.' Both considerations are vital to the doctrine of the atonement and to exploring its logic rather than what picture of God and ourselves will make us feel better in our own skins. Hence in this chapter we attend to the character of God, and in the following two, respectively, consider what we have become with the irruption of sin in creation and the problem it creates.

The divine perfections: a righteous holy love

The triune God of Scriptural revelation has perfections.[9] In other words God has a nature. Understanding that nature is crucial for understanding the course of the atonement. Karl Barth argues suggestively that love is the basic definition of who God is: 'God is the One who loves.'[10] He maintains, 'All our further insights about who and what God is must revolve round this mystery – the mystery of His loving. In a certain sense they can only be repetitions and amplifications of the one statement that "God loves."'[11] In fact, Karl Barth argues for two kinds of divine perfection: the perfections of *divine freedom* (unity and omnipresence, constancy and omnipotence,

---

[7] I am following Martin (2004), 'The translation "we reflect" removes the contrast of the Christians with the Jews, who because of their veil cannot see; so the rendering "we behold" is to be preferred' (comment on 2 Cor. 3:18); and also Hafemann 1996, comment on 2 Cor. 3:18.

[8] Anselm, *Cur Deus homo* 1.21, in Fairweather 1956: 138. Boso was Abbot of Bec (102, n. 3). Boso (138) was under the impression that he 'could blot out [a] sin by a single act of sorrow'.

[9] Some would say 'attributes' and others 'properties'. I am treating these terms as synonyms for the purpose of this study and will thus use them interchangeably. Strictly speaking, God is his perfections. We must not think of the divine nature as a pincushion, with the various perfections related to the divine nature being different pins in the cushion.

[10] *CD* II/1: 84.

[11] Ibid. 12: 283–284.

eternity and glory) and the perfections of *divine loving* (grace and holiness, mercy and righteousness, patience and wisdom).[12] Such dichotomizing for the sake of theological discussion is common.[13] Other theologians write of the natural and moral attributes of God; still others of his incommunicable attributes. In Barth's case it is clear though that the divine loving is the controlling idea. The Barthian dichotomy is highly suggestive, but perfections of divine loving are too specific and thus too restrictive. Is holiness, for example, a perfection of divine loving? Not in any obvious sense.

Each of the persons of the Trinity, however, is righteous, holy and loving, and always has been. The Barthian view is too narrow in making 'God is the One who loves' the basic definition of God.[14] Take how Jesus construes the Father as a case in point. According to John's Gospel, Jesus prayed in the garden to his 'Holy Father' (John 17:11) and to his 'Righteous Father' (John 17:25).[15] Although Jesus does not address the Father in this context as 'Loving Father', the references to the Father's love for the Son in the same prayer are indicative of the Father's loving character (John 17:23–26). Righteousness, holiness (understood in moral terms) and love are relational values. That God is a trinity helps us understand why righteousness, holiness and love have always been true of the Persons of the Godhead in their communion. It would be so much harder to see the sense in ascribing such perfections to an undifferentiated monad before there was a creation to which to relate.

Let us now explore each of these perfections in turn because they are particularly relevant to our understanding of the need and nature of the divine atoning project. Divine righteousness and holiness

[12] Ibid. 351–678.

[13] Not all theologians work with a dichotomy. Milne (1982: 64–71) has a fourfold schema: the Glory of God, the Lordship of God, the Holiness of God and the Love of God.

[14] Some contemporary writers also tend to be reductionist when it comes to the divine perfections. E.g. Chalke and Mann (2003: 63) maintain that love is 'the one, primary lens' through which all of God's interactions with the world ought to be viewed. The authority they cite for their view is Barth. No other attribute ought to be considered outside the context of divine love; otherwise the gospel is distorted and God's character misrepresented. Moreover, they claim that 'The Bible never defines God . . . as anything, other than love.' This claim, however, fails exegetically (e.g. cf. 1 John 1:5 and 4:8). To make one of the communicable attributes of God (love) do all this work is as fraught with question begging as is to make one of the incommunicable attributes (e.g. aseity) do so.

[15] Forsyth (1957: 3) rightly draws attention to this prayer as revealing Christ's 'central thought' of God. However, he highlights only holiness; whereas the passage is much richer.

inform the need for atonement. Divine love provides it, as I hope that this and subsequent chapters establish.

Divine righteousness

To say God is righteous is to claim that he acts as a relationship morally requires or allows. In other words, God gives every creature its due. It is no accident then that in the Old Testament the Hebrew term *ṣĕdāqâ* may be translated 'righteousness' or 'justice'. Likewise, in the New Testament the Greek term *dikaiosynē* may be translated 'righteousness' or 'justice'. According to M. A. Seifrid:

> In English usage, the term 'righteousness' is associated with the idea of individual moral rectitude. 'Justice', on the other hand, generally signifies a right social order, that is, the proper distribution of goods and honour, including retribution for evil. Thus the latter is often forensic, while the former is associated with personal ethics. Although such concepts are not foreign to the biblical authors, their concerns lie along other lines. The lexical distinction to which we are accustomed in English is absent from the Scriptures. The biblical terms often translated as 'righteousness' or 'justice' belong to a single word-group, that associated with the *ṣdq* root in Hebrew, or that based on the *dik-* root in Greek.[16]

A fascinating example in the Old Testament of the concept is found in the story of Judah and Tamar in Genesis 38. Tamar's husband, Er, dies (Gen. 38:7). Judah, her father-in-law, instructs Onan, Er's brother, to make Tamar pregnant. But he schemes to circumvent Judah's wishes. He, too, dies at God's hands (Gen. 38:8–10). Judah has had enough of this and fears that he will lose more sons. So he condemns Tamar to widowhood (Gen. 38:11). She knows where the relational responsibility lies.[17] So she disguises herself as a prostitute, seduces Judah and gets pregnant by him (Gen. 38:13–15). In the encounter she obtains a staff, seal and cord from Judah as a pledge of good faith (Gen. 38:18). Once the pregnancy becomes known, he is all for putting her to death (Gen. 38:24). However, she produces

---

[16] Seifrid 2001. Indeed, Seifrid adopts as a convention 'Righteousness/justice' in two of his main headings, which is illustrative of how aligned the terms are in Scripture: '"Righteousness/justice" as a creational concept"', and '"Righteousness/justice" as a forensic concept'.

[17] For details on the custom involved see Whybray 2000: 61.

the staff, seal and cord. Upon this revelation Judah declares, 'She is more righteous [*sĕdāqâ*] than I, since I wouldn't give her to my son Shelah' (Gen. 38:26). In this comparative statement Judah claims that Tamar has acted more appropriately in relationships than he has.

Isaiah 51 presents God as the righteous one. Israel needs rescuing from Babylon. God promises to comfort Zion (Isa. 51:3). Israel's hope lies in the righteousness of God (Isa. 51:5). He will act appropriately in relation to his now-disciplined people. From the Hebrew parallelism we learn that God's salvation will last for ever; so too his righteousness (Isa. 51:6, 8). This rescue will involve nothing less than a rerun, as it were, of the Exodus event (Isa. 51:9–10). The result of God's righteous action will be that

> The ransomed of the LORD will return.
> They will enter Zion with singing;
> everlasting joy will crown their heads.
> Gladness and joy will overtake them,
> and sorrow and sighing will flee away.
>
> (Isa. 51:11)

The righteousness of God on this occasion will also show itself in judgment upon the Babylonians:

> For the moth will eat them up like a garment;
> the worm will devour them like wool.
>
> (Isa. 51:8)[18]

The New Testament likewise affirms the righteousness of God in the context of divine judgment. Paul's address to the intelligentsia (Stoics and Epicureans) at a meeting of the Areopagus in Athens provides a notable example (Acts 17:16–34). Moved by the idolatry and concomitant ignorance of the living God evident in the city, he gives the meeting a lesson in Old Testament Doctrine of God 101, but sensitively, given the audience, without explicit biblical reference. The address climaxes on the note that in the past God overlooked such ignorance (i.e. did not judge whenever such ignorance showed itself), but now the day of reckoning is set. Paul proclaimed, 'In the past God overlooked such ignorance, but now he commands

---

[18] For a fine discussion of the righteousness of God see France 1970: 92–96.

all people everywhere to repent. For he has set a day when he will judge the world with justice [*dikaiosynē*, 'righteousness'] by the man he has appointed. He has given proof of this to all men by raising him from the dead' (Acts 17:30–31). The judge, as yet unnamed by Paul, has been appointed. The guarantee (*pistin paraschōn*) that this day is coming lies in the fact that God has raised the man from the dead. Significantly, the judgment to come will be done in righteousness. Perhaps judgment has this modifier because the fact that God has overlooked previous ignorance may raise the question of what kind of judgment this will be and how just. The response of the audience is mixed. Some sneer at the idea of resurrection, some want to know more and some become disciples (Acts 17:32–34).[19]

Divine holiness

To say God is holy in some biblical contexts is to claim that he is separate from creatures. In other words, God is transcendent: he is the incomparable one:

> 'To whom will you compare me?
> Or who is my equal?' says the Holy One.
>
> (Isa. 40:25)

In other biblical contexts, to say God is holy is a moral claim. To use the language of Habakkuk, God's 'eyes are too pure to look on evil' (Hab. 1:13). In context, Habakkuk predicates this claim on the nature of his God as 'my Holy One' (Hab. 1:12). Because of his holiness Habakkuk is puzzled why God has not yet judged 'the wicked' who 'swallow up those more righteous than themselves' (Hab. 1:13).

The *locus classicus* in the Old Testament for divine holiness is Isaiah's vision in ch. 6 of Yahweh in the heavenly temple. As R. T. France observes, 'to understand fully what is meant by the holiness

---

[19] I have heard it argued that Paul made a mistake in not preaching the cross at Athens. Consequently, he made sure he emphasized the cross when he preached at Corinth (1 Cor. 2:2). However, the argument is specious. Large numbers of converts are mentioned in the early chapters of Acts, where the audience is Jewish and therefore expecting a divine intervention in their affairs; but once the gospel is taken into the Gentile world, such numbers are no longer mentioned (see Acts 2:41; 4:4; 17:32–34). Fernando (1996), commenting on 'A Failed Mission? (Acts 17:22–34)', helpfully discusses the debate. He notes, 'those who work with non-Christians know that even a small number of converts from a highly intellectual audience can be considered a huge success'.

of God, we must turn to Isaiah, who *saw* what holiness means'.[20]
Isaiah recounts:

> In the year that King Uzziah died, I saw the Lord seated on a
> throne, high and exalted, and the train of his robe filled the
> temple. Above him were seraphs, each with six wings: With
> two wings they covered their faces, with two they covered
> their feet, and with two they were flying. And they were
> calling to one another:
>
> > 'Holy, holy, holy is the LORD Almighty;
> > the whole earth is full of his glory.'
> >
> > (Isa. 6:1–3)

His reaction to the vision is dramatic:

> At the sound of their voices the doorposts and thresholds
> shook and the temple was filled with smoke. 'Woe to me!' I
> cried. 'I am ruined! For I am a man of unclean lips, and I live
> among a people of unclean lips, and my eyes have seen the
> King, the LORD Almighty.'
> Then one of the seraphs flew to me with a live coal in his
> hand, which he had taken with tongs from the altar. With it
> he touched my mouth and said, 'See, this has touched your
> lips; your guilt is taken away and your sin atoned for.' (Isa.
> 6:4–7)

Here is a vision of both the holiness and the majesty of God. The
accent on holiness is emphatic in the trisagion 'Holy, holy, holy'
(Isa. 6:3). According to R. T. France, 'Repetition of a word in the
Old Testament is a way of laying emphasis upon it, and a threefold
repetition is rare indeed.'[21] Isaiah is before a greater king than any
Uzziah. The implied contrast is a pointed one. Under Uzziah,
Judah enjoyed fifty-two years of prosperity. But Isaiah is now in
the presence of the King of the creation. The divine king is seated,
which, according to William J. Dumbrell, is the posture of judgment.[22] In the presence of such holiness Isaiah's uncleanness

---

[20] France 1970: 62; original emphasis.
[21] Ibid. 62–63.
[22] I am indebted to Dumbrell's fine discussion (1988: 102–103).

becomes patent and must be addressed. The unclean must be cleansed, and he is.[23]

Divine holiness cannot be disregarded without peril, as Isaiah 5 demonstrates. Divine holiness and divine righteousness are not to be opposed to one another. In Isaiah 5:16 there is a remarkable claim:

> But the LORD Almighty will be exalted by his justice,
>   and the holy God will show himself holy [qādôš] by his righteousness [ṣĕdāqâ].

Geoffrey W. Grogan comments:

> Verse 16 is often treated as summing up the connection between holiness and righteousness in Isaiah (See, e.g., N.H. Snaith, *Distinctive Ideas of the Old Testament* [London: Epworth, 1944], pp. 51, 53.) God's separateness from human beings is not simply ontological but moral, his holiness not a simple synonym for his majesty (though majesty is an element in it; cf., e.g., Exodus 15:11) but the basis in his eternal character of his righteous judgments on sinners.[24]

The context is one of judgment. There is sin in the southern kingdom and not only among the rapacious well to do (Isa. 5:8–10). There is no due regard for the deeds of the Lord in general (Isa. 5:11–12). God will show his holiness by his righteousness through sending his people into exile (Isa. 5:13). Holiness acts appropriately (i.e. righteously) when faced with sin. A story from the Torah also shows the danger of disregarding divine holiness. Aaron's sons Nadab and Abihu discover this to their mortal cost. Despite a contrary divine command, they offer unauthorized fire before the Lord (Lev. 10:1). Fire comes out from the Lord's presence and they die (Lev. 10:2). Moses interprets the event in terms of the holiness of God. He recalls the divine revelation:

---

[23] Coggins (2000: 444) points out, 'No particular theory of atonement for sin is here implied; it is the fact of such cleansing that is all-important.'

[24] Grogan 1997, comment on Isa. 5:16. J. D. Watts (2004) maintains, 'The semantic spheres of "holiness" and "righteousness" are very different (cf. the theological dictionaries). The vision insists on merging them to define Yahweh's character and to understand how his acts of "righteousness" relate to his "holy" nature' (comment on Isa. 5:16).

> Among those who approach me I will show myself holy;
> in the sight of all the people I will be honoured.
>
> (Lev. 10:3)

Divine holiness can show itself with a fierce face. There is another side to holiness in action. God also may save because he is the holy one. He looks upon his broken people in Hosea 11 and, filled with compassion for their plight, although deserved, declares:

> How can I give you up, Ephraim?
> How can I hand you over, Israel?
> How can I treat you like Admah?
> How can I make you like Zeboiim?
> My heart is changed within me;
> all my compassion is aroused.
> I will not carry out my fierce anger,
> nor will I turn and devastate Ephraim.[25]
>
> (Hos. 11:8–9)

Instructively, the reason then given is:

> For I am God, and not man –
> the Holy One among you.
> I will not come in wrath.
>
> (Hos. 11:9)[26]

Like righteousness, in some contexts holiness expresses itself in wrath, but in others it saves. Indeed, to return to Isaiah for a moment, repeatedly we read with regard to Israel that Yahweh is 'your Redeemer, the Holy One of Israel' (Isa. 41:14; 43:3; 48:17; 49:7; 54:5, 8). And even wrath may have a positive aspect. God is not morally indifferent. As Terence E. Fretheim maintains, 'God's wrath means the deliverance of slaves (Exod. 15:7), the righteous from their enemies (Ps. 7:6–11), the poor and needy from their abusers (Exod. 22:21–24), and Israel from its enemies (Isa. 30:27–30).'[27]

---

[25] Day (2000: 577) rightly describes this passage as 'one of the most moving passages in the OT'.
[26] The Hebrew has *kî* for 'For', which may mean 'because' in response to questions. The LXX has *dioti*, which is rightly understood as 'because' or 'on account of'.
[27] Fretheim 2002b: 25–26.

There is no discontinuity between the older covenant and the new on this matter of the holy character of God, as John found. The trisagion ('Holy, holy, holy') is the cry heard in heaven too (Rev. 4:8). John's first letter also witnesses to the divine holiness and does so from the start. John writes:

> This is the message we have heard from him and declare to you: God is light [*phōs*]; in him there is no darkness [*skotia*] at all. If we claim to have fellowship with him yet walk in the darkness, we lie and do not live by the truth. But if we walk in the light, as he is in the light, we have fellowship with one another, and the blood of Jesus, his Son, purifies us from all sin. (1 John 1:5–7)

This message emanates from Jesus himself. Fundamental to it is the polarity between light and darkness. Perhaps the language is working at multiple levels, as so often is the case in Johannine writing. According to Stephen S. Smalley, 'The declaration, "God is light" [*ho theos phōs estin*], is a penetrating description of the being and nature of God: it means that he is absolute in his glory (the physical connotation of light), in his truth (the intellectual) and in his holiness (the moral).'[28] The light of God's truth does indeed dispel the darkness of ignorance. More probably though, the accent in this context is that God's moral purity (light) cannot abide moral impurity (darkness).[29] Without cleansing from defilement the impure cannot walk or fellowship with the pure. The sacrificial death of Christ (the blood) provides the requisite cleansing from sin. In fact, the sacrificial term 'blood', according to I. Howard Marshall, 'is used more often than any other expression to indicate the death of Jesus'.[30]

Divine love

The nearest thing to a systematic statement of the being and attributes of God to be found in Scripture is found in Exodus

---

[28] Smalley 2004, comment on 1 John 1:5–7.

[29] Burge (1996: 67) places the accent elsewhere: 'He [God] is pure, perfect, and utterly righteous. And above all, light is revealing. Light unveils our spiritual identity – whether we abide in the Son – and it identifies boldly those who live in darkness.' Calvin (2002b), on the other hand, emphasizes the idea of moral purity: 'Then the sum of what is said is, that since there is no union between light and darkness, there is a separation between us and God as long as we walk in darkness; and that the fellowship which he mentions, cannot exist except we also become pure and holy' (comment on 1 John 1:5–7).

[30] Marshall 1990: 82.

34:6–7.[31] Upon request, God reveals his name to Moses on the mountain of God. To reveal one's name is to reveal one's essential being. As Charles H. H. Scobie argues, *'God's name is an expression of his essential nature.'*[32] John Webster insightfully suggests, 'The divine attributes . . . are ways of offering a gloss on the divine name.'[33] As Moses stands hidden in the cleft of the rock, Yahweh passes him by and proclaims:

> The LORD, the LORD, the compassionate and gracious God, slow to anger, abounding in love and faithfulness, maintaining love to thousands, and forgiving wickedness, rebellion and sin. Yet he does not leave the guilty unpunished; he punishes the children and their children for the sin of the fathers to the third and fourth generation. (Exod. 34:6–7)

This is the covenant-making and covenant-keeping God who has set his love on Israel, but even so is not to be presumed upon. The only perfection accented twice is love (*ḥesed*), while the only perfection qualified is love. God abounds (*wĕrāb*) in steadfast love (*ḥesed*). In the Old Testament narrative such love led to the rescue of God's people from Egypt: 'But it was because the LORD loved [*'ahăbat*; LXX has *agapan*] you and kept the oath he swore to your forefathers that he brought you out with a mighty hand and redeemed you from the land of slavery, from the power of Pharaoh king of Egypt' (Deut. 7:8).

The New Testament tells us a similar story. According to 1 John 4:8, 16, 'God is love [*agapē*].' Judith Lieu rightly observes, 'That "God is love" (vv. 9, 16) is not a statement about the "divinity" of love or an abstract definition of God: it is God as experienced.'[34] This is a love that takes the initiative and provides for the other. It donates. And how did this love manifest itself? The epistle is clear: 'This is love [*agapē*]: not that we loved God, but that he loved us and sent his Son as an atoning sacrifice for our sins' (1 John 4:10).[35] This

[31] For a discussion of this passage and its importance for developing a doctrine of God see Cole 2008.

[32] Scobie 2003: 108; original emphasis.

[33] Webster 2003: 40.

[34] Lieu 2000: 1279. Unfortunately, she cites 1 John 4:9, when the relevant text is 1 John 4:8. Her point is unaffected by the slip.

[35] For an excellent treatment of the love of God in Scripture and its contemporary significance see Carson 2000.

love shows itself in a deed: the cross. Scripture does say that the divine love does on occasion discipline those who are his children (Heb. 12:5–11), but nowhere does it assert that the divine love judges.[36] This is one difference between how divine love acts, in contradistinction to divine holiness and righteousness. Yet, to be faithful to the Scriptural testimony and to understand the divine atoning project, all three perfections need to be predicated of the God of biblical revelation in requisite measure.

The theological conversion of P. T. Forsyth

It was the appreciation of the biblical presentation of the holy love of God that transformed theologian P. T. Forsyth's life. Up until that point he was conventionally liberal in his theology. He wrote in 1907:

> There was a time when I was interested in the first degree with purely scientific criticism. Bred among academic scholarship of the classics and philosophy, I carried these habits to the Bible, and I found the subject a new fascination, in proportion as the stakes were so much higher. But, fortunately for me, I was not condemned to the mere scholar's cloistered life. I could not treat the matter as an academic quest. I was kept close to practical conditions. I was in a relation of life, duty, and responsibility to others . . . And I was convinced that they were in no spiritual condition to have forced on them those questions on which scholars so delighted and differed.[37]

Then he movingly adds:

> *It also pleased God by the revelation of His holiness and grace, which the great theologians taught me to find in the Bible, to bring home to me my sin in a way that submerged all the school questions in weight, urgency, and poignancy. I was turned from*

---

[36] Lactantius thinks otherwise. He (2007: ch. 6) argues that 'These are the opinions entertained by the philosophers respecting God. But if we have discovered that these things which have been spoken are false, there remains that one last resource, in which alone the truth can be found [Scripture], which has never been embraced by philosophers, nor at any time defended: "*that it follows that God is angry, since He is moved by kindness*"' (my emphasis).

[37] Forsyth 1981: 281–282.

a Christian to a believer, from a lover of love to an object of grace.[38]

Strikingly, this transformation took place some years after his ministry began in 1876 at Shipley, which is located in Bradford.[39]

The cross as revelatory of the character of God

Although the cross of Christ will be discussed at some length in a later chapter with regard to the atonement, at this juncture it is important to draw attention – albeit briefly – to its revelatory power because, as Thomas F. Torrance argues, 'The cross is a window opened into the very heart of God.'[40] Just how it does so is the question before us.[41]

With regard to the divine love and righteousness in relation to the cross, Paul is the chief New Testament witness. In his letter to the Romans he contends that the divine love is demonstrated in the death of Christ. He notes how rarely anyone would sacrifice himself or herself for a righteous person. But in God's case Christ dies for us *while we are alienated from God*. Craig C. Hill comments, 'In their unreconciled state, humans are described as "weak", "ungodly", "sinners", and "enemies" of God (vv. 6, 8, 10), a portrayal that recalls the description in 1:18–32.' He concludes, 'A less pointed description, however, might undermine his [Paul's] argument concerning the absolute necessity of the atonement.'[42] Paul writes:

> You see, at just the right time, when we were still powerless, Christ died for the ungodly. Very rarely will anyone die for a righteous man, though for a good man someone might possibly dare to die. But God demonstrates his own love for us in this: While we were still sinners, Christ died for us. (Rom. 5:6–8)

---

[38] Ibid. 282–283; my emphasis. For a discussion of Forsyth's 'theological conversion' see McCurdy 1999: 29–31.

[39] Hunter 1974: 15.

[40] Torrance 1992: 112.

[41] For an excellent exploration of how the doctrine of God may be derived from the cross see Blocher in McCormack 2008: 125–141. He asks, in effect, the transcendental question 'If God was capable of the cross, what does it teach us about God?' His thesis is that only the God of trinitarian and Christological orthodoxy is capable of the cross.

[42] Hill 2000: 1094.

The Greek is instructive. The divine love is continually on view in the cross of Christ (*synistēsin*, present aspect, active). In this broken world of the groaning creation (Rom. 8:18–22), where is the divine love to be seen? The Pauline answer is to look to the cross as placarded in the gospel.

Paul is also a chief witness to the cross as revelatory of the divine righteousness. Let us turn to Romans once more. Paul claims that the cross demonstrates the righteousness or justice of God. The apostle writes:

> God presented him as a sacrifice of atonement, through faith in his blood. He did this to demonstrate his justice, because in his forbearance he had left the sins committed beforehand unpunished – he did it to demonstrate his justice at the present time, so as to be just and the one who justifies those who have faith in Jesus. (Rom. 3:25–26)

One of the purposes of the death of Christ on the cross was to display or to prove (*eis endeixin*, v. 25) that God is a righteous God (*tēs dikaiosynē*, v. 25; and *pros to einai auton dikaion*, v. 26) who does not overlook sin but judges it.[43] God takes his relationship to creation with the utmost moral seriousness. He behaves as he ought. Sin in creation is not a trivial matter. It is momentous. It requires a divine response.

The sacrifice of Christ on the cross reveals the holiness of God.[44] This is the logic of the book of Hebrews. A morally perfect high priest offers a morally unblemished sacrifice. Only he is qualified to be that high priest and to present that sacrifice that definitively deals with sin. In so doing, he ensures the holiness of those for whom he died. The writer tells his Christian readership:

> Day after day every priest stands and performs his religious duties; again and again he offers the same sacrifices, which can never take away sins. But when this priest had offered for all time one sacrifice for sins, he sat down at the right hand of

---

[43] This is the element of truth in the governmental theory of the atonement that is famously associated with Grotius. Grotius' theology of the cross will be explored in chapter 6.

[44] Blocher (2008: 138–141) argues that the cross reveals the sovereign singularity, righteousness and love of God, but fails to mention the holiness of God (esp. 138–141).

God. Since that time he waits for his enemies to be made his footstool, because by one sacrifice he has made perfect for ever those who are being made holy. (Heb. 10:11–14)

This important statement is part of a summation (Heb. 10:11–18) that draws together the themes of Hebrews 8:1 – 10:10.[45] In the passage quoted, a great contrast is drawn between the old order, on the one hand (*men*), which could not definitively address the problem of sin and unholiness because of the imperfections of the priests and Jesus, on the other hand (*de*), who alone can be the agent of the definitive divine action. Those caught up by his work are in a process. They are being made holy (*hagiazomenous*, present passive participle).[46]

In sum, the cross is of immense epistemic significance. There on display are the three perfections of God that we have been considering: righteousness, holiness and love.

Is divine love in conflict with divine wrath?

If the cross truly reveals the divine love and divine holiness, and if such love and holiness show themselves on the plane of history in mercy and wrath respectively, then a longstanding question merits some discussion. Is God internally conflicted? Is divine holiness at war with divine love? Does sin create a 'dilemma' for God?[47] The great Lutheran theologian Helmut Thielicke certainly thought so. He maintained, 'It is at the heart of the Lutheran view of God that God does contradict himself, that he sets his grace in opposition to his judgment and his love in opposition to his holiness; indeed, the gospel itself can be traced to this fundamental contradiction within God himself.'[48] So I must ask whether 'holy love' as a phrase is an

---

[45] Attridge 2000: 1250.

[46] An argument may also be made that the cross shows God's holiness because it reveals the divine wrath towards sin. Divine wrath is how holiness behaves in the presence of sin. Since the divine wrath is to be discussed at length in a subsequent chapter, I have chosen not to follow that line of argument here.

[47] Boyd and Eddy (2002: 116) appear to think that the penal substitutionary view of the atonement assumes that 'This sinfulness poses a dilemma for God, for he perfectly loves us, on the one hand, but he is perfectly holy and cannot have anything to do with sin, on the other hand.' Not all who hold to a substitutionary view of the atonement would be comfortable with the language of 'dilemma' because it seems too anthropomorphic, as though God is more like us than an accurate reading of Scripture suggests.

[48] Thielicke 1969: 575.

oxymoron. Let us consider an important attempt to answer the question.

In his *The Cross of Christ* John Stott criticizes the view of P. T. Forsyth, which asserts that 'there is nothing in the Bible about the strife of attributes'.[49] Hosea 11 provides Stott with evidence against Forsyth's contention. According to Stott:

> All parents know the costliness of love, and what it means to be 'torn apart' by conflicting emotions, especially when there is a need to punish the children. Perhaps the boldest of all human models of God in Scripture is the pain of parenthood which is attributed to him in Hosea, chapter 11.[50]

Stott maintains, 'Here [Hos. 11] surely is a conflict of emotions, a strife of attributes, within God.'[51] Thus there is duality in God, but not an irreconcilable one: 'For God is not at odds with himself, however much it may appear to us that he is.'[52] Thus when confronted with human sin a problem arises: 'The problem is not outside God; it is within God's own being.'[53] The cross of Christ provides the solution for Stott.

The problem with Stott's appeal to Hosea is that, as we saw previously, the prophet declares,

> For I am God, and not man –
> the Holy One among you.
> I will not come in wrath.
>
> (Hos. 11:9)[54]

---

[49] Quoted in Stott 1996: 129.

[50] Ibid.

[51] Ibid. 130.

[52] Ibid. 131.

[53] Ibid. 133. According to Lutheran theologian Helmut Thielicke, in the incarnation and cross we see the miracle of God's Yes (mercy) overcoming his No (judgment). He argues, 'The gospel is the wonder of this turning in God.' He describes the gospel as God's 'self-overcoming' (188). This is a bolder position than Stott's and shows his debt to Luther's Law–gospel dialectic. See Thielicke 1977: 187–190.

[54] Butterworth (2001) points out, 'The last part of v 9 means either "I will not come against a city" (see the NIV mg.), or "I will not come in wrath" or "burning". On either reading, divine holiness means in this context that God takes pity on undeserving Israel. Calvin (2002d) says, "This is what the Prophet means when he says, 'I will not enter the city'; that is, 'I will make war on you and subdue you and force you to surrender and that with great loss; but when the gates shall be opened, and the wall demolished, I will then restrain myself, for I am unwilling wholly to destroy you'"' (comment on Hos. 11:9).

Holiness on occasion does judge, but like righteousness it may also save.[55] Consequently, I am unconvinced that there is a conflict of attributes presented by the Hosea passage. Moreover, as D. A. Carson rightly contends:

> there is nothing intrinsically impossible about wrath and love being directed toward the same individual or people at the same time. God in his perfections must be wrathful against his rebel image-bearers, for they have offended him; God in his perfections must be loving toward his rebel image-bearers, for he is that kind of God.[56]

A distinction needs to be drawn between conceptual strife and the human experience of psychological strife. Holiness (expressed on occasion as wrath) and love (expressed on occasion as mercy) are not logically contradictory ideas.

Holy love then is not an oxymoron, unlike 'bittersweet'. Indeed, Hans Urs von Balthasar argues, 'There is no right love without wrath.' Why? Because 'God cannot love moral evil, he can only hate it. Of its very nature, it stands in complete opposition to God's essence.'[57] Now it may well be the case that, in our human psychology, to feel wrath and love towards the same object engenders enormous internal conflict. But who can say what 'divine psychology' is like? We must be careful not to fall into the Feuerbachian criticism of turning anthropology into theology, and projecting our thought and emotional life on to some notion of God. God is his perfections and they complement, not compete against, one another.[58]

Moreover, it is important to note that holiness is an essential attribute of God. Wrath is not. Wrath is an expression of holiness in certain contexts. Likewise, love is an essential attribute of God, but mercy is not. Mercy is how love acts in certain contexts. Some theologians make the category mistake of treating holiness, love and wrath as though all three were essential divine attributes. For example, Thomas Smail criticizes Stott's view along these lines: 'but how these two contradictory attributes [God's wrath and love]

---

[55] Webster (2003: 46–49) brings out the positive and negative aspects of holiness.
[56] Carson 2000: 69.
[57] Quoted in Oakes 2005: 244.
[58] See the useful discussions in Erickson 1993: 297–298; McCurdy 1999: 204–208; Marshall 1990: 46.

cohere in the same divine nature is left undefined'.[59] If wrath is an essential attribute of God, then God has eternally been wrathful. However, there is no biblical justification for this idea that wrath is an essential, and therefore an eternal, attribute of God.

Conclusion

The God of biblical revelation has a character. Divine action flows from that character. God is love and he is light. Moreover, he is righteous in all his ways. This is the story of both Old and New Testament. True, there is mystery. God is incomprehensible. We are finite, but God is not so limited. T. F. Torrance is right to contend, 'The reason for the atonement, its why and its how, is hidden in the holy love of God [I would say 'righteous holy love'], before which the very angels veil their faces and which they shield from our prying eyes.'[60] Even so, it is only as we grasp the righteous holy loving character of the God who has made us that we can begin to grasp in some measure the depths of the human plight outside Eden. And it is only against that dark backstory that the glory of the cross of Christ is revealed as the centre of God's plan to bring shalom. But to speak of the human plight raises the questions of just who we are as God's creatures, and what we have become that makes atonement so necessary. To these questions we turn next.

[59] Quoted in Jeffery, Ovey and Sach 2007: 286. The Jeffery, Ovey and Sach discussion of whether divine anger is compatible with divine love would be even sharper if the category distinction between divine holiness and love, on the one hand, and divine anger, on the other, were observed.

[60] Torrance 1992: xiii.

Chapter Two

The glory and garbage of the universe

Why are we such paradoxical beings? As a species, we are capable of acts of both great kindness and of unspeakable cruelty. It is not a recent phenomenon. In the seventeenth century Pascal captured the paradox in these startling words: 'What sort of freak then is man! How novel, how monstrous, how chaotic, how paradoxical, how prodigious! Judge of all things, feeble earthworm, repository of truth, sink of doubt and error, glory and refuse of the universe!'[1] Pascal further contended in another of his *pensées* that 'Man's greatness and wretchedness are so evident that the true religion must necessarily teach us that there is in man some great principle of greatness and some great principle of wretchedness.'[2] Contemporary theologian Daniel L. Migliore similarly observes:

> We human beings are a mystery to ourselves. We are rational and irrational, civilized and savage, capable of deep friendship and murderous hostility, free and in bondage, the pinnacle of creation and its greatest danger. We are Rembrandt and Hitler, Mozart and Stalin, Antigone and Lady Macbeth, Ruth and Jezebel. 'What a work of art,' says Shakespeare of humanity. 'We are very dangerous,' says Arthur Miller in *After the Fall*. 'We meet . . . not in some garden of wax fruit and painted leaves that lies East of Eden, but after the Fall, after many, many deaths.'[3]

Pascal further argued that a believable religion 'must also account for such amazing contradictions'.[4] The Christian doctrine of

---

[1] Pascal 1972: 64.
[2] Ibid. 76.
[3] Migliore 2004: 139.
[4] Pascal 1972: 76.

humanity as the image of God (theological anthropology) and the doctrine of sin (hamartiology) attempt to do just that.

The glory of creation: *imago Dei*

The Christian account begins where Scripture does; namely, the story of the creation. The language is simple, the ideas profound. The literary genre of the early chapters in Genesis remains a matter of debate, and with it the best way to characterize the writing. According to R. C. Sproul, 'The opening chapters of Genesis provide real difficulty to the person who wants to pinpoint the precise literary genre used. Part of the text has the earmarks of historical literature, yet part of it exhibits the kind of imagery found in symbolic literature.'[5] Sproul's observation is sound. In my view Genesis 1 – 3 deals with real personages and real events, but with much symbolic overlay.[6] Indeed, both the world of beginnings (protology) and the world of endings (eschatology) show symmetry in their use of symbolism. Both protology and eschatology speak of worlds we at present do not access: one lost and one still to come (cf. Gen. 1 – 2 and Rev. 21 – 22).[7]

Genesis 1:1 – 2:3 presents the creation of humankind in the divine image and likeness (Gen. 1:26–28).[8] This creature is unlike any other. No rock, dog, cat, angel nor neutrino is described as bearing the divine image. Man and woman are like God in some unique way that is not clearly defined in the Genesis text. Some have seen this uniqueness residing in certain attributes we have in common with God: rationality, moral sense, will and emotions (e.g. Millard J. Erickson).[9] Still others take the image to be relational in character. The polarity of male and female mirrors something of God's own inner relationality as triune (famously Barth).[10] Another view places

[5] Sproul 1977: 52–53.

[6] For a fine treatment of the complex relationship between the literal and symbolic in Gen. 1 – 3 see J. A. Thompson, accessed 16 June 2008.

[7] I am indebted to ibid. (esp. 19): 'In Particular, it is argued that in those areas which lie beyond the reach of man in the PROTON and in the ESCHATON, history writing is of a special kind' (original emphases).

[8] I understand 'image' and 'likeness' to be roughly synonymous in the light of Gen. 5:3. Wenham (2004) says, 'The interchangeability of "image"' and "likeness" (cf. 5:3) shows that this distinction is foreign to Genesis, and that probably "likeness" is simply added to indicate the precise nuance of "image" (comment on Gen. 1:26). The Orthodox Church takes a contrary view, and still maintains the distinction between image and likeness. See K. Ware 1996: 28.

[9] Erickson 1993: 513–514.

[10] *CD* III/1: 191–197; 291–292.

the accent on a Godlike function of exercising dominion (e.g. Gordon J. Spykman).[11] Millard J. Erickson wisely observes, 'The existence of a wide diversity of interpretations is an indication that there is no direct statement in Scripture to resolve the issue. Our conclusions then must necessarily be reasonable inferences drawn from what little the Bible does have to say on the subject.'[12]

In my view, Genesis 1:26–28 emphasizes the functional, but the theological concept of *imago Dei* needs to be much richer in content in that it synthesizes the total biblical testimony (*tota scriptura*). In other words, in theological use *imago Dei* acts as a master concept that catches up various elements in a biblical anthropology.[13] In so doing, it is clear that life, rationality, will and moral sense are necessary conditions for the right exercise of dominion that is done in concert with others, and thus the relational is an element in the theological story too.[14]

By the conclusion of the second chapter of Genesis we find that man and woman enjoy an idyllic existence in Eden. 'Eden' means 'delight'.[15] They are the kings and priests of creation, as the early church Fathers recognized.[16] Importantly, in the Genesis picture the rule of man and woman is not to be exploitive. Adam is to keep the garden like later priests were to tend the tabernacle (cf. Gen. 2:15; Num. 3:7–8; 4:23–24, 26).[17] The living creatures have been named (Gen. 2:19–20). The Adamic loneliness has been assuaged by the

---

[11] Spykman, 'It [*imago Dei*] is not to be sought in some ontic quality within us. It has rather dynamic, active, functional meaning' (1992: 228).

[12] Erickson 1993: 512–513.

[13] What is tricky is that the same English words 'image of God' appear both in translations (e.g. Gen. 9:6, NIV) and also as a technical expression in systematic theologies. The temptation that the systematician must resist is to read back into a given text of Scripture all the nuances of the technical term.

[14] I am reluctant to follow without qualification Erickson's commitment to the substantive view. If the image is found in communicable attributes, then the serpent too is the image of God. Aquinas even argues that angels are superior images to human beings since they are pure spirits. Aquinas (1963: 78) says, 'they bear a more perfect image of God than man does' (1a Qq 93). However, Scripture never makes this claim. In fact, according to Paul, believers will judge angels (1 Cor. 6:3). For a survey of contemporary views see Towner 2005: 341–356.

[15] Whybray 2000: 44.

[16] E.g. with regard to kingship see Gregory of Nyssa (c. 330–395), 'On the Making of Man', *NA* 2.1; and for priesthood see Maximus the Confessor (c. 580–662) in K. Ware 1996: 81. For contemporary advocates see Dumbrell's arguments in Hafemann 2002: 53–65.

[17] Christians may have played a role historically in the ecological problems of today. However, Scripture itself points in a very different direction – despite what secular critics such as philosopher Peter Singer might suggest. See Cole in Preece 2002: 95–105. For the affinities between Eden and the tabernacle see Wenham 2004, comment on Gen. 2:15.

woman's creation: 'It is not good for the man to be alone' (Gen. 2:18). Man and woman are naked but there is no shame (Gen. 2:25). Little is required of them. To be sure, there is a garden to care for, and they have permission to eat of any tree, except one. The tree of the knowledge of good and evil is off limits. The divine generosity is patent. However, there is a sober warning about the forbidden tree: 'for when you eat of it you will certainly die' (Gen. 2:17).

The primeval rupture

Then the serpent enters the story (Gen. 3:1).[18] We find in Genesis 3 that the serpent becomes the catalyst for what Augustine termed the fall, and for what more recently Jacques Ellul described as the Rupture.[19] Both terms are useful. The former term suggests that humanity has fallen away from its uprightness before God (traditionally understood as original righteousness). The latter accents the breaking of a network of relationships.[20] The relationship with God

[18] How evil arrives in God's good world is not explained in Scripture with any philosophical depth. Instead, a story is told of a paradisal garden zone and a malevolent serpent who enters from the outside and comes questioning the very character of God. From the canonical perspective it is clear that the Creator is not taken by surprise by these events. The New Testament tells us that Christ was slain from before the foundation of the world. See Blum 1997, comment on 1 Pet. 1:20. Blum writes, 'He was chosen before the creation of the world.' The Greek word for 'chosen' is *proegnōsmenou*, often translated 'know before'. The meaning, however, must be more than 'foresight'. For why would Peter at this point make the obvious statement that God knew before about Jesus and his death? Kelly (1977: 75) translates this as 'predestined before the foundation of the world'. 'The redemption was in the plan of God before Creation occurred.' Indeed, a minimal view of divine omniscience would maintain that God knows all possible worlds, including ones where evil erupts. How then could God ever be taken by surprise? We may float a theory as to why God has allowed evil in this actual world as long as its theory status is acknowledged. Any theodicy that specifies the divine rationale for allowing evil goes beyond what has been revealed. The 'secret things' still belong to the Lord (Deut. 29:29).

[19] Augustine 1958: 269; see Ellul 1985: ch. 7.

[20] Jensen (1997: 55) argues with regard to Gen. 3, 'Whether this is a strictly historical account or only the pictorial account of an historical event, the Bible's analysis of our present experience is undeniable: we simply and habitually assume all others to be like us, sinful.' However, others deny that Gen. 3 refers to any kind of space-time historical event. E.g. some argue that the story of Adam and Eve is a parabolic way of narrating the story of every one of us as creatures and fallen. Old Testament scholar M. D. Guinan (accessed 10 June 2008) takes this approach: 'The man and woman of Genesis 2–3, as well as other characters of the primal stories, are intended to represent an Everyman and Everywoman.' But, logically speaking, if the Genesis stories are about all of us *ex hypothesi*, then they are about the first of us, and consequently belief in real personages and a real space-time fall is unavoidable even on the parabolic or mythic view. Jensen (1997: 55) is sounder.

is ruptured. Fear and flight replace intimacy and fellowship (Gen. 3:8–10). The banishment from the garden dramatically shows the rupture, and the presence of the cherubim who bar re-entry to Eden underline the seriousness of what has taken place (Gen. 3:23–24). Death has come to the paradise of God. Death in Scripture is the severing of relationship. Indeed one of the vivid Old Testament ways of capturing the idea is that of being cut off from the people (*kārat*; e.g. Exod. 31:14). Man and woman have died in this sense just as the divine warning said. There is now too a self-consciousness that betrays a sense of shame (cf. Gen. 3:7 and 2:25). The relationship between male and female becomes difficult, as does the relationship to the environment. The man shifts blame to the woman and God for giving him such a companion (Gen. 3:12). Judgment does not fall only on the man and the woman. The serpent will be defeated, for that is the divine promise, and in that promise is hope. The so-called *protoevangelium* (first gospel) reads:

> And I will put enmity
>   between you and the woman,
>   and between your offspring and hers;
> he will crush your head,
>   and you will strike his heel.
>
> (Gen. 3:15)

If this promise is not understood, the rest of the biblical story becomes difficult to make sense of. The *protoevangelium* is programmatic. Moreover, the Creator does not leave the primeval pair naked but provides their clothing (Gen. 3:21). Even the banishment from the garden zone may have been a mercy, given the narrative logic of the account. Man and woman are prevented from eating of the tree of life and thus kept mercifully from being locked into their alienated state.

God's good creation has been spoiled.[21] Speaking of Adam and Eve, Karl Barth comments, 'They had allowed their peace with God to be broken.'[22] Man and woman are in exile. Indeed, according to

---

[21] N. T. Wright (2004: 94) rightly comments, 'Suffice it to say that the idea of a beautiful and good world, spoiled at one point in time by human rebellion, remains basic to all early Christian, as to all Jewish, thought.' Wright's point should not obscure the fact that Scripture assumes 'that evil in some way predates the human fall', as Gunton (2002: 60) notes. The first spoiling took place in the angelic realm.

[22] *CD* IV/1: 466.

I. M. Duguid, 'The expulsion of Adam and Eve from the garden of Eden is the archetype of all subsequent exile (Gen. 3:24).'[23] Genesis 4 – 11 tells the sorry story of humankind's decline into evil: Cain slays Abel, Lamech is a man of vengeance, the flood generation is full of wickedness, and Babel shows the overreach of human arrogance. However, even so humanity remains in the divine image (e.g. Gen. 9:6 and Jas 3:9), but, as Scot McKnight suggests, we are now 'cracked eikons'.[24] The Paulines provide further evidence that the image in some sense remains. The apostle argues the image (*eikōn*) requires renewal (*anakainoō*, Col. 3:10) rather than fresh creation, which suggests that it still exists in some way.[25]

The primeval sin

What exactly was the primeval sin that led to such unhappy consequences? The suggestions of theologians past and present are legion. According to Henri Blocher, the list of possibilities includes pride, sensuousness, selfishness, unbelief, greed, violence and inertia.[26]

Interestingly, when Paul discusses the sin of Adam in Romans 5, he uses a variety of ideas, which may be translated as in the ESV 'sin' (*hamartia*, v. 12), 'breaking a command' (*parabaseōs*, v. 14), 'trespass' (*paraptōma*, v. 15) and 'disobedience' (*parakoēs*, v. 19).[27] In fact, one of the contrasts between Adam and Christ that Paul draws is not one between pride (Adam) and humility (Christ), but the disobedience of

[23] Duguid 2001: 475. Is the judgment on Cain for slaying his brother, Abel, the next example of such exile? He is driven from his land to become a wanderer on the earth (Gen. 4:12–16).

[24] McKnight 2007: 51. Jesus nowhere describes human beings using image-of-God language, but with regard to Luke 12:24, Matt. 10:31 and 12:11–12, Wolterstorff (2008: 131) is probably correct when he argues, 'To be a human being is to have worth. Jesus does not indicate what that worth is, other than to say that it is much greater than the worth of birds and sheep and to suggest that it is a worth one has *qua* human being. Presumably, the worth he had in mind was that of bearing the image of God.'

[25] For a contrary view see Martin Luther's 'Commentary on Genesis', 'the image of God in us is lost' (Kerr 1974: 82).

[26] Blocher 2001: 783. Feminist theology has generally rejected as patriarchal the Augustinian claim that pride is the primeval sin, and claim that this is not relevant to women's experience. However, feminist alternatives are themselves diverse. For a useful survey and for her own proposal see McGougall 2006: 215–235. She follows Kathryn Tanner in positing 'blockage' and 'blindness' as the two metaphors that a feminist re-envisioning of the Christian doctrine sin may build upon. There is no appeal to Scripture at any point in her analysis.

[27] Much of the content of this paragraph comes from my 'Reinhold Niebuhr on Pride', in Cameron and Rosner 2007: 108–109.

Adam as opposed to the obedience of Christ (*parakoē* vs. *hypakoē*, Rom. 5:19). Indeed, given the Genesis narrative as it stands, pride is not obviously the sin of Adam, let alone Eve. Eve is seduced by the serpent's misrepresentation of God. Her attention is drawn to the tree of the knowledge of good and evil. Its fruit seems good to eat, it is a delight to the eyes and it can make one wise (Gen. 3:6). So many basic human needs seemed to be met by the tree and its fruit: the need for physical sustenance, the need for beauty and the need for knowledge (cf. Gen. 3:6 and 2 Cor. 11:3). As for Adam, all we learn is that he listened to his wife and did what she did (cf. Gen. 3:17). Accordingly, both disobeyed God's command. Arguably, behind the disobedience was not so much pride; rather, it was unbelief in God's word of command and in his goodness. After all, God's commandment and goodness are the serpent's targets (Gen. 3:1–5). As D. B. Knox argues, 'The problem Adam faced was, could God be trusted?'[28]

Whatever the right characterization of the primeval sin might be (as can be seen above, I incline strongly to the unbelief view), it is a separate question as to whether there is an essence to sin and that the Genesis story shows it. Scripture uses a multitude of descriptors for sin. There are fifty alone in the Old Testament, as we shall see in the next chapter. And, as we saw above, Paul uses four different descriptors of Adam's fall. Scripture is non-postulational. There is little if any interest in the Scriptures in speculating about the essences of things.[29]

Moreover, the primeval sin did not merely affect Adam and Eve. The ongoing effects are addressed classically in the notion of original sin. Following Augustine's account, original sin (*peccatum originale*) admits of two subconcepts. *Originating* original sin (*peccatum originale origans*) is the primeval sin of Adam. *Originated* sin (*peccatum originale originatum*) is the corrupt nature inherited by subsequent generations from Adam.[30] Infamously, in the early church period, Pelagius (c. 355 – c. 435) argued that Adam's sin hurt only Adam. Islam takes a similar view. Muslim academic Badru D. Kateregga maintains:

---

[28] Knox 1959: 9. If Knox is right, then there is no real difference between the sin of Adam and the sin of Eve. Both acted as unbelievers in the Word of God. Consequently, the attempt by some feminist theology to posit a difference fails to convince.

[29] See the discussion in Ramm 1967: 48.

[30] See Guinan, accessed 10 June 2008. Also see the comprehensive discussion of sin in Smith 1994.

As Muslims, we do not accuse Adam and Eve of transmitting sin and evil to the whole mankind. The two were absolved of their sin, and their descendents were immune from its effect. Sin is not original, hereditary, or inevitable . . . Muslims certainly believe that man is fundamentally a good and dignified creature. He is not a fallen being.[31]

If Pelagius and Kateregga are right, it is hard to understand why it is that as parents we need to teach our children to tell the truth. No lessons are needed, however, when it comes to lying.[32]

The dominical diagnosis

Who really understands the human heart, with its desires, motivations, intentions, manipulations, light and dark places? Sophocles? Shakespeare? Dostoevsky? The master of understanding the human heart is Jesus. According to John's account, Jesus knew what is in a person (John 2:24–25). The stories of his encounter with two very different people back up this claim. Nicodemus is a ruler of the Jews who, presumably to protect his reputation, comes to Jesus by night. Jesus strongly challenges him on the subject of the human necessity (*dei*) to be born anew (John 3:7). As a Pharisee, Nicodemus should understand this necessity. But he does not and Jesus knows it. The woman of Samaria is quite a contrast to Nicodemus. She has had five husbands and her current partner is not her husband. Jesus knows her moral history (John 4:18). She is astonished at his insight into her life and responds, 'I can see that you are a prophet' (v. 19). Jesus can read the human heart.

One incident in the Synoptic Gospels stands out as revelatory of Jesus' understanding of the human problem. The issue is purity. Some Pharisees and scribes from Jerusalem raise a question with Jesus about the failure of his disciples to observe the appropriate (according to them) purity protocols: 'Why don't your disciples live according to the tradition of the elders instead of eating their food with "unclean" hands?' (Mark 7:5). In the ensuing discussion Jesus points out how, through appealing to the tradition of the elders (the oral interpretation of the Torah), they actually set aside the Word of

---

[31] Kateregga and Shenk 1981: 107–108.
[32] For a more developed version of this argument see John Wesley in Burtner and Chiles 1954: 114–115. For stimulating studies of original sin see Blocher 1997 and Jacobs 2008.

God (vv. 6–13). His words are bracing: 'you hypocrites' (v. 6). Then, addressing the crowd, Jesus says, 'Listen to me, everyone, and understand this. Nothing outside a man [or woman, *anthrōpos*] can make him "unclean" by going into him. Rather, it is what comes out of a man [or woman, *anthrōpos*] that makes him "unclean"' (vv. 14–16). The saying is cryptic and Mark describes it as a parable (v. 17). Once inside, the disciples ask for an explanation. As so often is the case in Mark's Gospel, Jesus is not impressed with the disciples' obtuseness: '"Are you so dull?" he asked. "Don't you see that nothing that enters a man [or woman, *anthrōpos*] from the outside can make him 'unclean'?"' The reason is straightforward: 'For it doesn't go into his heart but into his stomach, and then out of his body.' What then is the problem? According to Jesus:

> What comes out of a man [or woman, *anthrōpos*] is what makes him 'unclean'. For from within, out of men's hearts, come evil thoughts, sexual immorality, theft, murder, adultery, greed, malice, deceit, lewdness, envy, slander, arrogance and folly. All these evils come from inside and make a man 'unclean'. (Mark 7:20–23)

Jesus' vice list is extensive. It covers both attitudes ('envy') and actions ('murder'). The human problematic is not a surface matter. Donald A. Hagner's comments on the parallel passage in Matthew 15:10–29 are apposite:

> The true problem of sin is not to be found in a failure to perform correctly some external minutiae of human making; sin is an interior matter that concerns the evil thought, words, and deeds that come from the heart. Moral righteousness is thus far more important than ritual purity. The fundamental problem of humanity is more basic than the Pharisees dreamed. The Pharisees simply failed to address sin as a radical human problem.[33]

The problem is not like rust on the surface of metal that the simple application of the file of the Mosaic law is able to remove (contra Pelagius).[34] The direction is from the inside (*esōthen*) to the outside

[33] Hagner 2004b, comment on Matt. 15:18–19.
[34] See Augustine's *Four Anti-Pelagian Writings* (1992: 9). Also see Carol Harrison 2000: 78–82. Interestingly, Harrison (81) maintains that Pelagius taught 'a theology of Christ's atoning, *vicarious*, sacrificial death for the forgiveness of [actual] sins' (my emphasis).

(*exōthen*). The heart (*kardia*) is the key. The core of what we are as thinking, feeling and willing creatures is flawed. According to Calvin, we are 'a perpetual factory of idols'.[35]

Neither Jesus nor Calvin has a romantic view of human nature. Neither did Shakespeare. Hamlet famously says:

> What a piece of work is a man, how noble in reason, how infinite in faculties, in form and moving how express and admirable, in action how like an angel, in apprehension how like a god! The beauty of the world, the paragon of animals – and yet, to me what is the quintessence of dust / Man delights not me – nor woman neither . . .[36]

Hamlet had his reasons for not delighting in man or woman: his uncle Claudius was responsible for the murder of his father, and his mother, Gertrude, had married the murderer.

The dominical diagnosis is not dated. More recently, Nobel prize-winning author Aleksandr Solzhenitsyn in his *The Gulag Archipelago* contended, 'Gradually it was disclosed to me that the line separating good and evil passes not through states, nor between classes, nor between political parties either – but right through every heart – and through all human hearts.'[37] And surprisingly, one of the great critics of Christianity, Bertrand Russell, came to a similar conclusion. He lamented, 'It is in our hearts that evil lies, and it is from our hearts that it must be plucked out.'[38]

The Pauline elaboration

The most sustained treatment of the human problem before God is found in Paul's letter to the Romans. His thesis is stark. None is righteous (Rom. 3:10). Whether Gentile or Jew, human beings have fallen short of the divine glory (Rom. 3:23). In Romans 1:18–32 he deals with the pagan world. Instead of glorifying the Creator and giving him thanks, there is idolatry:

> For although they knew God, they neither glorified him as God nor gave thanks to him, but their thinking became futile

---

[35] Calvin 2002e: 1.11.8.

[36] Hamlet, Act II, scene 2, lines 303–312, quoted in McCrone 1993: 110–111. McCrone discusses the debate on the sincerity of Hamlet's speech.

[37] Solzhenitsyn 1974: 615.

[38] Quoted in 'Bertrand Arthur William Russell', accessed 6 Sept. 2007.

and their foolish hearts were darkened. Although they claimed to be wise, they became fools and exchanged the glory of the immortal God for images made to look like mortal man and birds and animals and reptiles. Therefore God gave them over in the sinful desires of their hearts to sexual impurity for the degrading of their bodies with one another. They exchanged the truth of God for a lie, and worshipped and served created things rather than the Creator – who is for ever praised. Amen. (Rom. 1:21–25)

This unfortunate exchange (idols for God) brings moral confusion and judgment. Repeatedly, Paul argues that God gave idolaters up to the folly of their choices (Rom. 1:24, 26, 28). The consequences are sobering: foolishness, sexual impurity, degradation, unnatural lusts, depraved minds. In sum:

They have become filled with every kind of wickedness, evil, greed and depravity. They are full of envy, murder, strife, deceit and malice. They are gossips, slanderers, God-haters, insolent, arrogant and boastful; they invent ways of doing evil; they disobey their parents; they are senseless, faithless, heartless, ruthless. (Rom. 1:29–31)

As we shall see in a later chapter – a great and very different exchange to the one referred to by Paul in Romans 1 lies at the heart of the divine provision to remedy the malady.

Next Paul turns to the Jews (Rom. 2:1 – 3:20).[39] Despite their privilege (they have the oracles of God, Rom. 3:2), the Jews are in no position to censure the Gentiles: 'You, therefore, have no excuse, you who pass judgment on someone else, for at whatever point you judge the other, you are condemning yourself, because you who pass judgment do the same things' (Rom. 2:1). Bragging about the law is pointless unless one does the law. Using a diatribe style, Paul questions the Jew, 'You who preach against stealing, do you steal? You who say that people should not commit adultery, do you commit adultery? You who abhor idols, do you rob temples? You

---

[39] I am following Dumbrell (2005: 25–41) in viewing Rom. 1:18–32 as addressed to Gentiles, and Rom. 2:1 – 3:20 as addressed to Jews. Not all exegetes agree. For a contrary view see Keck in Meeks 1993: 2118, who argues that the 'whoever you are' (ō anthrōpe, 'O human being') of Rom. 2:1 must be allowed to have full non-specific force. On any of these views, the whole world stands under divine judgment.

who brag about the law, do you dishonour God by breaking the law?' (Rom. 2:21–23). His reflection on the human moral predicament before the Creator leads Paul to a startling conclusion: 'A man is not a Jew if he is only one outwardly, nor is circumcision merely outward and physical. No, a man is a Jew if he is one inwardly; and circumcision is circumcision of the heart, by the Spirit, not by the written code' (Rom. 2:28–29). The Pauline argument undermines any kind of Rousseau-like romanticism. It was Rousseau in the eighteenth century who famously said, 'Man is born free: and everywhere he is in chains.'[40] The psalmist took a very different view:

> Surely I was sinful at birth,
> sinful from the time my mother conceived me.
>
> (Ps. 51:5)

In Romans Paul, in the tradition of the psalmist, presents no noble savage born free but then spoiled by the civilization's structures. Instead, the whole world, without exception (none has escaped the problem of sin) and without distinction (both Jew and Greek), has defected from the will of God and lives contrary to the moral nature of God.

The C. E. M. Joad story

C. E. M. Joad (1891–1953) was a professional philosopher and head of the philosophy department of Birkbeck College, the University of London. He was also on a BBC radio panel, *The Brains Trust*. His role in the show made him a popular figure in British society for a time. Listeners supplied the questions and the panel would try to answer them and entertain at the same time. Invariably, Professor Joad would start an answer to a question with 'It all depends on what you mean by . . .'[41] He became famous for it. He was right to ask questions of the question, whether the question was stated or implied. For many years he was a self-described 'vocal and militant agnostic'.[42] However, on 12 April

---

[40] Jean-Jacques Rousseau, *The Social Contract*, Bk. 1, ch. 1, quoted in Flewelling 1946: 384. Also see the discussion of Rousseau's philosophy in R. Hooker, accessed 13 June 2008.

[41] Quoted in Symonds 2002.

[42] Joad 1952: 21.

1948 he was convicted of travelling on the London underground (the Tube) without paying his fare. He was dismissed from the BBC and suffered public humiliation. The incident led to deep reflection and he came to the view that he was morally flawed in a way that he had never faced. He concluded that he had been the victim of 'a shallow optimism in regard to human nature' because, like so many on the political left, he had rejected 'the doctrine of original sin'.[43] That growing moral self-awareness ultimately led him to consider the claims of Christ on his life. Joad learnt for himself the truth of Pascal's *pensée* that we are both the glory and garbage of the universe.

However, if sociologist Frank Furedi is to be believed, today Joad would have much more difficulty coming to moral self-awareness. The seven deadly sins of Christian tradition – lust, gluttony, avarice, sloth, anger, envy and pride – have become the seven deadly ills.[44] Morality has given way to therapy. In fact, so his argument runs, morality has been medicalized. Joad had an 'impulse-control disorder', not a moral flaw. Sins are now addictions. In Joad's case he was addicted to fare evasion. Instead of public humiliation, he might have become a suitable candidate for a role on *Big Brother*, *Celebrity Rehab* or some similar reality TV show. There is money to be made in recovery. Furedi confesses that 'as a humanist I don't much like the idea of sin'.[45] But there is a cost with the loss of the concept. Furedi argues, 'Addicts are told that they will never be completely cured. . . . No one ever really changes.'[46] However, Joad did change, as his book *The Recovery of Belief* shows.[47]

---

[43] Ibid. 81–82.

[44] Furedi's argument illustrates one of the three reasons that Erickson (1993: 563–564) adduces for the difficulty in speaking about sin in today's society; namely, sin is a foreign concept because our ills are seen as the product of 'an unwholesome environment'. He offers two other reasons in addition. Sin like death is an unpleasant topic and many moderns think in terms of sins as individual wrong acts disconnected from any understanding of a problematic underlying *nature* that gives rise to them. However, a caveat is in order. The failure to take seriously human fallenness is not a recent phenomenon. In the eighteenth century John Wesley wrote of how those who spoke of 'the fair side of human nature' were the ones 'most universally read, admired, applauded' (quoted in Watson 1984: 81).

[45] How right Whale (1957: 38) was to write, 'The congenital weakness of human nature is the submerged rock on which the claims of an optimistic humanism are shipwrecked.'

[46] For the substance of this paragraph I am indebted to Furedi (2002), who teaches at the University of Kent, England.

[47] Joad 1952: 243–248.

Conclusion

We human beings are paradoxes: capable of both greatness and unspeakable evil. This is unsurprising if the biblical story is believed. We remain images of God (the glory) structurally and functionally – albeit damaged though we are. Yet we are sinners (the garbage). Any account of human beings that does not reckon with the paradox is flawed. We are not devils, even though we can act like them. Christians ought not to be misanthropes. But we are not moral innocents either, even though we are capable of acts of great kindness and compassion. Natural disasters can bring out the best and worst in people. For example, hurricanes are common in the USA. As the news reports come in, so often we learn stories of wonderful other person-centred heroism. Neighbour cares for neighbour; stranger cares for stranger. Then there is the looting and the insurance fraud. A Christian anthropology that recognizes the great rupture combats both a facile optimism about human perfectibility and a despairing pessimism as to human value. Instead, there is realism about the human condition. Not only does the world need to be set right, but I too need to be set right. To these sobering needs we now shift our attention as we consider more deeply both the problem of sin and its problematic entailments.

Chapter Three

The great need: peace with God, with one another and for the cosmos

According to Scot McKnight, 'We cannot discuss atonement until we define the problem that atonement remedies.'[1] That problem is multifaceted. For the purposes of this book, however, I shall sum it up as the need for peace – given the way Paul uses the concept so globally in Colossians 1. I am not talking about peace understood merely as a state of mind. Living outside Eden as we do, our great need is peace in the rich biblical and relational sense of shalom: peace with God, with one another and for the cosmos itself. Two of these needs are obvious. War is a sorry feature of human life both past and present. Terrorism is a fact of global life these days. As for the cosmos, global warming is the current major ecological threat according to many. Peace with God, however, is not so obvious a need to increasing numbers in the West. The rise to prominence and the book sales of militant atheists such as Christopher Hitchens and Richard Dawkins provide evidence of this trend.[2] And yet, according to the biblical revelation, humanity's fundamental need is a religious one: to be in right relation to the God who created us and has a wise design for human flourishing. Maybe it is time to revisit Augustine's famous opening to his *Confessions*, the first Western autobiography. Augustine wrote in the form of a prayer, 'because you [God] made us for yourself and our hearts find no peace until they rest in you'.[3] But there are barriers to such rest and in this chapter we shall consider just what our problems are.[4]

---

[1] McKnight 2007: 23.
[2] Hitchens 2007, and Dawkins 2006.
[3] Augustine 1977: 21. 'Rest' for Augustine was not a glacial existence in the world to come, but rather 'There we shall rest and see, we shall see and love, we shall love and praise' (Augustine, *The City of God*, quoted in CCC, para. 428).
[4] Contra Marshall 1990: 80, I wish to accent that these are our problems, not God's. For a different view, Marshall argues that God is faced with 'problems' and

67

The problem of sin

In the last chapter we saw how sin entered human experience in the Genesis 3 story. We now explore in more detail the problem it constitutes for us. Sin is a religious category. We sin against God in the first instance, as Psalm 51 confesses:

> Against you, you only, have I sinned
> and done what is evil in your sight.
>
> (Ps. 51:4)

The traditional superscription to this psalm strikingly places it in the context of David's adultery with Bathsheba that led to what was in effect her husband Uriah's murder on the battlefield (cf. 2 Sam. 11 and Ps. 51). According to Henri Blocher:

> Preoccupation with sin is one of the hallmarks of biblical religion. Denunciation of sin and the announcement of ensuing woes occupies more than half of the prophetic books (cf. Mic. 3:8); the psalms and wisdom writings include many confessions of and reflections on sin; the sacred history emphasizes the consequences of disobedience on the part of rulers and people; the focus is basically the same in the NT, which has a frightening finale in the book of Revelation.[5]

Theologians use the concept of sin as a master concept to sum up the whole range of biblical ways of speaking of that state of being, those attitudes and actions displeasing to God, which contradict his character and sabotage the design for human flourishing (glory).[6]

Scripture has a multitude of descriptors of sin. For example, the semantic field for 'sin' in the Hebrew Bible contains no fewer than fifty terms.[7] The most important of these are often found clustered

---

'difficulties' posed by human sin, which he needs to solve. This language is question begging, unless carefully qualified as a way of speaking. However, he is right to see that 'It is at the cross that all barriers between God and man are broken down.'

[5] Blocher 2001: 781.

[6] N. T. Wright (2005: 24) helpfully points out that terms like 'atonement' (and I would add 'sin') are shorthands that 'are useful in the same way that suitcases are. They enable us to pick up lots of complicated things and carry them around all together.' However, some theologians see an essence to sin. Gunton (2002: 60) settles for 'Sin is for the creature to think and act as if it were the creator.'

[7] Blocher 2001: 782. Also see Shuster 2004: 263–265 for her useful Appendix 2, 'Biblical Vocabulary Relating to Sin'.

together ('missing the mark' [*ḥāṭāʾ*], 'iniquity' or 'lawlessness' ['*awôn*], and 'transgression' [*pešaʾ*]), as in Exodus 34:7; Psalms 32:1–2; 51:1–3; Daniel 9:24.[8] The cluster is not found as such in the New Testament but each of these ideas of sin is. For example, all three are found in the Paulines. The climax of Paul's argument concerning sin in the opening chapters of Romans is that all have missed the mark and fallen short of God's glory (*hamartia*, Rom. 3:23), transgression is the sin of Adam in Romans 5 (*parabasis*, Rom. 5:14) and lawlessness or iniquity is what God's people have been redeemed from in Titus 2 (*anomia*, Titus 2:14). Generally speaking, in the New Testament the two most commonly used terms to describe sin are *hamartia* (usually translated 'sin') and *adikia* (unrighteousness).[9]

How deep does the problem of sin go? Those who stand in the tradition of the Reformation and the Evangelical Awakening take a somber view: we inherit a corrupt nature. 'Total depravity' or 'entire depravity' is the term that speaks of this corruption. Calvinists hold to this view, as do Arminians. According to Calvin, 'Original sin, therefore, seems to be a hereditary depravity and corruption of our nature, *diffused into all parts of the soul*, which first makes us liable to God's wrath, then also brings forth in us those works which Scripture calls "works of the flesh".'[10] John Wesley preached, 'Know thou art corrupted in every power, in every faculty of thy soul; that thou art *totally corrupted* in every one of these, all foundations being out of course.'[11] Contemporary Arminian theologian I. Howard Marshall ably summarizes the view of both Calvinists and Arminians:

> Sin thus affects every relationship of man, to God, to his fellows and to himself. Its influence is seen in every part of his life. Its badness corrupts all that he thinks, says and does. This does not mean that he is as bad as he can be, but that no part of him is entirely free from the taint of sin. This is what theologians call 'total depravity'.[12]

---

[8] Shuster (2004: 264) contends, 'One can see the loss of nuance when the LXX uses only two words [*hamartia*] and [*adikia*], for almost the whole range of Hebrew terms.'

[9] Ibid. 263–265.

[10] Calvin 2002e: 2.1.8; my emphasis.

[11] John Wesley, 'Sermons: "The Way to the Kingdom", 2.1, in Burtner and Chiles 1954: 121; my emphasis.

[12] Marshall 1966: 42. Also for an Arminian view see Sanner 1983: 524–525.

Where Calvinists and Arminians differ is whether God through a universal act of prevenient grace (grace that goes before us) has remedied the corruption to the extent that a man or woman may freely choose to follow Christ (Arminians) or rather only those whom God regenerates (the elect) voluntarily follow Christ (Calvinists). That debate need not detain us.[13]

What is important to note is that the concept of total depravity – not the most fortunate of terms – ought not to be misunderstood. 'Entire' or 'total' in the phrase refers to extent. The idea is extensive not intensive. As Marshall argued above, the claim wrapped up in the concept is not that human beings as fallen creatures are as morally corrupt as a creature can be. We are not the devil. Rather, the idea is that no area of the human constitution is unaffected by the fall: reason, imagination, will, moral sense, emotion, physicality.[14]

We are sinners and sin invites divine wrath and divine judgment. Paul put it starkly to the Ephesians, 'we were by nature [*physei*] children [*tekna*] of wrath' (Eph. 2:3; my tr.: the NIV is too colourless here). Our sin creates true moral guilt before a righteous God for we have fallen short of the divine design for human flourishing and, in addition, ought to cause shame before a holy God for we are unclean. Sin spoils our relating to others and their relating to us. Sin is an instrument used by the god of this world to produce bondage in us. Sin can even get into the structures of society (e.g. unjust laws and government policies). Daniel 3 provides a biblical example of structural sin. King Nebuchadnezzar decreed a law that institutionalized idolatry and which Shadrach, Meshach and Abednego in conscience could not obey.[15] Sin spoils creation itself such that the created order too longs for a new start. We need a forgiveness that addresses our guilt and a cleansing that addresses

---

[13] For a very fine discussion of the issues see Demarest 1997: 143.

[14] Both the Eastern Orthodox Church and the Roman Catholic Church take the problem of sin with great seriousness. However, both reject the notion of total depravity. Fallen human beings are spiritually sick and wounded rather than spiritually dead. For the Eastern Orthodox view see K. Ware (1996: 28), 'we would not say with Luther or Calvin that our nature had undergone a radical depravity or total corruption'; and for the Roman Catholic position see CCC, paras. 405, 407. Para. 405 asserts, 'human nature has not been totally corrupted'. In contrast, Paul writes of our being dead in our transgressions and sins (Eph. 2:1).

[15] The idea of structural sin is a welcome contribution by liberation theology to hamartiology. For this perspective on sin see Boff and Boff 1989: 82.

our shame; only then can we lift up our faces in the presence of a holy and righteous God.[16]

How then can forgiveness and cleansing come?

The problem of wrath

Sin invites divine wrath because our sin offends God personally.[17] Famously, C. H. Dodd took a very different position with regard to the wrath of God, which he described as not 'the attitude of God to man, but . . . an inevitable process of cause and effect in a moral universe'.[18] In contrast, J. I. Packer maintains that understanding this connection between God, sin and wrath is vital to grasping the Christian gospel. He writes:

> Do you understand this? If you do, you are now seeing to the very heart of the Christian gospel. No version of that message goes deeper than that which declares man's root problem before God to be his sin, which evokes wrath, and God's basic provision for man to be propitiation, which out of wrath brings peace.[19]

But what exactly is divine wrath? Is it a celestial temper tantrum? Is it unworthy of God? How does it fit with a proper sense of *digno Dei*?

---

[16] The problem of shame has been somewhat neglected in Western theology. For a stimulating discussion of its importance see Tennent 2007: 77–103. Tennent (92) helpfully points out, 'the term *guilt* and its various derivatives occur 145 times in the Old Testament and 10 times in the New Testament, whereas the term *shame* and its derivatives occur nearly 300 times in the Old Testament and 45 times in the New Testament'. He (80) also argues, 'Virtually every culture in the world contains concepts of both guilt and shame.' In my view, the failure to recognize this fact leads to the one-sided discussions of the atonement, as in Green and Baker 2000: 153–170. If Tennent is right, then there is guilt even in shame-based cultures such as Japan, which Green and Baker use as a test case.

[17] Many attempts have been made to turn the personal language of Scripture into a way of speaking of the impersonal outworking of a principle of cause and effect in the moral realm (the principle of reaping what you sow). C. H. Dodd (as we have seen), K. Koch and C. Sticher are representative. But, as Carson shows, the arguments do not work for every biblical instance (e.g. Isa. 10:5–19). He (2008: 42–45) concludes, 'In short, there is no exegetically responsible way to dissolve the personal nature of God's wrath throughout the canonical Scriptures.'

[18] Quoted from Dodd's commentary on Romans in Yarbrough 2001: 390. For an updated version of Dodd's position on wrath see Fiddes 1989: 91.

[19] Packer 1973: 170–171.

Wrath is not an essential attribute of God.[20] Rather, wrath is how divine holiness justly expresses itself against human sin.[21] The sin may be that of God's people:

> When the LORD heard them [Israel complaining in the wilderness], he was very angry;
>> his fire broke out against Jacob,
>> and his wrath rose against Israel.

(Ps. 78:21)

Or the sin may be that of individuals, even those of the stature of Moses, who refuse to conform to the divine will: 'Then the LORD's anger burned against Moses' (Exod. 4:14). Or the sin may be that of a nation, as in the case of Egypt:

>> I will pour out my wrath on Pelusium,
>> the stronghold of Egypt,
>> and cut off the hordes of Thebes.

(Ezek. 30:15)

These temporal expressions of wrath presage the final expression of wrath on the Day of Judgment, or what Paul described as 'the coming wrath' (1 Thess. 1:10; Rom. 2:5–11), which is where the accent of the New Testament lies.[22]

Divine wrath does have an affective dimension. The God of biblical revelation is a passionate God.[23] Indeed, the Jewish Publication Society's translation of the Hebrew Bible (as used by the JSB) goes

---

[20] On this point I part company with Packer, 'And wrath, the Bible tells us, is an attribute of God' (ibid. 134), and A. W. Pink, whom Packer quotes with approval, 'The wrath of God is a perfection of the divine character on which we need to meditate frequently' (142). Packer and Pink need a clearer distinction between divine attributes or perfections and their contingent expressions.

[21] For the substance of this section I am heavily indebted to Carson's very fine treatment (2008: 37–63). Also see Jeffery, Ovey and Sach 2007: 294–300; Stott 1996: 102–110.

[22] Contra the idea found in W. P. Young's novel *The Shack* (2007: 119–120). The 'female' character, Papa, who represents God the Father, rejects the notion of divine wrath and instead states, 'I don't need to punish people for sin. Sin is its own punishment, devouring you from the inside' (120). There is some biblical truth for the second claim. In Scripture, one way God punishes sin is by giving us up (*didōmi*, Rom. 1:24, 26, 28) to our folly. Young's first claim, however, simply does not square with the Old Testament idea of the Day of the Lord (Amos 5:18–24) and the New Testament one of the last judgment (Rev. 20:11–15).

[23] See Cole 2000.

as far as to translate Exodus 34:14 in those terms: 'for you must not worship any other god, because the Lord, whose name is Impassioned, is an impassioned God'. God is not affect challenged. However, divine wrath is no celestial temper tantrum, as if divine emotion can subvert divine character. With regard to this point, D. A. Carson draws a helpful comparison between love and falling in love, and losing one's temper.[24] Scripture does speak of God's love for us (most famously John 3:16), but not of God's falling in love with us. Scripture commands us to love God (e.g. Deut. 6:5). But nowhere does Scripture speak of our falling in love with God – notwithstanding all too many contemporary Christian love songs to Jesus. Scripture does speak of the divine anger (e.g. Nah. 1:6). However, nowhere does Scripture speak of God's losing his temper. Put another way, Yahweh does not behave like Saul, who, in a jealous rage, loses his temper and attempts to kill David (cf. 1 Sam. 19:9–10 and David's interpretation of the king's behaviour in 1 Sam. 20:5–8). Divine jealousy is of another order. As R. T. France argues:

> But there is a right jealousy, the jealousy of the husband whose love for his wife brooks no rival, who will have nothing less than the best for her, a jealousy free of suspicion and restrictive possessiveness, the inevitable result of an exclusive love. God loves his people like that, and will brook no rival to their allegiance . . . (Dt. 6:14,15).[25]

Nor is Yahweh like Xerxes, who, on learning of Haman's plot to exterminate the Jews and seeing Haman seemingly attempt to molest Esther his queen, in rage has Haman hanged on the very gallows the official had prepared for Mordecai the Jew (Esth. 7:1–10). Only then does his fury subside. In neither Saul's nor Xerxes' case was holiness expressing itself. Hence the need carefully to distinguish divine wrath from human wrath.

For a proper sense of proportion though, the biblical language of divine wrath must be viewed in the context of the revelation of the divine name to Moses in the theophany on Sinai: 'The LORD, the LORD, a God merciful and gracious, slow to anger, and abounding in steadfast love and faithfulness' (Exod. 34:6 ESV). The text does not

---

[24] Carson 2008: 48.
[25] France 1970: 64.

read, 'God is angry (wrathful), slow to be merciful and gracious.'[26] Instead, Yahweh is long suffering as his dealings with Israel show. As the psalmist says:

> For his anger lasts only a moment,
> but his favour lasts a lifetime.
>
> (Ps. 30:5)

Even so, as Hebrews argues, 'It is a dreadful thing to fall into the hands of the living God' (Heb. 10:31). Packer offers this wise pastoral counsel: 'If we would truly know God, and be known of Him, we should ask Him to teach us here and now to reckon with the solemn reality of His wrath.'[27]

Lastly, is wrath unworthy of God? Francis Young certainly thinks so. On her view, notions of propitiating or averting God's wrath are misreadings of the Scriptures, especially passages such as Romans 3:25 and Hebrews 2:17.[28] In fact, such notions are the intrusion of 'pagan ideas and explanations' that were 'imported into the interpretation of both Old and New Testaments' by early church figures. John Chrysostom and his *Homilies on Hebrews* is her chief example.[29] However, in contradistinction I would argue that wrath seems unworthy of God only if our own sense of sin has become so atrophied that we think that it is God's business to forgive it. W. R. Dale captured the human reluctance to ascribe wrath to God in these perceptive words: 'it is partly because sin does not provoke our own wrath, that we do not believe that sin provokes the wrath of God'.[30] Or put another way, as Abraham Joshua Heschel argues, 'Is it a sign of cruelty that God's anger is aroused when the rights of the poor are violated, when widows and orphans are oppressed?'[31] If we remove

---

[26] For a discussion of this key passage see Cole 2008. Fretheim (2004: 26) goes too far in suggesting that such a passage ought to constitute 'a canon within a canon' by which other biblical texts are to be judged. Even so, see his very stimulating essay on God and violence in the Old Testament.

[27] Packer 1973: 142.

[28] F. Young 1975: 72. In many ways she undermines her own argument when she writes, 'It is true that the Greek word used [in Rom. 3:25 and Heb. 2:17] is usually translated "propitiation", and in both cases the general context of the surrounding chapters is an emphasis on God's wrath, his judgment against sin; it is a fearful thing to fall into the hands of the living God, who is a consuming fire (Heb. 10.31; 12.29).' Precisely!

[29] Ibid. 72–73.

[30] W. R. Dale, quoted in Stott 1996: 109.

[31] Quoted in Fretheim 2004: 23.

the wrath theme from Scripture, its storyline is eviscerated. That cost is too high.

Divine wrath needs to be addressed. But how is it to be assuaged?

The problem of judgment

Sin invites judgment because our sin puts us in the wrong before a righteous God. God's role as judge is an expression of his righteous character (e.g. Ps. 50:1–6).[32] The God of biblical revelation is not to be confused with 'Blind Justice', represented by so many statues outside Western law courts. The God of Scripture loves righteousness and hates wickedness, as the psalmist says (Ps. 45:7). In contrast, the concept of blind justice is best seen in the blindfolded figure that holds a sword in one hand and scales in the other.[33] The idea here is that of administering justice without passion. However, as J. I. Packer rightly observes, 'The modern idea that a judge should be cold and dispassionate has no place in the Bible.'[34]

Theologian Miroslav Volf movingly expresses the need for divine judgment in our broken world. He addresses those in the West, especially theologians, who find the idea of God's judgment too violent:

> To the person inclined to dismiss it [divine judgment], I suggest imagining that you are delivering a lecture in a war zone (which is where a paper that underlines this chapter was originally delivered). Among your listeners are people whose cities and villages have been first plundered, then burned and leveled to the ground, whose daughters and sisters have been raped, whose fathers and brothers had their throats slit. The topic of the lecture: a Christian attitude towards violence. The thesis: we should not retaliate since God is perfect noncoercive love. Soon you would discover that it takes the quiet of a suburban home for the birth of the thesis that human

[32] Surprisingly, Motyer (2001: 614) maintains, 'In all its aspects judgment is an outshining of the divine holiness (Ps. 50:1–6).' However, as we have seen, the psalm thematizes righteousness. He is right though to see a close link between divine righteousness and holiness, as in Isa. 5:16. Forsyth (1909: 53) links judgment and holiness very strongly: 'Do not think of God's judgment as an arbitrary affliction, but as the necessary reaction to sin in a holy God.'

[33] Lady Justice or Blind Justice has its origins in the Greek goddess Themis. The addition of a blindfold has been a feature since the sixteenth century, but not in every case. E.g. the statue that adorns the Old Bailey in London lacks a blindfold. See 'Blind Justice, Lady Justice, Scales of Justice, or Themis Statues', accessed 17 July 2008.

[34] Packer 1973: 128.

nonviolence corresponds to God's refusal to judge. In a scorched land, soaked in the blood of the innocent, it will invariably die. And as one watches it die, one will do well to reflect about many other pleasant captivities of the liberal mind.[35]

Volf's words remind us that all theology is situated in a time and a space.[36] Volf wrote these words as a Croatian who experienced war in the former Yugoslavia.

As soon as sin appears in the biblical storyline so too does the moral accountability motif. At the beginning of the biblical story, the primal couple is expelled from the garden in Genesis and all stand before the great white throne at the end of the story (Gen. 3 and Rev. 20 respectively). However, it is only in the New Testament that the name of the judge is revealed. Peter preached to Cornelius: 'He [Jesus] commanded us to preach to the people and to testify that he is the one whom God appointed as judge of the living and the dead' (Acts 10:42; likewise Paul, Acts 17:31). S. H. Travis observes:

In modern times the image of the great assize has for many people lost the power which it held throughout much of the church's history. But it serves to safeguard important truths: judgment is serious, just, inescapable. It is judgment under the searching gaze of holy love, judgment by Christ himself.[37]

All the major concepts of justice with regard to wrongdoing are found in the biblical testimony. There is deterrence as in Deuteronomy 13:6–11. The penalty is death for any who encourages the worship of other gods in Israel. Thus 'all Israel will hear and be afraid, *and no one among you will do such an evil again*' (Deut. 13:11; my emphasis). There is also reformative justice as in 1 Timothy 1:18–20. At Ephesus some had rejected holding on to faith and a good conscience. Two are singled out: Hymenaeus and Alexander. Paul writes, 'whom I have

---

[35] Volf 1996: 304. I thank my friend Dr Gordon Preece for pointing this statement out to me.

[36] Recognizing that theology is situated does not lead necessarily to postmodern conclusions. Quite the reverse! The fact that we recognize our situatedness (the insight of postmodernity) shows that there is something in our anthropology that transcends situatedness. Whether it is an aspect of reason or imagination (my guess), human beings have the ability to establish a critical distance between themselves and their own beliefs and values that on occasion enables their reform.

[37] Travis 2001.

handed over to Satan *to be taught* not to blaspheme' (1 Tim. 1:20; my emphasis). As well there is restorative justice as in the case of Zacchaeus the tax collector (Luke 19:1–10). Jesus calls him to discipleship. In response, he promises, 'Look, Lord! Here and now I give half my possessions to the poor, and *if I have cheated anybody out of anything, I will pay back four times the amount*' (Luke 19:8; my emphasis).

Lastly, there is retributive justice. The essence of retributive justice is getting what one deserves.[38] That God will render to every person according to their works is accented in both the Old Testament and the New. Judgment is according to works.[39] In the Old Testament, for example, wisdom asks, 'Does not he [Yahweh] who guards your life know it? Will he not repay each person according to what he has done?' (Prov. 24:12). The New Testament is even more insistent. Writing of the coming Day of Judgment, Paul affirms that God 'will give to each person according to what he has done' (Rom. 2:6).[40] The terrifying last judgment scene in Revelation strikes the same sobering note:

> Then I saw a great white throne and him who was seated on it. Earth and sky fled from his presence, and there was no place for them. And I saw the dead, great and small, standing before the throne, and books were opened. Another book was opened, which is the book of life. *The dead were judged according to what they had done as recorded in the books.* The sea gave up the dead that were in it, and death and Hades gave up the

---

[38] It is important to note that deterrence, reformative justice, restorative justice and retributive justice are not mutually exclusive. For a recent secular attempt to show how restorative justice can be integrated with retributive justice, reformative justice and deterrence see Roach 2000: *passim*. Roach contends that restorative justice is a partial theory and 'must be reconciled with retributive theories of justice'. From a theological perspective Blocher (2008: 140) wisely argues, 'Retribution and restoration are not mutually exclusive; the good news is the retribution, and the basis of restoration is in the person [Jesus] of the head and substitute.'

[39] Travis (2001) writes, 'Judgment will be "according to works" (Mt. 16:27; Rom. 2:6; Rev. 22:12). This does not conflict with justification by grace through faith. Although justification is a gift of God's free grace, it involves the obligation to work out our new status in practice. Thus, at the final judgment, a person's works will be the evidence of whether a living faith is present in him or not. It is not a question of earning salvation by good works: works are the evidence of the reality of the faith through which we are saved.'

[40] Green and Baker (2000: 54) take a contrary view. They argue with regard to Paul's theology that 'divine anger or retributive justice are alien concepts [to Paul]'. How this squares with Rom. 2:6 is not explained, and significantly this is one verse from Romans that is not treated by them, even though they cite Rom. 2:5 and 2:8.

dead that were in them, and each person was judged according to what he had done. Then death and Hades were thrown into the lake of fire. The lake of fire is the second death. If anyone's name was not found written in the book of life, he was thrown into the lake of fire. (Rev. 20:11–15; my emphasis)

With regard to the witness of Scripture, J. I. Packer rightly maintains, 'It shows us also that the heart of the justice which expresses God's nature is *retribution*, the rendering to men what they have deserved; for this is the essence of the judge's task.'[41] A universe without final retribution, even a hell, would be a morally indifferent one.[42] Given the horrendous nature of some of humanity's crimes against itself – one thinks of the Holocaust – such a universe would be a cause for despair. The 'How long, O LORD?' question of the oppressed and persecuted would find no answer (Ps. 13:1; cf. Rev. 6:9–11).

How then may we face the great white throne?

The problem of the human other

Sin brings strife because it spoils relationships between us. The classic example in the Old Testament is the primeval story of fratricide. Indeed, the first sin recounted after the expulsion from Eden is an interpersonal one. Cain slays his brother Abel (Gen. 4:1–5). Cain was enraged by the regard that Abel received from God because of his sacrifice ('fat portions from some of the firstborn of his flock') as opposed to that of his own ('some of the fruits of the soil').[43] As the biblical storyline unfolds, the primeval strife reaches a climax in the time of Noah. The Creator looks upon a world filled with 'wickedness', corruption' and 'violence' (Gen. 6: 5, 11–12). Grieved to his

---

[41] Packer 1973: 129; original emphasis. Packer has consistently maintained this conviction concerning retribution. For a recent affirmation see Packer and Dever (2007: 23), 'Both Testaments, then, confirm that judicial retribution from God awaits all whose sins are not covered by a substitutionary sacrifice: in the Old Testament, the sacrifice of an animal; in the New Testament, the sacrifice of Christ.'

[42] E. T. Oakes (in Pitstick and Oakes 2006: 30) says, 'When one of Ludwig Wittgenstein's graduate students allowed how much he regretted the Church's condemnation of Origen's doctrine that God would eventually abolish hell and redeem the whole world (including the devils), the philosopher shot back: "Of course it was rejected. It would make nonsense of everything else. If what we do now is to make no difference in the end, then all the seriousness of life is done away with."'

[43] The reference to 'fat portions' suggests that Abel offered the very best he had to God, whereas the text is silent concerning the quality of Cain's offering. See Wenham 2004, comment on Gen. 4:5.

heart God paradoxically uses the violence of divine judgment as it were to end the interpersonal violence through a mighty flood, preserving only Noah and his family (Gen. 6:6, 13).[44]

In the New Testament the classic example is that of the divide between Jew and Gentile described in various places in the New Testament. Think of Peter's problem in Acts 10 with visiting Cornelius' house. Peter has a vision of an opened heaven. A large sheet is let down containing, as far as the Torah is concerned, all sorts of unclean animals (Acts 10:11–12). He is instructed to kill and eat them but replies, 'Surely not, Lord! I have never eaten anything impure or unclean' (v. 14).The voice from heaven rebukes him: 'Do not call anything impure that God has made clean' (v. 15). This happens three times before the sheet is returned to heaven. He is puzzled as to the meaning of the vision. At this point emissaries from the Gentile Cornelius arrive on the scene. To cut the story short, at the behest of the Spirit he travels to Caesarea and enters the centurion's house (Acts 10:19–25). His words to those gathered in the house are illuminating: 'You are well aware that it is against our law for a Jew to associate with a Gentile or visit him. But God has shown me that I should not call any man impure or unclean. So when I was sent for, I came without raising any objection' (Acts 10:28–29).[45] The vision had done its work and Peter preaches the gospel to the Gentile world.[46] As Ajith Fernando rightly observes, 'A big shift has taken place in Peter's thinking, for he now realizes that no longer are the typical Jewish distinctions among people significant. They have been rendered void once and for all.'[47]

---

[44] Helmut Thielicke interestingly suggests that in a fallen world God uses 'a kind of higher homeopathy' by which violence is used to negate violence. Gen. 9:6 is his (1979: 570) example: 'Whoever sheds the blood of man, / by man shall his blood be shed; / for in the image of God / has God made man.' Boersma (2004: 37, n. 46) also recognizes that 'God's entry in restricted and inhospitable surroundings [the Old Testament world after the fall] required the use of violence.' I shall return to these ideas when I consider the issue of violence and the atonement in the appendix. On the matter of divine grief see Cole 2000: 16–27.

[45] Keener (2001a) says, 'Although many stories tell of Jewish teachers talking with Gentiles, strict Jews would not enter a Gentile's house or allow a Gentile in theirs. Thus Peter faces a problem in being invited to Cornelius's house. Although more lax Jews would probably not object (v. 23a), Peter has to be concerned about stricter elements within the Jewish church, which eventually included even Pharisees (15:5)' (comment on Acts 10:22).

[46] Israel was called in the Old Testament to be a distinct people ('my treasured possession', Exod. 19:5), but not a people disconnected from the nations ('my witnesses', Isa. 44:8). See C. J. H. Wright 2006. Peter had confused distinction with disconnection.

[47] Fernando 1996: 322.

Once back in Jerusalem, Peter had to explain himself: 'So when Peter went up to Jerusalem, the circumcised believers criticized him and said, "You went into the house of uncircumcised men and ate with them"' (Acts 11:2–3). Peter's story with regard to the Gentiles does not end there though, for Paul had occasion to rebuke Peter:

> When Peter came to Antioch, I opposed him to his face, because he was clearly in the wrong. Before certain men came from James, he used to eat with the Gentiles. But when they arrived, he began to draw back and separate himself from the Gentiles because he was afraid of those who belonged to the circumcision group. (Gal. 2:11–12)

These stories illustrate the barrier between Jew and Gentile, or what Paul in Ephesians describes as 'the dividing wall of hostility' (Eph. 2:14). The dividing wall of hostility is not restricted as phenomenon to Jew–Gentile relations, although those relations have a particular theological freighting.[48] One thinks of the recent history of Northern Ireland and Protestant–Catholic relations.

The dividing wall constituted by interpersonal hostility needs to be broken down, but how?

The problem of the god of this world

Sin brings bondage because the devil exploits it as the slanderer and uses it against humanity as an instrument of fear and oppression. The problem posed by the prince of this world – to use Johannine language – is not obvious from the Old Testament. For example, the serpent of Genesis 3 is nowhere in the Old Testament text identified with the Satan of Job 1 – 2.[49] However, once the incarnate Son

[48] According to A. T. Lincoln, there are two main possibilities as to what the writer was referring to. He could be drawing upon the architecture of the temple, with its balustrade separating Jew and Gentile. More likely though, it is a reference to the Torah. Lincoln 2004, comment on Eph. 2:14. It is important to note that I am more confident than Lincoln is that the writer was Paul.

[49] Whybray (2000: 44) comments on Gen. 3:1, 'The serpent (3:1) is neither a supernatural enemy threatening God's creation from outside nor some kind of inner voice within the woman urging her to disobedience. It is specifically stated that it is one of God's creatures.' Whybray's evidence for his assertions about the serpent that the serpent is 'one of God's creatures' does not establish his point. His claim fails to recognize the *tota scriptura* and the biblical presentation of Satan as a creature gone wrong. Indeed, in the light of the *tota scriptura*, the linkage between Gen. 3:1, Job 1 – 2 and Rev. 12 becomes irresistible.

walks the earth the prince of darkness comes into prominence in attacking the light (Matt. 4:1–11). In his parable of the weeds Jesus speaks of a landowner who sows good seed in his field (Matt. 13:14–30). But while everyone sleeps an enemy sows weeds among the wheat. The servants raise two questions: 'Sir, didn't you sow good seed in your field? Where then did the weeds come from?' (Matt. 13:27). The landowner responds, 'An enemy [*echthros*] did this' (v. 28). Jesus' point is that the kingdom of heaven is opposed and that the resolution of the conflict is eschatological. A day is coming when weeds and wheat will be definitively sorted. Jesus in his interpretation of the parable identifies the enemy as the devil (vv. 38–39).

Paul likewise saw opposition to the will and to the people of God as emanating from the devil. The dominion of darkness stands opposed to the kingdom of the Son (Col. 1:13). For example, Paul, in his celebrated passage about the armour of God, recognizes the problem the god of this world poses. The apostle writes:

> Finally, be strong in the Lord and in his mighty power. Put on the full armour of God so that you can take your stand against *the devil's schemes*. For our struggle is not against flesh and blood, but against *the rulers, against the authorities, against the powers of this dark world and against the spiritual forces of evil in the heavenly realms*. Therefore put on the full armour of God, so that when the day of evil comes, you may be able to stand your ground, and after you have done everything, to stand. (Eph. 6:10–13; my emphases)

This is no cartoon fight contemplated by Paul, but a genuine struggle requiring nothing less than the spiritual equivalent of the best military outfitting (that of the Roman soldier) of his day.[50]

According to Hebrews, the devil 'holds the power of death' (Heb. 2:14). Humanity is held in thrall through its fear of death. Comedian Woody Allen opined, 'It's not that I am afraid to die, I just don't want to be there when it happens.'[51] In 2 Corinthians alone, Paul

---

[50] We shall return to this important passage in a subsequent chapter when we explore how the Christian is to live between the time of the cross and the return of Christ.

[51] Allen 1976.

describes 'the god of the age' as the blinder of the minds of unbelievers lest they believe the gospel (2 Cor. 4:4), as the serpent seducer of Eve (2 Cor. 11:3) and as a masquerader posing as 'an angel of light' working through 'false apostles' (2 Cor. 11:13–14). Clearly, to the apostle to the Gentiles Satan is no abstract impersonal force of evil (the 'dark side of the Force' as in the film *Star Wars*), nor the product of mistaken mythology, but evil's all too personal face.[52] The apostle Peter sees no subtlety in the devil, whom he characterizes as, 'Your enemy the devil prowls around like a roaring lion looking for someone to devour' (1 Pet. 5:8).

By the end of the biblical story the identification of the serpent of Genesis 3 with Satan or the devil is clearly made (Rev. 20:1–2). The question arises, however, as to how the evil one is to be defeated.[53]

The problem of the groaning creation

Sin brings cosmic bondage because it distorts God's good creation. The Scriptures are not Manichean, as though spirit is good but matter is evil. Rather, the Creator has never abandoned his concern for creation. The *locus classicus* for this notion is found in Romans 8:18–22. Paul writes:

> I consider that our present sufferings are not worth comparing with the glory that will be revealed in us. The creation waits in eager expectation for the sons of God to be revealed. For the creation was subjected to frustration [*mataiotēti*], not by its own choice, but by the will of the one who subjected it, in hope that the creation itself will be liberated from its bondage to decay [*tēs douleias tēs phthoras*] and brought into the glorious freedom [*tēn eleutherian*] of the children of God.
>
> We know that the whole creation has been groaning as in the pains of childbirth right up to the present time.

---

[52] Contra liberal Protestantism, which, according to Harvey (1997: 216), abandoned the concept of a personal Satan 'as a relic of a prescientific mentality'. For an example see H. Berkhof 1979: 201. He argues that Satan is 'a picture' that 'expresses the relentless force of evil'.

[53] When we consider this problem in a later chapter, we will also see how seriously early Christianity took this problem in propounding the *Christus victor* understanding of Christ and his cross.

The key phrases and terms are 'subjected to frustration', 'bondage to decay', 'glorious freedom' and 'groaning'. J. D. G. Dunn argues that Paul sees a nexus between the fall of humanity and the present condition of creation (cf. Rom. 1:21 and 8:20). He comments, 'The reason why the created order awaits so longingly man's redemption is because creation itself is caught up in man's fallen state.'[54] The consequences are unhappy, to put it mildly: 'There is an out-of-sortness, a disjointedness about the created order which makes it a suitable habitation for man at odds with his creator.'[55] The creation needs liberation. It needs freedom from its frustration and decay.

How is creation to be set free?

Conclusion

There is then a great need for peace: peace with God, peace with one another and peace for the created order. Sin has created the problem. With regard to ourselves, many years ago J. S. Whale wrote:

> That man needs to be reconciled to Something; that there is a tragic disharmony in the human situation which cries to Heaven itself for adjustment – this is a conviction to which the literature of the world bears witness. Oedipus and King Lear are haunted by the same shadow. If you could take this away from Aeschylus, Dante or Goethe, there is little left but meaningless fragments. Take this away from the Bible, and there is nothing left.[56]

D. A. Carson argues similarly, 'In sum, we find ourselves fighting the Bible's entire story line if we do not recognize that our deepest need is to be reconciled to God (cf. 2 Cor. 5:11–21).'[57]

But this need for reconciliation creates four questions: (1) How can a righteous God of holy love win men and women away from their love of self to the love of God? (2) How can God forgive sinners without condoning their sin or denying his own implacable opposition as a holy God to it? (3) How can God set men and women free from their bondage to sin and evil? Finally, (4) how can the Creator

---

[54] Dunn 2004a, comment on Rom. 8:18–30.
[55] Ibid.
[56] Whale 1957: 71.
[57] Carson 2008: 56.

reclaim creation from its bondage to decay so that it too may enjoy peace?[58] Addressing these questions is our next task and as we do we will find merit in D. A. Carson's contention 'If that reconciliation turns, in substantial measure, on the setting aside of God's deserved wrath, we have arrived unavoidably at sacrifice, expiation, propitiation – in short, at penal substitution.'[59] These terms will indeed feature prominently in subsequent discussion, especially chapter 6.

---

[58] I have adapted these four questions from those raised by Marshall (1966: 80).
[59] Carson 2008: 56.

Chapter Four

Foundations and foreshadowings

The maker of heaven and earth has a project. By means of this project God will address the multifaceted problem posed by sin and its entailments. The project's goal is nothing less than the reclamation of creation, and the centrepiece of the project, as we shall see in the next two chapters, is the person and work of Christ, the Son, Saviour of the World. Realizing the goal requires that the various barriers constituted by sin and resulting from sin need to be removed. Importantly, this is a project grounded in God's own nature and its centrepiece has its backstory in God's dealings with Israel. It is vital to remember that in the Old Testament, although Israel is God's special concern, the whole of creation is ultimately in mind as Isaiah 65 – 66 shows.

To understand the atonement we first need to consider how atonement is grounded upon the loving nature of the triune God, and then how in the canonical presentation post-fall it is founded upon the promise of the Genesis 3:15 *protoevangelium* that the serpent will be defeated. We shall next need to explore the promises made to Abram that provide the framework for the project. After that we explore just how the story of Israel, which stems from the call of Abram, provides the crucial backstory and beginning superstructure for what was to occur through the coming, cross and victory of Jesus Christ, the prince of peace. He is the capstone of the building and instantiates the divine purpose. Both Israel's sacrificial system and its hope embodied in the Isaianic figure of the suffering servant ultimately point to him, as do the *protoevangelium* and the Abrahamic promises.

Foundations in the love of the triune God

We start this section of our study by reminding ourselves of the Christian doctrine of God, beginning with the Old Testament witness to God's oneness, then the Trinity and the concept of appropriations especially as applied to the atonement. Lastly, we consider the loving motivation of the triune God in providing atonement.

The Old Testament Scripture is adamant: there is only one God. This was Israel's creed, her 'central confession'.[1] So important in fact that Israel's children need to be taught this theology. Importantly, what a culture teaches its young is the true index of what it values. Deuteronomy says:

> Hear, O Israel: The LORD our God, the LORD is one. Love the LORD your God with all your heart and with all your soul and with all your strength. These commandments that I give you today are to be upon your hearts. Impress them on your children. Talk about them when you sit at home and when you walk along the road, when you lie down and when you get up. Tie them as symbols on your hands and bind them on your foreheads. Write them on the door-frames of your houses and on your gates. (Deut. 6:4–9)

God has revealed his very nature to Israel as the one God.[2] According to Jewish philosopher-theologian Abraham Joshua Heschel, this claim of oneness ('*eḥād*) asserts that the Lord is one and unique, and that he is without rival.[3] He only is God. No idol is his competitor. This passage of the Torah, specifically Deuteronomy 6:4, remains central to the various forms of observant Judaism to this today. As Bernard M. Levinson says of the Shema, 'During the late second temple period, this prayer rose to prominence both in the synagogue liturgy and in individual piety, a position it still maintains.'[4]Even so, it took many centuries for Israel to learn the hard lesson that idolatry is folly and that to love the Lord your God, as Deuteronomy insists, is to be loyal only to him and to no other claimant to deity.[5]

With the coming of Jesus, God's people now had to reckon with the need to nuance the divine name. The one God is now to be understood as Father, Son and Holy Spirit. Jesus both reaffirmed the Shema (e.g. Matt. 19:17 and Mark 12:28–32) and expanded our understanding of it. For example, the risen Christ commands

---

[1] Bultmann 2000: 142.

[2] The Hebrew allows several translation possibilities, as the mg. of the NIV shows: 'The LORD our God is one LORD'; 'The LORD is our God, the LORD is one'; 'The LORD is our God, the LORD alone.'

[3] Heschel 1951: 114–118.

[4] Levinson 2003: 379. In line with much of the literature, when referring to this verse I have not transliterated 'Shema'.

[5] Love as loyalty in Deuteronomy (e.g. Deut. 6:5) is finely explained by Kugel (2007: 353–355).

disciples to baptize in the name of Father, Son and Holy Spirit. Matthew's Gospel climaxes famously with the Great Commission:

> Then the eleven disciples went to Galilee, to the mountain where Jesus had told them to go. When they saw him, they worshipped him; but some doubted. Then Jesus came to them and said, 'All authority in heaven and on earth has been given to me. Therefore go and make disciples of all nations, baptiz-ing *them in the name of the Father and of the Son and of the Holy Spirit*, and teaching them to obey everything I have commanded you. And surely I am with you always, to the very end of the age.' (Matt. 28:16–20; my emphasis)[6]

Although Jesus speaks as a greater than Moses as he commissions his disciples to make disciples, he in no way repudiates the funda-mentals of the Old Testament presentation of God.[7] What is striking though is that now there is a complexity to the oneness that his coming has revealed. The name of God is singular (*to onoma*), but there is personal differentiation within the Godhead. To come to grips with this complexity was the subject of much early church dis-cussion and debate. Indeed, a new term, *trinitas*, was needed to do justice to it.[8]

This same complexity – unity in diversity – is in the Paulines. The Corinthian correspondence, for example, is instructive. 1 Corinthians 8 deals with the pastoral problem of food offered to idols. Paul reaffirms the Shema: 'We know that an idol is nothing at all in the world and that there is no God but one' (1 Cor. 8:4).[9] Even so Christian freedom is not to be abused at the cost of a fellow believer with a weak conscience who wrongly believes that idols are some-thing rather than nothing (1 Cor. 8:9–13). However, this affirmation of the oneness in 1 Corinthians does not conflict with the affirmation of the threeness, as can be seen in the famous passage about the gifting of the body of Christ in 1 Corinthians 12:4–6, 'There are

---

[6] For a helpful survey on the Great Commission in the various New Testament texts see Plummer 2005: 4–11. For the history of the phrase 'The Great Commission' see D. F. Wright 2007: 132–157. Hunsberger (1994: 135) prefers 'evangelizing warrant' to 'commission' language.

[7] The Mosaic typology at work informing Matt. 28 is well brought out by D. C. Allison (2000: 885).

[8] According to Kelly (1977: 113), Tertullian (c. 160–225) was the first to use *trinitas*.

[9] The debt to the Shema in 1 Cor. 8:6 is finely discussed by Barclay (2000: 1121).

different kinds of gifts, but the same Spirit. There are different kinds of service, but the same Lord. There are different kinds of working, but the same God works all of them in all men.' Nor does it conflict with the still widely used benediction of 2 Corinthians 13:14, 'May the grace of the Lord Jesus Christ, and the love of God, and the fellowship of the Holy Spirit be with you all.'

After Christ's first coming, to talk of the will of God is to speak of the undivided will of the holy Trinity. As Augustine taught, *omnia opera trinitatis ad extra indivisa sunt* (all the works of the Trinity to the outside are undivided).[10] 'Undivided' does not mean 'indistinguishable'. Father, Son and Holy Spirit are involved in all acts of God, whether creation, revelation or redemption, but not in the same way. Traditionally, the doctrine of appropriation has been deployed to explicate more precisely the roles of Father, Son and Holy Spirit in relation to creation, redemption and atonement. Alister McGrath explains the term 'appropriation' in the following useful way: 'A term relating to the doctrine of the Trinity, which affirms that while all three persons of the Trinity are active in all the outward actions of the Trinity, it is appropriate to think of those actions as being the particular work of one of the persons.'[11] In this view, it is appropriate to ascribe to one or other person of the Trinity the prominent role in a particular divine activity. Thus the Father is the chief figure in the story of creation, as in the first article of the Nicene Creed: 'We believe in one God, the Father, the Almighty, maker of heaven and earth, of all that is, seen and unseen.'[12] The Son is the key figure in the story of redemption, as in the second article of the same creed: 'We believe in one Lord, Jesus Christ . . . For us and for our salvation he came down from heaven.'[13] Finally, the Holy Spirit is the main player in the story of sanctification, as in the third article of this creed: 'We believe in the Holy spirit, the Lord, the giver of life.'[14]

With regard to the story of the atonement some theologians have developed this approach further, especially in the Reformed tradition.[15] Briefly put, the Father is viewed as the architect of the atonement. The Son is seen as the accomplisher of atonement. The Holy

---

[10] Augustine 2005: 2.1.4; 5.3.

[11] McGrath 2007a: 487.

[12] *A Prayer Book for Australia* 1999: 123.

[13] Ibid.

[14] Ibid.

[15] E.g. L. Berkhof (1969: 266), 'Now we find that in the economy of redemption there is, in a sense, a division of labor: the Father is the originator, the Son the executor, and the Holy Spirit the applier.'

Spirit is regarded as the applier of the atonement. The Gospel of John provides exegetical footing for this approach.[16] According to John 5:36, it is the Father who sends ('the Father who sent me', *apestalken*). Jesus is thus the agent of the Father's will: 'For I have come down from heaven not to do my will but to do the will of him who sent me' (John 6:38). He has been given a work to accomplish by the Father. Jesus prays to the Father, 'I have brought you glory [*edoxaso*, aorist aspect] on earth by completing [*teleiōsas*, perfect aspect] the work [*to ergon*] you gave me to do' (John 17:4). The pinnacle of that work is the cross, the place of his glorification. The Father and the Son send the Spirit, who is the agent of new birth, leads disciples into the truth about Jesus, and convicts the world of guilt, sin, righteousness and judgment (cf. John 14:26; 15:26; 3:5–8; 16:7–11).

The Fourth Gospel is clear as to the divine motivation that impelled the work Jesus was sent to do as 'the Lamb of God, who takes away the sin of the world' (John 1:29). Why then has the triune God provided the atonement? Is it for his glory? Is it for his praise? Is it to display divine wisdom? All these ideas may be supported biblically (e.g. in Eph. 1:3–14, with regard to praise and glory, esp. v. 14; and 3:1–10 for wisdom). John's Gospel, however, tells its readers of another motivation for the project in probably the Bible's most famous verse. This motivation springs from who God is in himself. We read, 'For God so loved [*ēgapēsen*] the world that he gave [*edōken*] his one and only [*monogenē*, 'unique'] Son, that whoever believes in him shall not perish but have eternal life' (John 3:16). John Murray wisely comments in relation to this verse, 'Any doctrine of the atonement is misdirected from the outset if it does not take account of the fact that the atonement is the provision of God's love.'[17] Donald Guthrie adds to our understanding of the depths to John 3:16 by helpfully drawing out three significant aspects of this Johannine claim: 'The statement in v 16 concisely expresses three truths – the universal character of God's love, its sacrificial nature and its eternal purpose. It is no wonder it has been described as "the gospel in a nutshell".'[18] In his tractate 110 on John's Gospel, Augustine adds an important observation:

---

[16] The schema finds support in the Paulines too. E.g. in Galatians the Father sends the Son (Gal. 4:4), the Son redeems (Gal. 4:5) and the Spirit enables the prayer of the adoptees (Gal. 4:6).

[17] J. Murray 1976: 9.

[18] Guthrie 2001, comment on John 3:16. Kieffer (2000: 966) similarly describes the verse as the 'gospel in miniature'.

The love, therefore, wherewith God loves, is incomprehensible and immutable. For it was not from the time that we were reconciled unto Him by the blood of His Son that He began to love us; but He did so before the foundation of the world, that we also might be His sons along with His Only-begotten, before as yet we had any existence of our own. Let not the fact, then, of our having been reconciled unto God through the death of His Son be so listened to or so understood, as if the Son reconciled us to Him in this respect, that He now began to love those whom He formerly loved, in the same way as enemy is reconciled to enemy, so that thereafter they become friends, and mutual love takes the place of their mutual hatred; but we were reconciled unto Him who already loved us, but with whom we were at enmity because of our sin.[19]

The loving provision of the atonement is not reluctantly wrung out of a hostile deity by the cross.

Why the roles are as the doctrine of appropriation suggests has led to a number of theories. For example, Aquinas thought that anyone of the Godhead could have become incarnate: 'Had it been the will of God (the undivided will of God in Trinity), the Father or the Holy Ghost might have become incarnate.'[20] However, since the Son is the agent of this creation, 'it is most fitting' that the Son became the incarnate one with the task of repairing creation. Like many in the Reformed tradition, B. B. Warfield suggests that behind the plan of salvation stands a covenant of redemption.[21] Persons of the Trinity in this covenant voluntarily assume one of the roles. Still others insist that only the Son could be the incarnate one because, as there is a certain order of authority in the Godhead that is observed in divine activity, only the Son could be the sent one. Bruce Ware is a proponent of this view.[22] Adjudicating between these theories, however, would take us well beyond the scope of this work.

In sum, Thomas F. Torrance is entirely right to maintain, 'Thus we cannot but think of the atonement as a threefold act grounded in and issuing from the triune being of God.'[23] We shall return to the

[19] Augustine 2007: tractate 110.6.
[20] Aquinas 1963: 315.
[21] Warfield 1968: 54–55.
[22] B. A. Ware 2005: 81–82.
[23] Torrance 1992: 113.

need to understanding the atonement in trinitarian perspective when we come to consider the death of Christ in particular.

The foundational promise: the *protoevangelium*

With regard to the unfolding story of the divine project as canonically presented, post the fall the foundation of atonement lies in the *protoevangelium* of Genesis 3:15. The promise is found among the judgments of the Creator pronounced upon the serpent, the woman and the man in the immediate post-fall context (Gen. 3:14–19). The serpent is addressed as follows:

> So the LORD God said to the serpent, 'Because you have done this,
>
> > 'Cursed are you above all the livestock
> > and all the wild animals!
> > You will crawl on your belly
> > and you will eat dust
> > all the days of your life.
> > *And I will put enmity*
> > *between you and the woman,*
> > *and between your offspring and hers;*
> > *he will crush your head,*
> > *and you will strike his heel.'*
> >   (Gen. 3:14–15; my emphasis)

The word of blessing in the creation story is now counterbalanced by the words of cursing post-fall (cf. Gen. 1:22, 28; 2:3, 14, 17). More specifically, Gordon J. Wenham suggests that the reference to the serpent's eating dust is freighted with significance: '"Eat dust." This is not to say that snakes live on dust, rather it is figurative for abject humiliation, especially of enemies (cf. Ps 72:9; Isa 49:23; Mic 7:17).'[24] Moreover, with regard to Genesis 3:15 he argues, '"Hostility" ['enmity', NIV]: Both this context and other passages suggest that long-lasting enmity is meant (cf. Num 35:21–22; Ezek 25:15; 35:5).'[25] In biblical perspective the resolution of the conflict will not be coming quickly.

---

[24] Wenham 2004, comment on Gen. 3:14.
[25] Ibid., comment on Gen. 3:15.

How the serpent's fortunes are to be reversed is not revealed in any depth in Genesis 3.[26] A male descendant of the woman will be involved. That is clear. Suffering will be involved for both the male offspring and the serpent:

> he will crush your head,
> and you will strike his heel.
>
> (Gen. 3:15)

That too is clear. The serpent will lose definitively, a crushed head versus a struck heel. Both Jewish translators and early Christian commentators saw in the progeny of the woman a messianic hope.[27] To anticipate discussion to come, Paul writes to the Romans, 'The God of peace will soon crush Satan under your feet' (Rom. 16:20). The apostle thus links 'peace' (shalom) with the outworking of the *protoevangelium*.[28]

In sum, without some understanding of the *protoevangelium* the canon of Scripture loses its narrative coherence. Indeed, according to James Hamilton in his study both of Genesis 3:15 and of its resonances throughout the rest of Scripture, 'from the moment God uttered his judgment against the serpent, *the* seed of the woman (the collective of those who trust God) were hoping for the seed of the woman (the man who would achieve the ultimate victory over the serpent)'.[29]

---

[26] It is highly unlikely that there is an anticipation of the atonement in the provision of clothing for Adam and Eve, on the grounds that some animal must have shed its blood to provide the skins (Gen. 3:21). Wenham (2004) says, 'In this context [Gen. 3:21] God's provision of clothes appears not so much an act of grace, as often asserted, but as a reminder of their sinfulness (cf. Calvin 1:182)' (comment on Gen. 3:21). For a more positive interpretation of the provision of clothing see Bartholomew and Goheen 2005: 44.

[27] According to Dumbrell (2001b: 27–28), 'Such [interpretation], in fact, is found in the Septuagint, a very early witness to a traditional interpretation, where the neuter noun seed of verse 15 is treated syntactically as masculine to refer to the messiah. In the Palestinian Targums, Aramaic translations of the Hebrew noun *'āqēb* (heel, end) leads to a messianic understanding. The verse is taken to mean that the serpent and his descendents will bite the women's descendants on the "heel" but also that there will be a remedy at the "end," in the day of the messiah. (There is no evidence in rabbinic sources of a messianic interpretation.) According to Irenaeus and the early church fathers, the woman's seed refers to humankind generally and then to Christ specifically.'

[28] See the discussion by Seifrid (2007: 692).

[29] Hamilton 2006: 43; original emphasis. Gunton (in Webster and Schner 2000: 116) argues that the act of creation itself was a victory over 'the darkness and chaos'. I find his argument unconvincing.

The Abrahamic framework

For our purposes, the call of Abraham is the next crucial event in the unfolding project of reclamation. In the call and promises made to him we find that greater specificity is developing about who the male offspring will be. He will be someone descended from Abram. For it is through Abram that God will bless his world. In contrast to the Tower of Babel story, where rebellious humanity attempted to make a great name for itself, in Genesis 12:1–3 we read how God himself will make Abram's name great:

> The LORD had said to Abram, 'Leave your country, your people and your father's household and go to the land I will show you.

> > 'I will make you into a great nation
> >   and I will bless you;
> > I will make your name great,
> >   and you will be a blessing.
> > I will bless those who bless you,
> >   and whoever curses you I will curse;
> > and all peoples on earth
> >   will be blessed through you.'

Christopher J. H. Wright rightly describes Genesis 12:1–3 as 'a pivotal text'.[30] In this foundational passage the fivefold cursing found in Genesis 3 – 11 (Gen. 3:14, 17; 4:11; 5:29; 9:25) is counter-balanced by the fivefold blessing in the promises. According to Craig G. Bartholomew and Michael W. Goheen, 'Genesis 12:1–3 declares that through Abraham, God is at work to reverse the effect of judgment on his creation.'[31] Indeed, as they rightly say, 'Abraham is to be the medium of divine restoration for the whole world.'[32]

Christopher J. H. Wright argues that in the light of Genesis 3:15,

---

[30] C. J. H. Wright 2006: 194.

[31] Bartholomew and Goheen 2005: 55.

[32] Ibid. They quote Wenham to good effect: 'The promises to Abraham renew the vision for humanity set out in Genesis 1 and 2. He, like, Noah before him, is a second Adam figure. Adam was given the garden of Eden: Abraham is promised the land of Canaan. God told Adam to be fruitful and multiply: Abraham is promised descendants as numerous as the stars in heaven. God walked with Adam in Eden: Abraham was told to walk before God. In this way the advent of Abraham is seen as the answer to the problems set out in Genesis 1–11: through him all the families of the earth will be blessed.'

'Attentive readers will have been wondering who this serpent crusher will be. From Genesis 12:1–3 onward we know it will be one of the seed of Abraham. A son of Abraham will be a blessing for the sons of Adam.'[33] The *protoevangelium* and the Abrahamic promises are programmatic and without an understanding of both, the Bible's grand narrative remains unlocked.

Foreshadowings: the backstory of God and Israel

I am using the metaphor of 'backstory' drawn from the world of screenwriting to suggest that one cannot really understand what God has done in Christ without another story informing it. That story is Israel's. Abraham's children did indeed multiply as God had promised. But, instead of life in the land of promise, the Israelites found themselves in the Egyptian house of bondage. But God! God did not forget his promises. He honoured his covenant, redeemed Israel from bondage and brought them to himself at Sinai. Israel was given a startling identity and task:

> Then Moses went up to God, and the LORD called to him from the mountain and said, 'This is what you are to say to the house of Jacob and what you are to tell the people of Israel: "You yourselves have seen what I did to Egypt, and how I carried you on eagles' wings and brought you to myself. Now if you obey me fully and keep my covenant, then out of all nations you will be *my treasured possession*. Although the whole earth is mine, you will be for me *a kingdom of priests and a holy nation*." These are the words you are to speak to the Israelites.' So Moses went back and summoned the elders of the people and set before them all the words the LORD had commanded him to speak. (Exod. 19:3–7; my emphases)

This people is to be unique, 'a display-people, a showcase to the world of how being in covenant with Yahweh changes a people nation'.[34] Distinct from the wider world as 'God's treasured

---

[33] C. J. H. Wright 2006: 212.

[34] Durham 2004, comment on Exod. 19:6. Torrance (1992: 7) says, 'In his desire to reveal himself and make himself known to mankind, he selected one small race out of the whole mass of humanity, and subjected it to intensive interaction and dialogue with himself in such a way that he might mould and shape this people in the service of his self-revelation.'

possession', but not disconnected as 'a kingdom of priests'. In the latter expression a task is implied. The Israelites' response shows that they understand the implication: 'The people all responded together, "We will do everything the LORD has said"' (Exod. 19:8).

The task implied by the expression 'kingdom of priests' is that of priestly mediation between Yahweh and the nations. Christopher J. H. Wright helpfully captures the importance of the descriptor:

> It is thus richly significant that God confers on Israel as whole people the role of being his priesthood in the midst of the nations. As the people of YHWH they would have the historical task of bringing the knowledge of God to the nations, *and bringing the nations to the means of atonement with God.*[35]

Wright further argues that carrying out this task is how Israel is to fulfil the Abrahamic one of bringing blessings to the nations. In claiming this he follows John Goldingay's suggestion that 'Exodus 19:3–8 is a reworking of Genesis 12:1–3.'[36]

The question arises, however, as to how the righteous, holy and loving God can dwell in the midst of an all too flawed Israel with a view to Israel being the conduit of blessing to the wider creation. To answer that question we turn first to reflect upon Israel's sacrificial system. As R. W. Yarbrough rightly states, 'Sacrifice to atone for sins was at the heart of the religious system which God instituted for his people and as a witness to the surrounding world.'[37]After that, we shall consider Israel's hope as embodied in the suffering-servant figure of Isaiah's prophecy before drawing a conclusion.

Sacrifice in Israel

The canon speaks of the practice of sacrifice well before Israel's emergence as a nation. For example, Cain and Abel offer their respective sacrifices to God as early as Genesis 4. In fact, as David Peterson suggests, 'Sacrifice was common in the ancient world and it is regularly mentioned in the book of Genesis in connection with key individual and significant moments in the outworking of God's purposes for his world (e.g. 8:20–22; 12:7–8; 22:1–19).'[38] One of those

---

[35] C. J. H. Wright 2006: 331; my emphasis.
[36] Ibid.
[37] Yarbrough 2001: 389.
[38] Peterson in Peterson 2001b: 2.

key moments had to do with covenant-making (Gen. 15), another with faithful obedience (Gen. 22). Yet there is little in the Genesis stories, with the possible exception of Noah's sacrifice in Genesis 8:21, that connects sacrifice with addressing the problem of sin per se.[39] However, it is with the story of the exodus that sacrifice becomes clearly an 'essential part of God's plan for Israel as nation' and the problem posed by sin, wrath and judgment come into plain view.[40] To that story found in the book of Exodus we next turn.

In the Exodus account the Israelites had multiplied in Egypt, but are oppressed by Pharaoh. God hears their cries and acts in covenant faithfulness to keep his promises to Abraham (Exod. 2:23–25). God's stratagem was to raise up Moses to be his covenant agent and through him challenge Pharaoh's power and that of Egypt's gods (Exod. 3 – 15). The famous ten plagues follow, culminating in the deaths of Egypt's firstborn, including Pharaoh's son. But the Israelites are protected from that climactic judgment through sacrifice. The plague is clearly climactic because Yahweh declares, 'On that same night I will pass through Egypt and strike down every firstborn – both men and animals – and I will bring judgment *on all the gods of Egypt*' (Exod. 12:12; my emphasis). The Passover itself involves the blood of a sacrificed lamb sprinkled on the door frame of an Israelite dwelling. The destroyer passes over the Israelite households. Importantly, the shedding of blood averts the divine wrath: 'when I see the blood, I will pass over you' (Exod. 12:13). So important is this event that it was to be celebrated in a feast from that point on as 'a lasting ordinance' (Exod. 12:14). Indeed, the exodus is, as Christopher J. H. Wright maintains, 'the Old Testament model *par excellence* of Yahweh's acting in redemption to put things right'.[41]When God acts to set things right, there is both liberation and judgment (liberation for Israel and judgment for Egypt). As we shall see in a later chapter, the cross of Christ has a similar double effect. William J. Dumbrell is right to suggest, 'The New Testament presentation of the death of Christ builds upon this duality.'[42]

The language of atonement features prominently in the third book of the Torah. These sacrifices did not establish Israel's relationship to Yahweh. God's gracious rescue of the Israelites did that: 'I am the

[39] Well pointed out by C. J. H. Wright in Tidball, Hilborn and Thacker 2008: 73.
[40] Peterson 2001b: 2.
[41] C. J. H. Wright 2008: 73.
[42] Dumbrell 1988: 32.

LORD your God, who brought you out of Egypt, out of the land of slavery' (Exod. 20:2). Rather, the various divinely prescribed sacrifices delineated in Leviticus provide the means by which rescued Israel could live with Yahweh in her midst, maintain the covenant and repair it when necessary. In broad strokes, the logic of the sacrifices suggests the following sequence. Sin and guilt offerings are offered to make atonement (*kipper*) in Leviticus 4:1–35 and 5:14 – 6:7 respectively. Next the burnt offering represents the dedication of the Israelite to God (Lev. 9:7–17), leading to the peace offering. David Peterson sums up the process of atonement in the following way: 'It appears the making of full atonement normally requires sin and/or guilt offerings and a burnt offering. Peace offerings finally symbolized the fellowship thus restored or maintained between God and his people (e.g. Lev 9:18–21).'[43] The shedding of blood was involved in each of the four kinds of animal sacrifice.

One day each year, however, was especially important with regard to atonement.[44] The Day of Atonement was, as William J. Dumbrell suggests, 'perhaps the most significant day in the national calendar . . . on which the national sins were symbolically atoned for by cleansing the sanctuary'.[45] According to Leviticus 16:11–22, a bull and two goats were involved. The high priest took the blood of the sacrificed bull and goat into the holy of holies. Both sanctuary and people needed cleansing. Of particular significance, as we shall see in a later chapter, some of the blood was sprinkled on the mercy seat (Hebr., *kappōret*; Gr., *hilastērion*) on the top of the ark. The other goat, the scapegoat, was set free and sent into the desert, but not

---

[43] I am much indebted for this paragraph to Peterson's account (2001b: 5–6). Dumbrell (1988: 42) provides much more extensive biblical evidence for Peterson's sequencing, drawn from the Torah, the Prophets and the Writings. Argument is needed because in Lev. 1:1 – 6:7 the order appears to be different: burnt, cereal, peace, sin and lastly guilt offerings.

[44] Kugel (2007: 325) appears to disagree. He notes that scholars (but does not say who they are) observe that the Day of Atonement is not mentioned in the book of Exodus or in the list of holidays in Deut. 16:1–17. He says, 'as far as these books are concerned there is no such holiday'. Kugel makes a simple mistake here: the absence of evidence is not necessarily the evidence of absence. On his principle the book of James shows that James did not know about the Lord's Supper because he failed to mention it in his letter! Kugel (125–126) also appears to follow, albeit cautiously, those 'modern scholars' who argue that Lev. 16 is about the priestly matter of purging the sanctuary and 'originally had nothing to do with forgiving people their sins once a year'. This notion is based on analogies with other ANE ceremonies (e.g. in Babylon), but this assumes that there was nothing unique about Israel's historical experience (e.g. revelation from God).

[45] Dumbrell 1988: 45.

before Aaron had laid his hands on its head and confessed Israel's wickedness and rebellion over it.[46] Thus Israel's sins were carried away in a highly dramatic but publicly recognizable way. Again Wright is helpful: 'The effect of this highly complex ritual was not solely to atone for sin but was to restore harmony between God and Israel.'[47] Put another way the Day of Atonement ensured shalom.

The key term for atonement in the Hebrew Bible is *kipper* (the piel form of *kpr*; LXX *exilaskomai*). However, its translation is a matter of much debate. Does it mean 'conceal' or 'cover'? Does it mean 'purge', 'wipe' or 'clean'? Does it mean 'ransom'? Most likely *kipper* and cognates mean 'purge', 'wipe' or 'clean' (synonyms) in some contexts (e.g. Isa. 27:9), ransom in others (e.g. Exod. 32:30) and even 'forgive' in others (Ps. 78:38).[48] A crucial usage is that found in Leviticus 17:11, 'For the life of a creature is in the blood, and I have given it to you to make atonement for yourselves on the altar; it is the blood that makes atonement for one's life.' Christopher J. H. Wright convincingly argues that in this statement 'to *kipper* for your lives' means 'ransom'.[49] He contends that the verse speaks of 'an exchange, an equivalence, that provides a substitute for the life of the Israelite'.[50] David Peterson usefully expands the picture: 'Atonement here [Lev. 17:11] is not simply a matter of removing guilt or defilement by purging, but of averting the wrath of God by offering the life of a substitute.'[51] The significance of the text is underlined by the fact that Leviticus 17:11 is the only place in the Old Testament where sacrificial blood is said to be a ransom for human life.[52]

---

[46] Scobie (2003: 585) rightly contends, 'laying hands on a victim, [was] a practice that suggests "not simply identification or ownership, but that the victim was a vicarious substitution for the donor himself, or that the worshipper's sins were symbolically transferred to the animal"'.

[47] C. J. H. Wright 2008: 79.

[48] Peterson 2001b: 9–10. The references cited in the main text are only some of Peterson's biblical examples. For an important study of the linguistic detail of *kpr* see Averbeck 1996. Also see the recent study by Sklar (2005). With regard to the noun *kōper*, in ch. 2 Sklar argues that 'ransom' and appeasement' are the best English translations depending on context.

[49] C. J. H. Wright 2008: 75. Schwartz (2003: 249) takes the same view as to the best translation: 'to serve as a ransom for your lives'. He maintains that the verse is referring to 'a symbolic payment in exchange for one's life which would otherwise be forfeit'. Finlan (2007: 12) has little sympathy for the Old Testament portrayal of God (too violent) but, interestingly, recognizes that Lev. 17:11 may indeed be substitutionary.

[50] C. J. H. Wright 2008: 76.

[51] Peterson 2001b: 11.

[52] Grabbe 2000: 102.

Israel's hope: the messianic child and the suffering servant

The faithful in Israel not only looked back to the exodus deliverance as a time of salvation, but also as a time of judgment upon their enemies. They also looked forward to a time of shalom. God would deliver his people again and bring them peace. Indeed, T. J. Geddert argues:

> *Peace was central to the eschatological expectations of the OT prophets.* The messianic child would be a 'Prince of Peace' (Is 9:6). He was expected to come in peace, to end warfare and to proclaim peace throughout the land (Zech 9:9–12). He would reunite families (Mal 4:6); he would decimate Israel's enemies in order to bring lasting peace to Jerusalem (meaning 'city of peace') (cf. Is 66:10–16).[53]

For our purposes, Isaiah's prophecy provides an especially important window on Israel's hopes for deliverance and peace. However, the messianic child of Isaiah 9:6 mentioned by Geddert above is not the only figure that Isaiah's prophecy deals with. There is also the mysterious figure of the servant in Israel's future, and the two are connected.

Most scholars recognize that there are four servant songs in Isaiah's prophecy.[54] Identifying the servant has proved challenging and the subject of much debate past and present. The Ethiopian eunuch in the book of Acts still asks the question of many when he says to Philip, 'Tell me, please, who is the prophet [Isaiah] talking about, himself or someone else?' (Acts 8:34).[55] The first song (Isa. 42:17) appears to present the servant as Israel with the task of bringing the light to the whole world, Israelite and Gentile alike. The second (Isa. 49:1–6) seems to narrow the profile to a purified Israel with a mission both to

---

[53] Geddert 2001; my emphasis.

[54] Scholars in the main identify the following as servant songs: (1) Isa. 42:1–7 or to v. 9 or to v. 12; (2) 49:1–6 or to v. 7 or to v. 13; (3) 50:4–9 or to v. 11; and (4) 52:13 – 53:12; see Scobie 2003: 406. Scobie himself (277) maintains that the speaker of Isa. 61:1–3 ought 'probably also to be identified with the Servant'. Dumbrell (2001b: 124) describes the speaker in Isa. 61 as servant-like.

[55] Scobie (2003: 407–409) usefully discusses the four options: an individual, a collective, an ideal or messianic. According to him (409), these notions are not mutually exclusive, and he sees that 'there is clearly a progression from a collective toward a more individual understanding of the servant, especially in Song IV [Isa. 52:13 – 53:12]'. Also see S. Groom in Tidball, Hilborn and Thacker 2008: 100. With regard to development in the songs, Groom draws on the earlier work of H. H. Rowley (1954).

the rest of God's people and the Gentiles. The third song (Isa. 50:4–9) tells how the servant will suffer and experience shame. In this song it is not obvious whether the servant is a collective or an individual. The final song (Isa. 52:13 – 53:12) describes an individual. The last song is particularly relevant to our task.

The fourth song is often described as the song of the suffering servant, although some prefer triumphant servant.[56] The trajectory of the poem is striking in its chiastic form: the servant's exaltation (52:13–15), the rejection/suffering of the servant (53:1–3), the significance of the servant's suffering (53:4–6), the rejection/suffering of the servant (53:7–9) and the servant's exaltation (53:10–12).[57] The servant sprinkles the nations, an idea with sacrificial overtones (Isa. 52:15).[58] He takes on our infirmities and carries our sorrows (Isa. 53:4). (Is 'our' Israel speaking, or the nations, the prophets or most likely anyone who has gone astray?)[59] He is pierced for our transgressions, crushed for our iniquities and bears our punishment (Isa. 53:5). He substitutes for others.[60] But in so doing he brings peace (Isa. 53:5). His wounds heal (Isa. 53:5). All this when we mistakenly thought it was God who was afflicting him for his iniquities (Isa. 53:4). But in fact the Lord laid on him our iniquities (Isa. 53:6). He suffers for the sins of others, not his own.[61] He is like a sacrificial lamb going to slaughter (Isa. 53:7). His conduct is exemplary (Isa. 53:7). Experiencing violence, he returns none (Isa. 53:9). He even intercedes for the transgressors (Isa. 53:12). He bears our iniquities ('*āwōnōtām*) and in fact bears the sins of many (Isa. 53:11–12). He becomes a guilt offering (Isa. 53:11). This is the offering ('*āšām*) that wipes out guilt (cf. Lev. 5:1–19; Num. 5:8; 1 Sam. 6:3–8).[62] David

---

[56] Groom (2008: 96) is attracted to the triumphant servant designation. But, in my view, suffering servant and triumphant servant are not mutually exclusive.

[57] See Gentry 2007: 24 for a stimulating coverage of critical issues and illuminating exegesis. S. G. Dempster (in Hafemann and House 2007: 157) has a similar but simpler analysis: exaltation–humiliation–exaltation. Also see J. A. Groves (in Hill and James 2004: 61–89) for a technical discussion of the exegesis of this fourth servant song.

[58] Groom 2008: 101.

[59] Groom (ibid. 98–99) discusses the possibilities.

[60] This point is finely made by Peterson (2001b: 19–23).

[61] Dempster (in Hafemann and House 2007: 156, n. 88) is right to argue that 'the most straightforward meaning of Isaiah 53 indicates that the servant was not suffering for his own sins'.

[62] For 'guilt offering' as the best translation (as in the NIV) in this context see Groom 2008: 111 and Gentry 2007: 36. Others argue for 'sin offering' (as does incidentally the ESV and NRSV); e.g. Scobie 2003: 585 and Coggins 2000: 477. In either view sacrifice is required and sin creates the need that is so addressed.

Peterson maintains, 'The novelty of Isaiah 53 is the claim that one person's obedient service may be accepted by God as an atoning sacrifice for others.'[63] His faithfulness leads to triumph (Isa. 53:10–12) and beneficial consequences, which in subsequent chapters show that through his life poured out even to death will come the renewal of God's people and God's world.[64] Through it all God's will is being done. For it is Yahweh's stratagem to make the willing servant's life a guilt offering. (R. Coggins rightly criticizes those scholars who raise the question whether the servant actually dies in the poem: 'The picture in these verses is clearly of the death of the servant.')[65] The wills of both Yahweh and the servant are aligned in the task.[66]

As mentioned previously, the messianic child and suffering servant of Isaiah are connected. Seeing a connection is evidenced as early as the LXX rendering of Isaiah 53:2, which translates *yōnēq* (tender shoot) by *paidion* ('child' or 'servant'). According to Peter J. Gentry, this shows that for the ancient translator there was a nexus between Isaiah 9:5 and Isaiah 53:2.[67] The servant is both royal and Davidic. The shalom Israel longs for will come not through their own efforts but through an agent who truly and selflessly represents their interests and embodies God's concern.

Conclusion

We have explored the foundations to and foreshadowings of the triune God's loving provision in Christ to bring shalom to creation. This consideration led us to focus first on the foundational promise of the *protoevangelium*. Victory over the serpent has been promised. Next we examined the formative promises to Abraham that are programmatic for the biblical story of salvation. Then we looked at the backstory of God's dealings with Israel that foreshadow what God accomplished in Christ. With regard to the latter, Thomas F. Torrance insightfully says:

> Israel was the people which became so intimately locked into the holy presence of God that it was completely spoiled for

[63] Peterson 2001b: 22.
[64] Dempster 2007: 159–160.
[65] Coggins 2000: 477.
[66] Groom 2008: 102.
[67] I find both Gentry 2007: 24 and Zimmerli and Jeremias 1979: 41 convincing on this point. Also see Dumbrell 2001b: 120, 'In the Aramaic translation, the Targums, of Isaiah 53, the Servant is defined as the messiah.'

any naturalistic existence as an ordinary nation, but became the means through which God worked out in the midst of the nations a way of reconciliation with himself in which the tensions embedded in man's alienated existence are resolved and the peace of God is built into the whole of his creation. Israel became the people impregnated with the promise of *shalom* for all humankind.[68]

The *protoevangelium*, the Abrahamic promises, the point of Israel's' sacrificial system, the messianic child born of the house of David and suffering servant figure of Old Testament expectation will find their instantiation in God's faithful Son. That embodiment in Jesus we explore next. He, after all, is the centrepiece of God's atoning project.

---

[68] Torrance 1992: 27; original emphasis.

Chapter Five

The faithful Son

The linchpin of the divine plan and the central figure in the divine project is God's faithful Son, Jesus Christ. This can easily be seen in the fact that there are four accounts of his person and work in the canon of Scripture. No other biblical character is treated from so many angles. Even the Synoptic Gospels support this point. There are commonalities between Matthew, Mark and Luke to be sure, but each has its own distinctive and complementary theological approach. Stephen Neill was warranted in entitling one of his books *Jesus through Many Eyes*.[1] An outstanding characteristic of Jesus is that here is one who really does live by every word that proceeds out of the mouth of God. Adam did not, nor did Israel; yet this Son did. To help in underlining these crucial contrasts we turn to the seminal contribution of the early church Father Irenaeus before considering the faithfulness of Christ.[2]

Irenaeus: a pioneering contribution

Irenaeus (130–200) was a pioneering biblical theologian. That is to say, he sought to understand Scripture as a whole and in terms of its own inner dynamics. He was the one who coined the terms 'Old Testament' and 'New Testament'. But he did not write out of mere personal curiosity; he wrote to combat those Gnostic and Marcionite heresies that removed the Old Testament from the category of Christian Scripture and did so on the assumption that the Old Testament was the work of a lesser god. He wrote as a bishop of the church with the responsibility of protecting God's flock. According to Irenaeus, Scripture presents God as a great educator. As such he used Old Testament persons, events and institutions to prepare the

---

[1] Neill 1976.
[2] Others too have found Irenaeus' theology important for their own theology of the cross. E.g. Hans Boersma (2004).

way for the coming of the Son. Irenaeus was an early Christian exponent of a typological approach to the Old Testament. He wrote in his classic work *Against Heresies*:

> Thus it was, too, that God formed man at the first, because of His munificence; but chose the patriarchs for the sake of their salvation, and prepared a people beforehand, teaching [the divine pedagogy] the headstrong to follow God; and raised up prophets upon earth, accustoming man to bear His Spirit {within him}, and to hold communion with God: He Himself, indeed, having need of nothing, but granting communion with Himself to those who stood in need of it, and *sketching out, like an architect, the plan of salvation* to those that pleased Him. And He did Himself furnish guidance to those who beheld Him not in Egypt, while to those who became unruly in the desert He promulgated a law very suitable {to their condition}. Then, on the people who entered into the good land He bestowed a noble inheritance; and He killed the fatted calf for those converted to the Father, and presented them with the finest robe. *Thus in a variety of ways, He adjusted the human race to an agreement with salvation.*[3]

Irenaeus thus believed that there was a unity to Scripture. Marcion, on the other hand, infamously split the Old Testament from the New. According to Irenaeus, 'Marcion therefore himself, by dividing God into two, maintaining one to be good and the other judicial, does in fact, on both sides, end deity.'[4] Irenaeus' seminal contribution in terms of our study of God's atoning project lies in his unified approach to reading Scripture. He took seriously the storyline of Scripture.[5] In other words, he worked with some idea of salvation history. With some merit, Justo L. González describes Irenaeus as 'among the greatest theologians of all times'.[6]

Materially speaking, Irenaeus had a profound understanding of the divine project and of Christ as its linchpin. As Justo L. González

---

[3] Irenaeus, *Against Heresies*, quoted in González 1989: 71–72. The italics are González's. Only the square brackets are mine.

[4] Stevenson 1970: 99. Also see Bettenson and Maunder 1999: 41.

[5] Irenaeus could be theologically fanciful though. Is Jesus' mother, Mary, really the antitype to the Old Testament's Eve? Irenaeus, *Against Heresies* 3.21.10 (Bettenson 1978: 83).

[6] González 1987: 170.

observes, 'Christ is the center of Irenaeus' theology.'[7] Irenaeus argued that Jesus recapitulates in his own person (*in seipso recapitulavit*) all that Adam should have been and failed to be.[8] At every stage of life Jesus was the obedient one as opposed to Adam with his primal and catastrophic disobedience.[9] Jesus lived out a truly faithful human life from cradle to grave.[10] Thus, to use Pauline language, Irenaeus rightly saw the great contrast between the first and the last Adam (1 Cor. 15:45). The strength of Irenaeus' recapitulation idea lies in the notion that at every stage of human development Christ was the faithful and obedient Son of God, whether in the temple as boy or on the cross as a mature adult. Irenaeus, however, runs too far with the idea and has Jesus living to old age, presumably to cover all the ages of human life. Consequently, Irenaeus goes far beyond what is written because of the gravitational pull of his own theory. This is a perennial temptation for the theologian.

Calvin too saw the theological importance of the Adam–Christ connection. However, he wrote with more restraint and less theological speculation than Irenaeus:

> The second requirement of our reconciliation with God was this: that man, who by his disobedience had become lost, should by way of remedy counter it with obedience, satisfy God's judgment, and pay the penalties for sin. Accordingly, our Lord came forth as true man and took the person and the name of Adam in order to take Adam's place in obeying the Father, to present our flesh as the price of satisfaction to God's righteous judgment, and, in the same flesh, to pay the penalty that we had deserved.[11]

This statement from Calvin's *Institutes* is theologically rich with insight into the atonement and we shall return to his insights in a later chapter.

Writing in the tradition of Calvin, Robert Letham is a contemporary theologian who recognizes the role not only of obedience in the Adam–Christ contrast but also of faithfulness. He writes:

[7] Ibid. 165.

[8] Irenaeus, *Against Heresies* (McGrath 2007b: 344).

[9] Irenaeus, *Against Heresies* 3.18.6–7 (Bettenson 1978: 78–79).

[10] Ibid.

[11] Calvin 2002e: 2.13.3. The first requirement mentioned by Calvin in the quotation is that the mediator must be truly God and truly human (2.12.2).

As man, *he trusted* his heavenly Father. His worship of God was pure and sinless. He obeyed God's law totally, fulfilling its precepts and suffering its sanctions on our behalf. All that he did is on our behalf, *throughout his life as well as on the cross.* He himself was and is the active, human, bodily expression of God's faithfulness, of 'God with us' (Mt. 1:23). But as man, *he was and is active human faithfulness*, the second Adam whose obedience has overthrown the first Adam's disobedience.[12]

A particular strength of Letham's discussion is the way he links Christ's faithfulness to the idea of covenant: 'It is [Christ's] response, not ours, which fulfills the covenant.'[13] Christ is both the covenant-making God (along with Father and Son as the holy Trinity) and the covenant-keeping man.

Irenaeus', Calvin's and Letham's analyses may be usefully extended to Old Testament Israel.[14] In many ways Israel became God's pilot scheme.[15] William J. Dumbrell captures the connection between Adam and Israel well:

> The creation account, while indicating the universality of Yahweh, also reveals Israel's understanding of Yahweh and of her own background through Abraham; thus, we are not surprised to find direct connections between the prime narratives and the history of Israel. Vocational and functional correspondences between Adam and Israel prepare us for the continuance of God's governmental purposes for our world through Israel . . . Israel resumed the role, initially given to Adam, of God's regent in a world that needs order.[16]

---

[12] Letham 1993: 49; my emphases. Letham (117) speaks warmly of Irenaeus: 'This is the great insight Irenaeus had (for all its undertones of universalism), that Christ's whole history was a recapitulation of Adam's.'

[13] Ibid. 49.

[14] Letham's fine study of the work of Christ would be the stronger if Israel were factored into it. E.g. he (ibid. 76–77) takes the temptations of Matt. 4:1–10 in terms of an Adam–Christ contrast, whereas it is much more likely an Israel–Christ contrast, as I shall shortly argue.

[15] H. Berkhof (1979: 244–249) uses a different metaphor. Drawing on the biblical idea of Israel as vineyard, he describes Israel as God's 'experimental garden', which ultimately proved unfruitful.

[16] Dumbrell 2001b: 9–10. According to D. G. Reid 2001, there is intertestamental evidence that some in Israel understood Israel as the new Adam (e.g. 1QS 4.23; CD III/20; 1QH 17.15).

According to Dumbrell, 'The priestly/king role that Adam exercised in Genesis 1–2 devolved upon Israel at Sinai.'[17] On this view, the Promised Land flowing with milk and honey becomes the analogue of Eden. However, Israel as a nation forfeited that role because of disobedience.[18]

As the Old Testament concludes, we see a world needing a new Adam and a new Israel. But where is faithfulness to be found?

The faithful/faith-filled Son

In contrast to both Adam and Israel, Jesus comes before us in the New Testament as God's faithful son. In his humanity he is all that Adam should have been and the embodiment of all that Israel's covenant faithfulness should have been. His faithfulness is evident in how he meets the tempter in the wilderness, in how even his mockers recognize what animated him, in the way that diverse New Testament writers see him in faith/faithfulness categories.

In the Gospel accounts the first great test of Christ's faithfulness comes in the wilderness immediately after his baptism at the hands of John the Baptist. His messianic calling is soon challenged by the devil. In Mark the language is breathlessly direct: 'The Spirit immediately drove [ekballei] him into the wilderness' (Mark 1:12; my tr.). There he encounters Satan. He is with the wild beasts and ministered to by angels (Mark 1:13). The reference to 'the wild animals' may be signally the restoration of harmony between the new Adam and an alienated animal kingdom, alienated because of the great rupture of Genesis 3.[19] Compared with Mark's account, Matthew expands the story considerably. In this Gospel we learn of Jesus' hunger and the exact nature of the temptations. The devil attempts to lure Jesus into unfaithfulness by Jesus' pursuing a different will to God's by providing for himself in the wilderness rather than relying on God's provision (Matt. 4:3), by putting God to the test by jumping from the temple top (Matt. 4:5–7) and by accepting the devil's offer of gaining the world with its kingdoms in exchange for worship (Matt. 4:8–9).[20] But Jesus stays faithful to the Father's will throughout the

---

[17] Dumbrell 2001b: 45.
[18] Ibid. 11.
[19] Montague 1976: 243.
[20] Dumbrell (2001b: 163) points out that the wilderness, temple and mountain were all key sites in Israel's eschatological expectations.

temptations. And in this account the angels come at the end of the ordeal to minister to Jesus (cf. Matt. 4:1, 11).

The Matthean and Lucan accounts are resonant with Old Testament echoes. Matthew's genealogy takes us back to Abraham as its starting point (Matt. 1:1–17) and with its overall Jewishness. It is not too speculative to see Jesus' triumph through the testing as the very reverse of Israel's experience in the wilderness. Israel, God's son (Exod. 4:22), was tested in the wilderness. God's Old Testament son, however, failed.[21] If only Israel had lived the theology of Deuteronomy, the very theology of faithfulness that Jesus drew on to combat the devil as seen in his quotes, Israel would presumably not have fallen. The Lucan account of the temptations is also preceded by a genealogy (Luke 3:23–38). This genealogy goes all the way back to Adam, who is described significantly as 'the son of God' (Luke 3:38). It is not too speculative to see in the Lucan account of the temptations an allusion to Adam's test in the paradise of God as God's son, and subsequent failure in contrast to the testing of this son of Adam, Jesus, who in a very different setting – not a garden but a wilderness – does not fall to temptation.[22]

Jesus is all that Israel should have been as God's Son and all that Adam and Israel should have been as God's sons. In other words, Jesus is the faithful Adam and the faithful Israel.

The scorn at the cross

The passion narrative in Matthew provides some unlikely witnesses to the role of faith in the life of Christ. At the cross the soldiers cast lots for Christ's clothing (Matt. 27:35) and those who pass by mock him: 'You who are going to destroy the temple and build it in three days, save yourself! Come down from the cross, if you are the Son of God!' (Matt. 27:40). The chief priests, the teachers of the law and the elders join the scornful chorus (Matt. 27:41). Even the robbers crucified with him add their insults (Matt. 27:44). Of these groups it is the chief priests, teachers of the law and elders who are our witnesses.

---

[21] Ibid. Also see Hagner 2004a, comment on Matt. 4:1–11.

[22] For the Adam–Christ contrast see Dunn 1977: 31. Also see Nolland 2004, who is more cautious than Dunn: 'In the final analysis Jesus is tempted neither as second Adam, nor as true Israel, but as Son. There is a touch of Adamic typology and considerable exodus typology, but that is because the experiences of Adam and Israel are paradigmatic cases of the testing of God's Son. Jesus's temptations are not uniquely messianic, though it is clear that his sonship is of a uniquely exalted kind' (comment on Luke 4:1–13).

They mock as follows: '"He saved others," they said, "but he can't save himself! He's the King of Israel! Let him come down now from the cross, and we will believe in him"' (Matt. 27:42). Then they add, 'He trusts in God. Let God rescue him now if he wants him, for he said, "I am the Son of God"' (Matt. 27:43).

'He trusts [*pepoithen epi*] in God' is the key. The verb 'trusts' is in the perfect aspect: trust is what characterizes Jesus. These scorners are not pointing to an isolated case as though only now in the light of an extreme situation does Jesus trust in God. No! This is his way of life and the scorners want to see if it does him any good. In fact, whether intentional or not their mocking is alluding to Psalm 22:8, where the psalmist speaks of his mockers as those who insult him with words such as

> He trusts in the LORD;
> let the LORD rescue him.[23]

What this evidence shows is that even Jesus' fiercest opponents recognized that he was a believer. Jesus' confidence in his Father comes out most clearly in the Lucan passion account. In the garden, with the prospect of the agony of the cross before him, he prays, 'Father, if you are willing, take this cup from me; yet not my will, but yours be done' (Luke 22:42).[24] On the cross he assures the repentant thief, 'today you will with me in paradise' (Luke 23:43). He dies with these words issuing from his lips: 'Father, into your hands I commit [*paratithemai*, 'entrust'] my spirit' (Luke 23:46).

---

[23] Wilkins (1996) comments in n. 16 that if these members of the Sanhedrin are consciously alluding to a well-known messianic psalm, then they are mocking what they consider to be Jesus' messianic pretensions; if unconscious, then it is unintentionally prophetic, like Caiaphas was. Blomberg (2007: 98) regards Matt. 27:43 to be more than an allusion to Ps. 22:8 but less than a quotation. He regards it as perhaps 'a paraphrase'. The LXX, interestingly, uses *elpizō* (hopes) and not *peithō* (trusts).

[24] Some MSS add, 'An angel from heaven appeared to him and strengthened him. And being in anguish, he prayed more earnestly, and his sweat was like drops of blood falling to the ground' (Luke 22:43–44). Many scholars regard these verses as an addition. E.g. Nolland (2004) argues, 'However, the tradition here was certainly known by the time of Justin Martyr (see *Dial.* 103.8). The arguments for and against inclusion are finely balanced. Both addition and removal are explicable in terms of arguments over Christology . . . After an earlier move in critical opinion toward accepting the verses, the more recent trend has been to question their presence in the original text of Luke. I have excluded them primarily on the basis of the emotional tone of the verses and secondarily on the basis of the chiasm' (comment on Luke 22:39–46). At the very least, these verses show that early Christians understood the garden experience as an ordeal. Jesus stayed true to his heavenly Father just as he had done in the wilderness (Luke 4:1–13).

The witness of Hebrews

The book of Hebrews provides two lines of evidence concerning Christ's faithfulness or faith-filledness. The first line of evidence lies in the contrast the writer draws early in the letter between Jesus and Moses. The second is provided by the parade of believers found towards the end of the exhortation. We shall consider each in turn.

In Hebrews 3:1–6 the writer compares the faithfulness of Moses with that of Christ. He writes:

> Therefore, holy brothers, who share in the heavenly calling, fix your thoughts on Jesus, the apostle and high priest whom we confess. *He was faithful to the one who appointed him*, just as Moses was faithful in all God's house. Jesus has been found worthy of greater honour than Moses, just as the builder of a house has greater honour than the house itself. For every house is built by someone, but God is the builder of everything. Moses was faithful as a servant in all God's house, testifying to what would be said in the future. *But Christ is faithful as a son over God's house.* (My emphases)

Both Moses and Christ are faithful to the one who appointed them (*piston onta tō poiēsanti*) to their respective tasks and roles.[25] However, on the one hand (*men*), Moses is but a servant in (*en*) God's household. Christ, on the other hand (*de*), is the son over (*epi*) that house. Jesus is clearly then the superior of the two. In fact, as George H. Guthrie suggests in regard to Hebrews 3:1–6, 'we are challenged to consider Jesus as the paradigmatic image of faithfulness'.[26]

Towards the end of the letter the writer parades before the readers a long list of Old Testament worthies who were men or women of faith. His list is predicated on the claim that 'without faith it is impossible to please God' (Heb. 11:6). These Old Testament characters did please God, and for some at quite a personal cost. He starts the cavalcade with Abel and, interestingly, connects faith and righteousness: 'By faith he was commended as a righteous man' (Heb. 11: 4).

---

[25] Calvin (2002c) says with regard to Christ, 'For we say of Christ, that as he is clothed with our flesh, he is the Father's minister to execute his commands. To the calling of God is added the faithful and upright performance of duty on the part of Christ; and this is required in true ministers, in order that they may obtain credence in the Church' (comment on Heb. 12:2).

[26] Guthrie 1996.

Enoch, Noah, Abraham, Sarah, Isaac, Jacob, Joseph, Moses, Israel, Rahab – each gets some discussion, albeit some more than others (Heb. 11:5–31). If the writer had more time, then Gideon, Barak, Samson, Jephthah, David, Samuel, the prophets and other men and women whom he does not name would have been given their due (Heb. 11:32–40). The writer is clear that one expression of faith is obedience. By faith (*pistei*) Abraham obeyed (*hypēkousen*) God's call, 'even though he did not know where he was going' (Heb. 11:8).

The division of Scripture into chapters and verse is a very great aid to the serious student of Scripture. However, these divisions may mislead. The parade of the faithful culminates in Christ, whom the writer describes in the following striking way in Hebrews 12:1–3:

> Therefore, since we are surrounded by such a great cloud of witnesses, let us throw off everything that hinders and the sin that so easily entangles, and let us run with perseverance the race marked out for us. Let us fix our eyes on Jesus, the author and perfecter of our faith, who for the joy set before him endured the cross, scorning its shame, and sat down at the right hand of the throne of God. Consider him who endured such opposition from sinful men, so that you will not grow weary and lose heart. (My emphasis)

The 'so therefore' (*toigaroun*) of Hebrews 12:1 logically connects the passage to the forgoing presentation of believers. Jesus is the climax of the story of faith. He is the founder (*archēgos*) and perfecter (*teleiōtēn*) of the faith (*tēs pisteōs*), according to Hebrews 12:2.

What does it mean to describe Jesus as the pioneer and perfecter of the faith? (Contra the NIV, both ESV and NRSV note that 'our' is not in the text at this point.) David Peterson comments, 'Jesus is the perfect example of the faith we are to express. The word translated *author* (Gk. *archēgos*, as in 2:10) literally means that he is pioneer or leader in the race of faith.'[27] Peterson's comment is apposite. Like so many listed in the previous chapter of Hebrews, Jesus knew suffering, shame and opposition, but he endured (e.g. cf. Heb. 11:35–38 and 12:2–3). In fact, he triumphed and finished the task given him: he 'sat down at the right hand of the throne of God' (Heb. 12:2). He is the paradigmatic believer. However, William Lane rightly nuances the exegesis:

---

[27] Peterson 2001a, comment on Heb. 12:1–13. Keener (2001c) entitles his section on Heb. 12:1–3 'The Ultimate Hero of Faith'. W. L. Lane (2001) exegetes Heb. 12:2 similarly.

The primary reference in 12:2*a* is to the exercise of faith by Christ himself. Jesus, however, is not simply the crowning example of steadfast faithfulness, whose response to God is cited to encourage the community to persevere in faith. His attainment of exaltation glory by way of faithful obedience in suffering was unprecedented and determinative, and not merely exemplary.[28]

Even so, exemplary it clearly is.

The witness of Revelation

The book of Revelation contains many descriptors of Jesus: 'the firstborn from the dead', 'the ruler of the kings of the earth', 'the First and the Last' and 'the Living One'. Those are drawn only from the first chapter. Also in that first chapter the seer identifies Jesus as 'the faithful witness' (*ho martys ho pistos*, Rev. 1:5; also see 3:14 and 19:11). Revelation has three other references to 'witness' (*martys*, 2:13; 11:3; 17:6). According to David E. Aune, these other references always have 'those who die for their faith' in view.[29] The question is whether the Revelation 1:5 reference to faithful witness has in view Jesus' earthly ministry pre-resurrection or Jesus' heavenly ministry as the conqueror of death. Aune argues for the latter.[30] However, not all agree. Craig S. Keener, for example, takes a different view:

> Jesus is the 'faithful witness,' who provided the ultimate witness of the Father (John 3:11) and stood faithful in his witness when on trial before Pilate (1 Tim. 6:13). Because he is the 'faithful and true witness' (Rev. 3:14), believers can depend on his promises (Prov. 14:5, 25); in fact, he fulfills a divine role (Jer. 42:5). But more important here, Jesus provides the perfect model for Christians who will bear witness for him (Rev. 19:10) and suffer for that witness (17:6). Thus the only named martyr in the book of Revelation is likewise called a 'faithful witness' (2:13).[31]

---

[28] W. L. Lane 2004b, comment on Heb. 12:2.

[29] Aune 2004, comment on Rev. 1:5.

[30] Aune (ibid.) speaks of 'weighty reasons' for his view, but I do not find them compelling.

[31] Keener 1996.

In either view, Jesus is the faithful witness. If Keener is correct, then the seer is drawing the reader's attention to Jesus' public ministry that ended in his death but exhibited his faithfulness in the face of persecution and suffering. If Aune is right, then the exalted Christ continues to be the faithful witness.[32]

The Pauline witness: Christ's faithfulness or faith in Christ?

There is present debate whether in some Pauline passages the apostle is referring to the faithfulness of Christ or to faith in Christ. As we have seen, there is enough evidence to show that Christ is seen by a number of New Testament writers and even by some of his critics as someone who trusted God. The debate therefore does not touch this point. However, if it can be shown that Paul in some contexts thematizes Christ's faithfulness, then there is even more evidence for the claim that Christ's faithfulness is fundamental to understanding the importance of his active and passive faith to his atoning work.

A case in point is Romans 3:22. The traditional exegesis of the phrase 'through faith of Jesus Christ' (*dia pisteōs Iēsou Christou*) understands Jesus Christ to be the object of faith. For example, the NIV translation runs, 'through faith in Jesus Christ' (Rom. 3:22). 'Faith of' is taken to be an example of an objective genitive. D. A. Carson takes the genitive this way for the following reasons.[33] First, he needs to deal with the apparent tautology. For on the objective view there seems to be needless repetition of the idea of believing in Jesus: 'through faith in Jesus Christ to all the believing' (his tr.). He argues that the repetition is periphrastic. Secondly, following with acknowledgment J. D. G. Dunn, if the faithfulness of Christ is Paul's point, then why introduce Abraham as an example of a believer in the next chapter? Christ would be illustration enough.[34] Thirdly, the

---

[32] I incline to Keener's position on the matter. Rev. 1:5 seems to show a progression in its descriptors of Jesus. In this view 'the faithful witness' refers to his public ministry, including his death, 'the firstborn from the dead' highlights the resurrection, and 'the ruler of the kings of the earth' accents his exaltation to the place of executive power at the right hand of God. Beasley-Murray (2001) says, 'Jesus worshipped, loved, *trusted* and obeyed *his God and Father*, as all Christians should' (comment on Rev. 1:5; my emphases).

[33] Carson in Hill and James 2004: 126–127.

[34] Dunn (2004a) says, 'But Christ's faithfulness is not something which Paul draws attention to elsewhere in the extended exposition of Romans, even where it would have been highly appropriate – particularly chap. 4, where Abraham's *pistis* is the model for the believer, *not* for Christ, and 5:15–19, where the antithesis *apistia/pistis*

traditional exegesis fits better contextually with the argument of Romans 1:18 – 3:20, and fourthly, with the final clause of Romans 3:26. However, Carson acknowledges that the linguistics is complex and 'usually judged to be far from conclusive'.[35]

D. B. Knox takes a different view.[36] His argument is exegetical and theological. In his view, Romans 3:22, Galatians 3:22 and Philippians 3:9 are speaking of Christ's faith, not our own. He maintains that Jesus' faith is 'the ground of our salvation'.[37] Indeed, he contends, 'The chief example that our Saviour has left us is the example of faith' and that Jesus' faith expressed itself in his obedience to the Father's will.[38] He acknowledges that the usual English translations point in another direction. However, the tautologies involved are to him real and not merely apparent.[39] For example, to avoid tautology he translates Philippians 3:9 as 'The righteousness which is through the faithfulness of [pisteōs] Christ, that is, the righteousness which comes from God upon our faith [epi tē pistei].'[40] Theologically, he argues that Christ's faith contrasts with the sin of Adam, which was 'he failed to believe the truth of God's Word and

---

would have been very natural, had Christ's faith been a factor in his thought' (comment on Rom. 3:22). Dunn's argument is interesting but not compelling. Abraham is the appropriate example of faith in Rom. 4 because he needed to be justified, as do both Jew and Gentile. Christ did not. As for Rom. 5, the contrast between Adam's disobedience and Christ's obedience does not exclude faith but presupposes it or the lack of it.

[35] Carson in Hill and James 2004: 126–127. Carson also appears to be concerned that taking the genitive to be a subjective one 'through the faithfulness of Jesus Christ' could be used to support the 'New Perspective on Paul' (e.g. N. T. Wright), a school of thought with which he profoundly disagrees.

[36] N. T. Wright (2002, 10: 473–474) takes a similar view to Knox: 'Granted the importance of Jesus' faithfulness in the argument of this passage [in Romans], stated proleptically in 3:22 . . . it is more likely that what he means here, stated still in condensed form, is that God justifies the one whose status rests on the faithful death of Jesus. Even there, of course, the notion of the believer's own faith is not absent, since it is this faith that precipitates God's announcement of the verdict in the present time. But the basis for this faith is precisely the faithfulness of Jesus seen as the manifestation of the covenant faithfulness of God.'

[37] Knox in Payne 2000: 111.

[38] Ibid. 102–105.

[39] I am unconvinced that Carson sufficiently addresses the tautology issue given the other putative Pauline examples (Gal. 3:22 and Phil. 3:9).

[40] Knox in Payne 2000: 111. Knox (112) also argues that in Rom. 1:17 the phrase 'The righteousness of God from faith to faith' should be understood as follows. The first reference to faith in the text is to Christ's own faith, while the second is to ours. This is certainly possible, but so too is the idea of faith in both instances referring to our faith ('faith from first to last'). For a helpful discussion of the issues see Dunn 2004a, comment on Rom. 1:17.

the goodness of God in giving him that command'.[41] In his view 'Jesus reversed mankind's sin'.[42]

Deciding between these views, however, is beyond the scope of this study.[43] Furthermore, both positions may find other New Testament texts to support their conflicting claims concerning the specific texts discussed above. For example, Hebrews 12:2 highlights that Jesus is the pioneer of believing, while John 3:16 is clear that eternal life comes through believing in him. D. A. Carson comments with regard to Romans 3:22:

> Even if the subjective genitive were to prevail, the traditional interpretation of the paragraph as a whole remains plausible: after all, some NT writers, especially John and Hebrews, make much of the obedience, and thus the faithfulness of Jesus Christ in accomplishing his Father's will, even though they *also* insist that Jesus is the object of our faith.[44]

Wisely and finely said.

The faith/faithfulness of Christ or the obedience of Christ?

The 'obedience of Christ' (*obedientia Christi*) is a traditional category some use in discussing the significance of Christ's life and death. This category admits of two sub ones: the active obedience of Christ (*obedientia activa*) and the passive (meaning suffering) obedience of Christ (*obedientia passiva*). Scholastic Protestant theology, whether Lutheran or Reformed, made much of these categories and those indebted to them.[45] For example, Robert Murray McCheyne preached:

---

[41] Knox in Payne 2000: 230.

[42] Ibid.

[43] Note the cautious way that Letham (1993: 253, n. 17) enters the debate: 'There may be some justification for reading a subjective genitive in Rom. 3:22; Gal. 2:16; 20; 3:22.' There are good arguments on both sides of the question. Letham himself appears sympathetic to the subjective genitive argument.

[44] Carson in Hill and James 2004: 125–126; original emphasis.

[45] See the fine discussion of these categories and their scholastic context in Muller 1986: 205–206. There is also an emphasis on dominical obedience in Roman Catholic theology, CCC, para. 623: 'By his loving obedience to the Father, "unto death, even death on a cross" (*Phil* 2:8), Jesus fulfills the atoning mission (cf. *Isa* 53:10) of the suffering Servant, who will "make many righteous; and he shall bear their iniquities" (*Isa* 33:11; cf. *Rom* 5:19).'

When he [Jesus] came into the world, he came not only to suffer [passive obedience], but to do [active obedience] – not only to be the dying Saviour, but also a doing Saviour – not only to suffer the curse which the first Adam had brought upon the world, but to render the obedience which the first Adam had left undone. From the cradle to the cross he obeyed the will of God from the heart.[46]

In the light of these traditional categories some may wonder why the discussion has not accented the obedience of Christ in contrast to the disobedience both of Adam and that of Old Testament Israel. However, I want to ask whether the faithfulness of Christ, the active faith of Christ and the passive faithfulness of Christ provide an even more fundamental set of categories for theologians to employ. For example, Paul in his most sustained discussion of Israel in Romans 9 – 11 does not draw as much attention to empirical Israel's disobedience as he does to its unbelief. Using the image of an olive vine and its branches he writes, 'But they were broken off because of unbelief [*apistia*, 'unfaithfulness' or 'unbelief'], and you stand by faith [*pistei*]' (Rom. 11:20). The writer to the Hebrews describes the wilderness generation's failure to enter the Promised Land in the same terms: 'So we see that they were unable to enter, because of their unbelief [*apistian*]' (Heb. 3:19). Speaking of Israel's history, Paul does refer in Romans 10:16 to some Israelites disobeying the gospel. Even in this reference, however, Paul quotes the prophet Isaiah in evidence and the quote speaks of faith not obedience. Paul writes, 'But not all the Israelites accepted [*hypakousan*, 'obeyed' as in the NRSV] the good news. For Isaiah says [Isa. 53:1], "Lord, who has believed our message?' Paul appears to understand the link between unbelief and disobedience.

How then are the faithfulness and obedience of Christ to be related? Are they independent principles of action? Is one subordinated to the other in importance? Are they coordinate principles? The obedience of Christ, so essential to atonement, I suggest, issued from his faithfulness. The exegetical basis for this claim I examined previously. However, there is also a logical point to be made. Obedience begs the questions of obedience to whom (e.g. a parent) and obedience to what (e.g. a law). In either case, there is someone or something to be believed. It is odd, to say the least, to assert that

---

[46] McCheyne 1961: 102–103.

I obeyed the police but I don't believe they exist. Such belief is logically necessary for obedience to exist. However, such belief is insuf-
ficient: one might obey out of fear or some other motive and not out
of faithfulness (e.g. a political prisoner). Thomas Becket in T. S.
Eliot's play *Murder in the Cathedral* recognizes the importance of
motive when he says, 'The last temptation is the greatest treason: To
do the right deed for the wrong reason.'[47] Faithfulness involves a
belief as to the value of the word to be obeyed and/or the person to
be obeyed. Though necessary, belief as to value is still not sufficient.
Faithfulness as an attitude issuing in action also requires a commitment to a person or task and that is maintained over time, especially
in the face of testing. Paul describes the Roman Christians as those
who had 'become obedient [*hypēkousate*] from the heart [*ek kardias*]
to the form of teaching to which you were entrusted [*paredothēte*]'
(Rom. 6:17 NRSV). The apostle was not interested in mere outward
conformity. He also wrote in the same letter of 'the obedience of
faith' (Rom. 1:5 and 16:26 NRSV).[48] If there is merit in the above
reflections, Jesus paradigmatically instantiated the obedience sourced
in faith.[49]

Jesus' faithful life and atonement

This study takes a broad approach to God's atonement project,
rather than the more traditional and narrow one that focuses on
the cross. Consequently, we have considered the faithfulness/
faithfilledness of Christ as seen in his life. The question, however,

---

[47] Eliot 1935: 44.

[48] There is ambiguity here, as C. C. Hill points out. Paul could be writing of faith
as an expression of obedience or of obedience as an expression of faith (2000: 1088).
The NRSV is to be preferred to the NIV in translating both Rom. 1:5 and 16:26. E.g. the
NIV in Rom. 1:5 decides the interpretative question for the reader: 'the obedience that
comes from faith' (presumably taking *pisteōs* as a genitive of source). This translation
is certainly possible as is 'the obedience which is faith', as Hawthorne (2001) maintains. Moo (2001) says, 'Believing and obeying are two different activities, but for
Paul they were always inseparable: people cannot truly obey God without first
bowing the knee to the Lord Jesus in faith; and people cannot truly believe in that
Lord Jesus without obeying all that he has commanded us (Mt. 28:20)' (comment on
Rom. 1:5; original emphasis).

[49] N. T. Wright (2004: 54) suggests, '"Faithfulness" and "obedience" turn out to be
two ways of saying much the same thing. "Faithfulness" highlights Jesus' role in fulfilling Israel's commission; "obedience" highlights his submission to the Father's
will.' This is both helpful and puzzling. Helpful because he distinguishes the difference
in what is highlighted. The puzzling part is how 'fulfilling Israel's commission' and
'submission to the Father's will' are then conceptually much the same.

arises as to how Christ's faithful life connects with the work of atonement. Does it connect at all? Calvin's Geneva Catechism for children of 1545 thinks not. The master asks, 'Why do you make the transition forthwith from birth to death, omitting all the story of his life?' The scholar replies, 'Because nothing is dealt with here, except what so pertains to our redemption, as in some degree to contain the substance of it.'[50] However, another Reformation era catechism takes the more expansive view followed in this study. The Heidelberg Catechism of 1563 asserts, 'That *during his whole life on earth*, but especially at the end, Christ sustained, in body and soul, the wrath of God against the sin of the whole human race.'[51]

In anticipation of subsequent discussion we shall briefly reflect on Christ's faithfulness and the imputation of righteousness to us. There are current debates to engage here, which we shall do in a later chapter. Next we shall consider the importance of Christ's faithfulness for his high priestly vocation, which shall be discussed more expansively in the next chapter. Both themes deserve some consideration here to provide some backdrop to what is to come.

Christ's faithfulness and imputation

Christ's faithfulness issued in obedience. His obedience constituted his righteousness. His righteousness is put to our account, if we are believers, as the traditional doctrine of imputation maintains. It is put to our account not because of a mere reckoning so by God, but because we are really united to Christ by the Spirit. We are in Christ (*en tō Christō*). Without such righteousness we cannot be at-one with a holy and righteous God. This union is a matter of faith, not sight, and is unimaginable, but not inconceivable.[52] We shall return in chapter 7 to this key idea of our union with Christ, when we consider the 'peace dividend' the cross brings.

Christ's faithfulness and his high priestly ministry

In general terms, Christ perfectly fulfilled the vocation to be human. Christ's perfect faithfulness meant that he lived a perfectly pleasing

---

[50] Quoted in H. Berkhof 1979: 300, Q. and A. 55.

[51] Ibid., A. 37; my emphasis.

[52] In my view, imagination (at least in part) has to do with our ability to form a mental picture. Conceivability, on the other hand, has to do with our reason's capacity to form a non-contradictory notion. E.g. I can imagine a pregnant bull, but I cannot form a coherent concept of one. A square circle I can neither imagine nor conceive of. Many a Christian idea and doctrine (e.g. the Trinity) are conceivable, but unimaginable.

life to God in his humanity. No unfaithfulness could be found in him, unlike Adam and unlike Israel. In particular terms, Christ was thus qualified to be the perfect offerer and offering with regard to human sin. In other words, he was qualified in the particular calling of great high priest. The book of Hebrews makes much of this.

Conclusion

Jesus, God's faithful Son, in contrast to unfaithful Adam and unfaithful Israel, lived by every word that proceeds out of the mouth of God. He was and is perfect. Irenaeus was right to see in Christ the very reverse of Adam's behavior. Jesus' perfect faithfulness can be seen in the Gospels at a number of critical points in the narrative. The temptations and the cross are just two. His faithfulness is thematized by New Testament witnesses as diverse as Paul, the writer to the Hebrews, Peter and the John who wrote the book of Revelation. Even his critics recognized his trust in God at the cross – albeit mockingly. His perfect faithfulness and his perfect obedience stand in the closest of connections. One trusts a person. One obeys the command of a person. He trusted God. He obeyed God. His faith issued in the obedience that is the ground of our righteousness. He did not merely assent to the will of his father; he did it from the heart. Without his perfect righteousness imputed to us we cannot be at one with God. In addition, without his perfect righteousness he could not be the perfect offerer and offering for our sins, as we shall explore in the next chapter. His high priestly ministry as articulated by the book of Hebrews is predicated on this double perfection.

Chapter Six

The death and vindication of the faithful Son

In the previous chapter we examined Christ's faithfulness as the Son who lived by every word that proceeds out of the mouth of God. His faithfulness showed in his obedience. Calvin was right to argue, 'Christ has redeemed us through his obedience, which he practiced throughout his life.' But how so? Calvin's answer is couched in terms of Christ's obedience but makes better sense, in my view, if 'faithfulness' is substituted for obedience. He asks the question 'Now someone asks, How has Christ abolished sin, banished the separation between us and God, and acquired righteousness to render God favorable and kindly toward us?' And then answers, 'To this, we can in general reply that he has achieved for us by the whole course of his obedience [I would say 'faithfulness'].'[1] Calvin, however, saw the need for more precision in his answer: 'Yet to define the way of salvation more exactly, Scripture ascribes this as peculiar and proper to Christ's death.'[2] Christ's death and its vindication through the resurrection are the concerns of this chapter.

Humanist European intellectual and famed novelist Umberto Eco offers a startling idea as he ponders Christianity's great claim concerning Christ. He illustrates too how someone outside the church can be theologically astute and independently support Calvin's point:

> If I am a believer, I find it sublime that God asked his only son to sacrifice himself for the salvation of all mankind . . . But if I think that God does not exist, then the question becomes even more sublime: I have to ask myself how a section of humanity possessed enough imagination to invent a God who was made man and who allowed himself to die for the love of humanity. The fact that humanity could conceive of so sublime and paradoxical an idea, on which mankind's

---

[1] Calvin 2002e: 2.16.5.
[2] Ibid.

intimacy with the divine is founded, inspires me with great admiration for it.[3]

Eco clearly recognizes the astounding nature of the Christian claim. Of course, for the believer, the sacrifice of Christ is no human invention, no mere cultural artefact, but divine provision.

For all their differences, both Arminian and Calvinist theologians have recognized the importance of the divine provision of the atoning death of Christ. From the Arminian side John Wesley said, 'Nothing in the Christian system is of greater consequence than the doctrine of the atonement.'[4] And from the Reformed ranks, B. B. Warfield articulated the importance of the cross to Christianity as follows:

> This is as much to say that not only is the doctrine of the sacrificial death of Christ embodied in Christianity as an essential element of the system, but in a very real sense it constitutes Christianity. It is this which differentiates Christianity from other religions. Christianity did not come into the world to proclaim a new morality and, sweeping away all the supernatural props by which men were wont to support their trembling, guilt-stricken souls, to throw them back on their own strong right arms to conquer a standing before God for themselves.

What then, according to Warfield, did Christianity have to offer the world?

> It came to proclaim the real sacrifice for sin which God had provided in order to supersede all the poor fumbling efforts which men had made and were making to provide a sacrifice for sin for themselves; and, planting men's feet on this, to bid them go forward.[5]

'Sin and sacrifice' were for Warfield the key terms and, as we shall see, rightly so. For in our broken world no shalom can come without sacrifice.[6]

---

[3] Eco 1999: 215–216.

[4] John Wesley in Watson 1984: 99.

[5] Warfield 1970: 425–426.

[6] Given the literature that the story of the sufferings of Christ has generated, my account will need to be highly selective. E.g. Jeffery, Ovey and Sach (2007) devote 373 pages to expounding and defending only penal substitution.

Sacrifice

When we use the term 'sacrifice' in common speech in the West, it typically refers to some act that results in personal cost to ourselves and done for the benefit of another. For example, a woman sacrificed her time last weekend for the firm. She went into the office and got the report ready early. Or parents sacrificed the house to pay for the operation for their daughter. A soldier sacrificed himself for his comrades by throwing himself on a grenade in Afghanistan. This is not the language of offering. In Scripture, however, the language of sacrifice has a religious meaning: it is the language of offering. A sacrifice is that which is offered to God.

As we saw in an earlier chapter, the Old Testament speaks of various sacrifices: sin, guilt, burnt and peace. In the New Testament, 'sacrifice' is on occasion used in an extended sense in that it can refer to all that we offer to God in response to the gospel, as in Romans 12:1: 'Therefore, I urge you, brothers, in view of God's mercy [the gospel], to offer your bodies as living sacrifices [*thysian*, lit. a 'living sacrifice', sg.], holy and pleasing to God – this is your spiritual act of worship.' Likewise, in Hebrews 13:15 we find this invitation: 'Through Jesus, therefore, let us continually offer [*anapherōmen*] to God a sacrifice [*thysian*] of praise – the fruit of lips that confess his name.' The next verse extends the usage even further: 'And do not forget to do good and to share with others, for with such sacrifices [*thysias*] God is pleased.'

However, in the New Testament the language of sacrifice chiefly has to do with Christ and his death, not ourselves. According to I. H. Marshall:

> The New Testament takes over the sacrificial language of the Old and uses it to express in bold metaphor the significance of the death of Jesus. The sacrificial term 'blood' is used more often than any other expression to indicate the death of Jesus (Mk.14:24; Jn. 6:53–56; Acts 20:28; Rom. 3:25; 5:9; Col. 1:29; Heb. 9:14; 13:11ff.; 1 Jn. 1;7; Rev. 1:5). This is all the more remarkable when we recall that death by crucifixion did not involve the shedding of blood to any significant extent.[7]

---

[7] Marshall 1990: 82. Likewise, Swinburne (1989: 152), who says, 'To my mind, by far the most satisfactory biblical model for what was effected by the life and death of Christ is the model of sacrifice.'

The apostle Paul captures eloquently the nexus between Christ, his death, his sacrifice and its benefit for the sake of others in the following graphic way: 'Christ loved us and gave himself up for us as a fragrant offering and sacrifice to God' (Eph. 5:2).

The question before us is how Christ's sacrifice is integral to God's atoning project in the narrow sense of dealing with our sins. Here Christ's work as our great high priest comes to the fore, or, more broadly speaking, his work defeats the forces of evil that oppose shalom. Here Christ's work as our King comes into sharp relief. Indeed, J. S. Whale maintains, 'Christ's sacrifice is represented throughout the New Testament as a cosmic necessity.'[8]

Let us consider the broader picture next.

Divine victory through sacrifice

As noted in a previous chapter, after the fall the very first hint of good news in the canon of Scripture speaks of victory over the serpent that worked such mischief in the garden:

> And I will put enmity
>   between you and the woman,
>   and between your offspring and hers;
> he will crush your head,
>   and you will strike his heel.
>
> (Gen. 3:15)

---

[8] Whale 1957: 89. Christ's death is not only integral to the work of atonement but, in addition, Jesus as Prophet made it plain that it was necessary (*dei*) for him to die (Mark 8:31). Yet what kind of necessity attends the cross? Learned discussion canvasses the merits of hypothetical necessity versus absolute consequent necessity. In the former view, a sovereign God could have elected a different way to save than one involving the sacrifice of the Son. This position protects the freedom of God. In the latter view, consequent upon the divine election of some sinners for salvation, it was absolutely necessary for the Son to die as an atonement for their sins. There was no other way. This view protects the wisdom and freedom of God. See the discussion in J. Murray 1961: 11–12. Vanhoozer (2005: 384–389) provocatively embraces the 'consequent necessity' position, but also describes the cross as an 'improvisation' and 'eternal improvising'. How these ideas comport is not immediately clear. These debates need not detain us. However, at the very least we must assert that a prophetic necessity was in play. Jesus 'said to them, "How foolish you are, and how slow of heart to believe all that the prophets have spoken! Did not the Christ have to [*edei*] suffer these things and then enter his glory?" And beginning with Moses and all the Prophets, he explained to them what was said in all the Scriptures concerning himself' (Luke 24:25–26). God stands by his promises!

Jesus himself described his work as binding the strong man (Mark 3:27; Satan in the context). In the book of Acts, Peter preached to Cornelius:

> You know the message God sent to the people of Israel, telling *the good news of peace* through Jesus Christ, who is Lord of all. You know what has happened throughout Judea, beginning in Galilee after the baptism that John preached – how God anointed Jesus of Nazareth with the Holy Spirit and power, and how he went around doing good and *healing all who were under the power of the devil*, because God was with him. (Acts 10:36–38; my emphases)

Significantly, the above passage of Scripture highlights both the peace theme ('good news of peace') and victory over the devil ('healing all who were under the power of the devil').

The early church Fathers were especially attracted to the idea of victory over the devil and some of them developed strange ways of elaborating the concept.[9] For example, Rufinus of Aquileia (c. 345–410) wrote:

> [The purpose of the incarnation] was that the divine virtue of the Son of God might be like a kind of hook hidden beneath the form of human flesh [. . .] to lure on the prince of this world to a contest; that the Son might offer him his human flesh as a bait and that the divinity which lay underneath might catch him and hold him fast with its hook.[10]

One may applaud Rufinus of Aquileia for taking the defeat of Satan so seriously. But his imagination took him into the realm of the

---

[9] It was the Swedish Lutheran theologian Aulén (1931) who made the term 'Christus Victor' famous in theology. He argued that this understanding of the atonement was the classic view of the Fathers of the early church and of Luther too. He may have overstated his thesis, but in so doing recovered a key aspect of the New Testament witness. Pelikan (1971: 149) offers this caution: 'To be sure, other ways of speaking about the atonement were too widespread even among the Greek fathers to permit us to ascribe exclusive or even primary force to any one theory, but Christ as victor was more important in orthodox expositions of salvation and reconciliation than Western dogmatics has realized.' Pelikan's observation is borne out by the amazing absence of the Christus Victor theme from Roman Catholicism's most recent official catechism, CCC, as both the table of contents and subject index show.

[10] Quoted in McGrath 2007b: 349. Augustine preferred the mousetrap version of the theory, with Christ as the innocent bait (352–353).

fanciful and dubiously moral. Is such deception of Satan compatible with divine goodness? I think not.

This 'fish hook' theory of the atonement is an example drawn from a family of theories known as Christus Victor. In general terms many theologians of the first millennium (e.g. Irenaeus, Origen, Gregory of Nyssa and Gregory the Great) believed that Satan through his deception of Eve and Adam in the garden of Eden had secured some kind of right over their destinies and with them all humanity.[11] After all, Scripture does describe Satan as 'the prince [*archōn*, 'ruler'] of this world' (e.g. John 12:31). Christ's death provided a ransom that set the captives free. He died as an innocent and, in some way or another, in so doing outsmarted the evil one and broke his power over humanity.[12]

A contemporary evangelical advocate of Christus Victor is Gregory A. Boyd. His elaboration though exhibits none of the grotesqueries of Rufinus'. Boyd concludes his argument with this *confessio fidei* (confession of faith) in which he boldly asserts, 'I believe the Christus Victor model of the atonement should be considered more foundational to our thinking about Jesus than other atonement models.'[13] Moreover, in a qualified way, he is even prepared to follow the fathers in viewing Jesus as 'in a sense, "bait"'.[14] His belief

[11] Unsurprisingly, Eastern Orthodoxy with its veneration of the Fathers has never resiled from the Christus Victor view. K. Ware (1996: 52) writes, 'Each year we Orthodox relive Christ's saving victory with particular vividness in the triumphant service of Easter midnight.' He (52) also endorses Aulén's judgment that Christus Victor is 'the classic approach to the atonement so far as the Christian East is concerned'.

[12] For the substance of this paragraph I am indebted to Beilby and Eddy (2006: 12–13). Their introduction provides a handy, albeit brief, treatment both of the history of the doctrine of the atonement and contemporary discussions.

[13] Boyd in ibid. 23–49. I prefer the thick terms 'interpretation' or 'tradition' to those of 'theory', 'model' or 'metaphor'. I am using some of Carson's terminology here as found in McCormack (2008: 60). Carson is comfortable with the term 'theory' but not as comfortable with 'model'. Like Carson I believe that the terms 'model' and 'theory' are now so widely used that both will continue to feature in the literature. Consequently, they will appear on occasion in this book. In my view, an interpretation of the atonement elaborates a biblical fact about the death of Christ and the language it is couched in by teasing out its presuppositions and entailments. E.g. assuming that penal substitution is biblically grounded, what theory of justice does it presuppose? Does the biblical fact of penal substitution (and with it propitiation) presuppose retributive justice? Or is there more than one theory of justice that comports with Scripture's testimony to the death of Christ? A strong interpretation would claim that its proposals are *demanded by* the text, while a weak interpretation would claim that its proposals are *consistent with* the text. 'Metaphor' in my view is too thin as a descriptor of what is on offer in an atonement tradition or interpretation to be of much use as a master concept.

[14] Boyd in Beilby and Eddy 2006: 37. Boyd (101) also sees in C. S. Lewis's *The Lion, the Witch and the Wardrobe* 'a marvelous parable of the Christus Victor understanding of Christ's substitutionary role in redeeming humanity'. Lewis was deeply read in the Fathers of the early church.

rests on a wide induction of biblical testimonies that cover the warfare motif in Scripture and Christ's victory over the powers. How right is he? Is the Bible on his side? That is one question. The other concerns the claim that Christus Victor is foundational. To that question we shall return when we examine the claim that the penal substitution theory is central to the atonement.

The idea that one key aspect of the work of Christ on the cross is to deal with Satan and evil has firm biblical grounding. The *proto-evangelium* of Genesis 3:15 signals the divine intent to defeat evil, and the cross constitutes the blow. Paul tells the Colossians:

> When you were dead in your sins and in the uncircumcision of your sinful nature, God made you alive with Christ. He forgave us all our sins, having cancelled the written code, with its regulations, that was against us and that stood opposed to us; he took it away, nailing it to the cross. *And having dis-armed the powers and authorities, he made a public spectacle of them, triumphing over them by the cross.* (Col. 2:13–15; my emphasis)

Indeed, this Christus Victor theme connects the incarnation and the cross as far the letter to the Hebrews is concerned:

> Since the children have flesh and blood, he too shared in their humanity so that by his death he might destroy him who holds the power of death – that is, the devil – and free those who all their lives were held in slavery by their fear of death. For surely it is not angels he helps [*epilambanetai*, 'lays hold of'],[15] but Abraham's descendants. For this reason he had to be made like his brothers in every way, in order that he might become a merciful and faithful high priest in service to God, and that he might make atonement for the sins of the people. Because he himself suffered when he was tempted, he is able to help those who are being tempted. (Heb. 2:14–18)

---

[15] I am following P. T. O'Brien here ('Hebrews 2', unpublished MS, 34): 'The verb used to describe Christ's action, *epilambanomai*, basically means to "seize, lay hold of" something. Although it has been understood metaphorically to mean "assume the nature of", "prefer", "be concerned about" or even "help", it is best taken in a literal sense depicting Christ, the pioneer, as taking hold of his followers on the way to glory, a notion that exactly fits the imagery of the whole passage.'

Christ's high priestly work is predicated upon his humanity and that work is the work of the cross, as the letter to the Hebrews proceeds to establish. (More on this below.) Finally, the last book in the canon reveals that it is the slain Lamb whose shed blood enables martyrs to overcome (*enikēsan*) the devil (Rev. 12:11).[16]

The idea of ransom too has solid biblical warrant. Jesus himself famously described his work in ransom categories: 'Just as the Son of Man did not come to be served, but to serve, and to give his life as a ransom [*lytron*] for many' (Matt. 20:28 NIV). There is a cost: his death. However, Jesus does not elaborate. This did not stop Origen in the early church period from doing so. In his Commentary on Matthew (16:8) he asks:

> To whom was the ransom paid? Certainly not to God; can it be to the evil one? For he had power over us until the ransom was given to him on our behalf, namely the life of Jesus; and he was deceived thinking he could keep his soul in his power; not seeing that he could not reach the standard required so as to be able to keep it in his power.[17]

Origen's theological imagination was both his great strength (he is the great speculative theologian of the early church) and his great weakness, because in this case his reflections on the idea of ransom fly unfettered from the wider Matthean context.

In its Matthean context the ransom idea is not linked to the defeat of the devil either explicitly or implicitly. What then does ransom mean in the context? Donald A. Hagner says:

> 'Ransom,' although drawn from the background of purchasing the freedom of a slave or captive (i.e., to free by payment), is here used in a metaphorical sense for a setting free from sin and its penalty at the cost of the sacrifice of Jesus. This is the

---

[16] Aune (2004) says, '"And they conquered him through the blood of the Lamb." The verb *nikaō*, "to conquer, be victorious," occurs seventeen times in Revelation; when Christ is the subject of this verb (5:5), it means that he conquered *through death*, and it means precisely the same thing when it is used eleven times of Christians, explicitly in 12:11 and implicitly in the other references (cf. 2:7, 11, 17, 26; 3:5, 12, 21 [2×] . . . There is a close parallel to v 11a in 1 Cor. 15:57, "Thanks to God who gave us victory [*nikos*] through our Lord Jesus Christ," where in the context of the entire chapter it is likely that the resurrection of Jesus is meant. Nevertheless, in both passages, one emphasizing Christ's death and the other his resurrection, victory is achieved by means of Christ (*dia*)' (comment on Rev. 12:11).

[17] Bettenson 1978: 224.

service performed by the suffering servant of Isa 53 (see esp. Isa 53:10–12, where the servant [v. 11] gives himself up to death as an offering for sin and bears the sin of 'many' [v. 12]).[18]

Origen would have been on firmer biblical ground if he had considered Paul's Colossian letter. Paul writes, 'For he has rescued us from the dominion of darkness and brought us into the kingdom of the Son he loves, in whom we have redemption, the forgiveness of sins' (Col. 1:13–14). Peter O'Brien elaborates, 'Negatively, God has delivered us . . . from the tyranny of darkness and, positively, he has placed us under the rule of his beloved Son.'[19] There are echoes here of those Old Testament texts that speak of 'Deliverance from an alien power'.[20] The principalities and powers are in view implicitly in Colossians 1:14–15 and come into explicit view in Colossians 2:15. Even so Colossians gives Origen no licence to pursue his question 'To whom was the ransom paid?'

The Scriptures are obviously addressed to us as creatures. Paul did not write his letters to angels, principalities and powers. As a consequence, we can lose sight of the wider canvas. Job did not know of that wider canvas, nor did his 'friends'. Hence the 'friends' made an all too easy moral equation between suffering and personal sin in Job's life. But we as readers do know because of the first two chapters that reveal the cynicism of Satan expressed before the divine council: 'A man will give all he has for his own life. But stretch out your hand and strike his flesh and bones, and he will surely curse you to your face' (Job 2:4–5). Job's integrity is under test against a cosmic backdrop. If we lose sight of the bigger picture, we can shrink the achievement of Christ's work down to how it affects us at the personal level alone.[21] Yet the New Testament draws the veil aside on occasion to reveal that God has a cosmic point to make. Paul writes to the Ephesians:

His intent was that now, through the church, the manifold wisdom of God should be made known to the rulers and

---

[18] Hagner 2004b, comment on Matt. 20:28.

[19] O'Brien 2004, comment on Col. 1:13–14.

[20] Ibid., 'Deliverance from an alien power was an important theme in the OT (the Lord rescued his people from the hand of the Egyptians [Exod. 14:30; Judg. 6:9], from bondage [Exod. 6:6] and from all her enemies [Judg. 8:34]).'

[21] The personal must not be played off against the cosmic. Christ commissioned his disciples to proclaim the forgiveness of sins in his name, not the defeat of the devil (Luke 24:46–49; Acts 2:38; 10:38; 13:38; 26:16–18).

authorities in the heavenly realms, according to his eternal purpose which he accomplished in Christ Jesus our Lord. In him and through faith in him we may approach God with freedom and confidence. (Eph. 3:10–12; my emphasis)

The eternal purpose, of which Paul writes, concerns the wisdom of the cross that brings peace between Jew and Gentile (Eph. 2:14 – 3:9). The Christus Victor theme then helps to remind us of the bigger canvas in a way that some other interpretations of the cross (e.g. exemplarist theories) might not.

However, just how the victory over the devil and evil is secured by the death of Christ ultimately requires our consideration of other aspects of the cross. In particular, we shall need to reflect on how the cross as a sacrifice removes the fear of death and addresses the accusations levelled against us as sinners by the evil one. In other words, how the cross breaks Satan's power.[22] (More on this in the next chapter.)

The idea of satisfaction

The idea of satisfaction, understood variously, has had a long history in Christian thought and practice. In Roman Catholic theology, for example, the term may mean, as in the medieval period, 'the compensation for a debt or offense', or, as in the sacrament of penance, that which is voluntarily accepted by the penitent 'to expiate the temporal punishment of sin', or 'the penance imposed by a superior in a religious institute'.[23] In Protestant scholastic theology *satisfactio* (satisfaction) refers to 'making amends or reparation; specifically the making amends for sin required by God for forgiveness to take place'.[24] The definition, which I shall shortly propound, subsumes the Protestant scholastic one but is not exhausted by it.

At this point it is worth observing that there is a whole family of atonement theories known as 'satisfaction' theories that go back most notably to Anselm in the medieval period. In these theories

---

[22] There is a weakness in Vanhoozer (2005) on this point. The idea of drama that he magnificently works with assumes conflict. However, there are no references in his subject index to 'Satan', 'devil' or 'demons'. The Christus Victor theme, while present in the work, is muted.

[23] Broderick 1987: 542. Also see Muller 1986: 271.

[24] Muller 1986: 271.

Christ's death makes amends for human sin. In many ways, Anselm is the father of satisfaction theories. For him Christ's death satisfied the divine honour that had been offended by human sin. Christ rendered that honour with a surplus of merit that may be put to our account if we embrace the Son. Thus amends are made. To explore Anselm's debts to his feudal context and his rationalism would take me too far from my brief. Two comments are in order though. First, we need to note that for Anselm divine love motivated the provision of atonement.[25] From some discussions of his theology one could gain the impression that only the 'mechanical' pursuit of divine honour was God's motive. Secondly, it is important to note that Anselm argued that the atonement satisfied divine justice and not merely divine honour. Moreover, in so doing, as E. R. Fairweather suggests, 'Anselm avoids the slightest suggestion that the atonement is the placating of an angry God, the satisfaction of an offended Father by the punishment of a loving Son.'[26] How then do honour and justice relate? Formally, the Creator must be given what he is owed. This is only just. Materially God is owed honour.[27] Giving God his honour is to do justice to God. Anselm has much to teach us still, even though we do not live in his feudal world of honour and shame. Even so I want to propose a concept of satisfaction that takes us beyond Anselm's.[28] Whether it is as culture bound I shall leave the reader to judge. The language of satisfaction per se is used typically in Scripture of human satisfaction and not of God's satisfying himself in some way. One's hunger is to be satisfied at a feast (e.g. Deut. 14:29). The Lord satisfies the earth 'by the fruit of his work' (Ps. 104:13). In a notable instance the Servant of the Lord is satisfied at the completion of his task (Isa. 53:11). However, B. B. Warfield's wise words on the term 'Trinity'

[25] Anselm in Fairweather 1956: 104, 106.

[26] Fairweather 1956: 57. In contrast, A. W. Bartlett (2001: 84) argues that 'a relentless vision of divine honor' animates chs. 11–24 in *Cur Deus homo* and that violence is the beating heart of Anselm's work. How this claim squares with Anselmic statements such as the Father 'did not love the Son's suffering' is unclear (Anselm in Fairweather 1956: 117).

[27] Anselm in Fairweather 1956, Bk 1, ch. 24, and Bk 2, ch. 20, esp. For the history see G. Allison 2007: 8–10; and for an analysis, Letham 1993: 164–165.

[28] Interestingly, Leanne Van Dyk (in Placher 2003: 218) also calls for 'an expanded conception of satisfaction'. Her (216) expanded version of satisfaction includes the notion that 'Jesus Christ satisfied God – satisfied God's determination to be God-for-us in full human form.' However, her proposal materially speaking differs significantly from my own. E.g. she explicitly refuses to allow any penal dimension in her account.

and the doctrine it represents have application here. He argues, 'A doctrine so defined, can be spoken of as a Biblical doctrine only on the principle that the sense of Scripture is Scripture.'[29] I am contending that there is a biblical doctrine of divine satisfaction. Satisfaction is meeting the divine desires, longings, expectations and wants as well as realizing divine purposes and intentions. Desires, longings, expectations, wants, purposes and intentions are the characteristics of a person. In human experience to have a project successfully realized where one's desires, expectation, and wants are met is satisfying in the extreme. Now someone might ask, 'Is this not construing God too anthropomorphically, projecting our experience on to God?' Fair question. However, given the biblical teaching about *imago Dei* it may not so much be that to do so is to project something alien on to the Creator. Rather, it may simply be that our experiences of satisfaction are theomorphic. We are persons (lower-case 'p'), while God is Personal (capital 'P'). Satisfaction is thus a fitting idea for our purposes because the triune God revealed in Scripture is clearly Personal. Indeed, the idea of satisfaction, as I have defined it, is found as early in the canon as Genesis 1. For example, we see it in the repeated refrain 'And God saw that it was good' (Gen. 1:10, 12, 18, 21, 25 and the climax, 31, 'very good'). Creation fulfils the divine intentions. According to T. E. Fretheim, 'In this remarkable and recurring phrase, God responds to the work, making evaluations of it . . . This statement carries the sense of achieving the divine intention, which includes elements of beauty, purpose, and praise.'[30]

With that conceptual work behind us the question becomes, 'How then is God satisfied when it comes to realizing the project of reconciliation?'[31]

Satisfaction of divine holiness through sacrifice

Jesus' sacrifice satisfies the divine holiness because he offers himself as a lamb without spot or blemish to God in our place.

---

[29] Warfield 1958: 79.

[30] Fretheim 2002a: 343–344.

[31] Weaver would presumably find even my expanded understanding of the concept of satisfaction repugnant: 'my argument exposes the divine violence intrinsic to any and all forms of satisfaction atonement, and shows that no amount of redefining or interpreting or supplementing or amending or enriching the satisfaction motif overcomes that violence. It should be abandoned' (in Sanders 2006: 1–2). In the appendix I attempt to address the question of violence and the atonement.

Holiness requires no less. In a context in which the holiness of God is prominent, 1 Peter 1:18–19 presents Christ in these sacrificial terms: 'For you know that it was not with perishable things such as silver or gold that you were redeemed from the empty way of life handed down to you from your forefathers, but with the precious blood of Christ, a lamb without blemish or defect.'[32] The references to 'blood' and 'lamb' take us back to the Old Testament and, in particular, Leviticus 22:21, which speaks of an acceptable offering as one 'without defect [*amōmou*] or blemish [*aspilou*]'.[33] There may also be an allusion to the Passover lamb and the suffering servant of Isaiah 53, but J. Ramsey Michaels is probably right to argue:

> Although Peter's metaphor recalls the regulations for the Passover lamb according to Exod 12:5, his terminology is drawn not from the LXX of that verse . . . where Exod 12:5 is restated in the terminology of 1 Peter, and probably not exclusively from traditions about the Passover lamb, but in a more general way from the LXX and from Jewish sacrificial language.[34]

Likewise, the letter to the Hebrews presents Christ's death in sacrificial terms. In a contrast between the old order and the new, if the blood of goats and bulls sanctified the ceremonially unclean a fortiori, 'How much more, then, will the blood of Christ, who through the eternal Spirit offered himself unblemished [*amōmou*] to God, cleanse our consciences from acts that lead to death, so that we may serve the living God!' (Heb. 9:14).

Theologically speaking, the sinlessness of Christ is vital to his sacrificial work. Without such sinlessness he could not be the ultimate high priest because, as the letter to Hebrews argues, if he were like all his predecessors, then he would need regularly to offer a sacrifice for his own sins as well as those of the people (Heb. 10:1–14). However, as the letter to the Hebrews demonstrates, Jesus' priesthood was not Aaronic but Melchizedekian. His priesthood is unique. He was not caught up in the sorry track record of so much of the Aaronic line.[35] W. H. Griffith-Thomas pithily makes the point, 'As Priest, Christ is

---

[32] Puzzlingly, Finlan (2007: 43) cites 1 Peter as 'Deutero-Pauline'.
[33] D. L. Bartlett 2002: 258–259.
[34] Michaels 2004, comment on 1 Pet. 1:18–19.
[35] Finely discussed by Letham (1993: 106–108).

our Representative, but as Sacrifice He is of necessity our Substitute.'[36] The necessity lies in the fact that only an unblemished offering can constitute the definitive sacrifice.

The Hebrews' accent on the finality of Christ's sacrifice underlines its definitive nature, especially the language of *hapax* ('once for all' NIV, Heb. 9:26; 'once' NIV, Heb. 9:28) and *ephapax* ('once for all', e.g. Heb. 9:12; 10:10).[37] The definitive nature of Christ's sacrifice is also signalled in the Matthean account of the rending in two of the temple curtain (Matt. 27:50–51): 'And when Jesus had cried out again in a loud voice, he gave up his spirit. At that moment the curtain of the temple was torn in two from top to bottom.' Access to the divine presence has been opened up to all by the death of Christ. Donald A. Hagner says, 'With the atoning death of Jesus, toward which the sacrificial cultus pointed, this system has come to an end. From that time on, every believer, Jew and Gentile, has immediate and unrestricted access to God and to the forgiveness of sins accomplished through the death of Jesus on the cross.'[38] An unholy Christ would have accomplished nothing.

P. T. Forsyth rightly captures the importance of satisfying the divine holiness in the following way: 'By the atonement, therefore, is meant that action of Christ's death which has *a prime regard to God's holiness*, has it for its first charge, and *finds man's reconciliation impossible except as that holiness is divinely satisfied once for all on the cross.*'[39]

Satisfaction of divine righteousness through sacrifice

Paul is crystal clear: 'the wages of sin is death' (Rom. 6:23). In saying this to the Romans he has firm Old Testament backing. The warning in the garden in Genesis 2:16–17 runs, 'And the LORD God

---

[36] Griffith-Thomas 1963: 59. Denney (1973: 196) argues that there is a sequence in the New Testament. Christ does his work on the cross as our sacrificial substitute and only then can he do his work as our representative. However, it is as our great high priest that he, according to Heb. 8 – 10, offers that sacrifice. To do justice to the New Testament we need both the language of representation (Christ has my interests at heart) and substitution (Christ died in my place).

[37] Surprisingly, Letham (1993: 128) wrongly cites Heb. 10:12 and 10:14 as examples. However, neither *hapax* nor *ephapax* appears in these texts.

[38] Hagner 2004b, comment on Matt. 27:51. Like Hagner, Boring (2002: 492–493), comment on Matt. 27:51) sees the apocalyptic elements in the passage but misses its full import. He reduces its message to a signal of the temple's coming destruction.

[39] Forsyth 1909: 5; my emphases.

commanded the man, "You are free to eat from any tree in the garden; but you must not eat from the tree of the knowledge of good and evil, for when you eat of it you will surely die."' Ezekiel declares, 'The soul who sins is the one who will die' (Ezek. 18:4). For Paul, Adam is the key to understanding why this is so, as the following phrases drawn for Romans 5:12–18 indicate:

> Therefore, just as sin entered the world through one man [Adam], and death through sin, and in this way death came to all men [and women, *pantas anthrōpous*], because all sinned . . . Nevertheless, death reigned from the time of Adam . . . The judgment followed one sin and brought condemnation . . . by the trespass of the one man, death reigned through that one man . . . the result of one trespass was condemnation for all men [and women, *pantas anthrōpous*] . . .

Patently, Paul sees a causal connection between Adam's folly and subsequent humanity's moral status before a righteous/just holy God.[40]

How may a righteous/just holy God deal with human sin? Is there a way that sin may be dealt with and the one who sins not face the consequences of it? According to Scripture, there is. Jesus' sacrifice satisfies divine righteousness/justice: perhaps the key biblical testimony pertinent to the claim is Romans 3:21–26. In fact, D. A. Carson describes the significance of the passage in the following way: 'Romans 3:21–26 has for a long time been a focal text for debate about the atonement.'[41] Paul writes:

> But now a righteousness [*dikaiosynē*] from God, apart from law, has been made known [*pephanerōtai*, 'manifested'], to which the Law and the Prophets testify. This righteousness [*dikaiosynē*] from God comes through faith in Jesus Christ to all who believe. There is no difference, for all have sinned and fall short of the glory of God, and are justified freely by his grace through the redemption that came by Christ Jesus. God presented him as a sacrifice [*hilastērion*] of atonement, through faith in his blood. He did this to demonstrate [*endeixin*,

---

[40] I have adopted Seifrid's (2001) convention (mentioned in chapter 1) in this opening sentence to indicate that in this section I am treating righteousness and justice as synonyms.

[41] Carson in McCormack 2008: 119.

'display'] his justice [*dikaiosynē*], because in his forbearance
he had left the sins committed beforehand unpunished – he
did it to demonstrate [*endeixin*, 'display'] his justice [*dikaio-*
synē] at the present time, so as to be just and the one who
justifies those who have faith in Jesus. (Rom. 3:21–26)

This crucial passage is replete with references to righteousness/
justice and their relation to Christ's death understood in sacrificial
terms. Indeed, if N. T. Wright is correct about the relevance of 4
Maccabees 17.21–22 as the Second Temple period background to
the text, 'It was, then, thinkable in Paul's period that the suffering of
the righteous Jew might in some way atone, as a sacrifice did, for
Israel.'[42]

What have theologians made of this Romans passage and its
accent on God's character, righteousness, and the cross of Christ?
Henri Blocher for one writes of Romans 3 in these terms:

> In the light of convincing scholarly statements, I reach the
> conclusion that the root meaning of 'righteousness,' 'justice'
> in the Bible is *conformity to a norm*, with an irreducible
> retributive element, and that *dikaiosynē* exhibited on the
> cross according to Romans 3 is *the satisfaction of the*
> *demands of retributive justice*. Through the *sacrificial substi-*
> *tution* of the Redeemer for those who had deserved to die –
> through Christ's death on the cross – *God shows himself*
> *righteous* (inflicting the retribution of sins) and the justifier
> (acquitter) of the guilty who benefit from Christ's
> intervention.[43]

Blocher's conclusion rightly introduces two important notes sounded
in the text: substitution and showing righteousness. Each note lies at

---

[42] N. T. Wright 2002, 10: 475. E.g. 4 Maccabees 17.21–22: 'the tyrant [Antiochus]
was punished, and the homeland purified [*katharizō*] – they have become, as it were, a
ransom for the sins of our nation. And through the blood of those devout ones [the
martyrs at Antioch] and their death as an atoning sacrifice [*hilastērion tou thanatou*],
divine Providence preserved Israel that previously had been mistreated' (NRSV).
Finlan (2007:16) argues, contra the NRSV, that 'death as an atoning sacrifice' ought to
be translated 'atoning death'. 4 Maccabees is probably to be dated between the
middle of the first to early second century AD, according to Tobin (1993: 1815). Tobin
(1835) notes that 'vicarious atonement' is in view.

[43] Blocher in McCormack 2008: 139; my emphases. By 'convincing scholarly statements' Blocher is drawing upon the work of M. A. Seifrid, S. G. Gathercole, D. J.
Moo and M. Silva (ibid. n. 40).

the heart of a historic interpretation of the atonement. The first we shall consider in due course is penal substitution, or what Karl Barth describes as 'The Judge Judged in our Place'; the second is moral government theory, made famous by Grotius.[44] Blocher also draws out a Pauline assumption informing the text; namely, the notion of retributive justice.[45]

With regard to the history of discussion of the atonement, the classic expression of penal substitution is found in Calvin's *Institutes*:

> Accordingly, our Lord came forth as true man and took the person and the name of Adam in order to take Adam's place in obeying the Father, to present our flesh as *the price of satisfaction to God's righteous judgment*, and, in the same flesh, *to pay the penalty that we had deserved* . . . He offered as a sacrifice the flesh he received from us, that he might wipe out our guilt by his act of expiation and appease the Father's righteous wrath.[46]

Here are emphases on a 'price' and 'penalty' paid for the 'satisfaction to God's righteous judgment', and appeasing 'the Father's righteous wrath'. Here is the biblical theology perspective that places the atoning work of Christ in a framework that covers Genesis to Revelation. Importantly, Calvin does not disconnect the death of Christ from his incarnation. No incarnation, no atonement. No atonement, no gospel.

---

[44] *CD* IV/1: 273: 'He [Jesus] took our place as Judge. He took our place as the judged. He was judged in our place. And he acted justly in our place.' This is a profound insight. Letham (1993: 171) describes Barth's position as 'a vigorous and ingenious exposition of the penal substitutionary view of the atonement'. Also see Bromiley 1955: 179–180. A weakness in Jeffery, Ovey and Sach (2007) is their failure to treat Barth. Indeed Barth is not even listed in the index of names. I am grateful to Scott Harrower for drawing my attention to this gap. Stott (1996: 160–161) does not make the same mistake. Interestingly, Pannenberg (1982: 78–89) is comfortable with the language of substitution, representation and expiation. He writes, 'Jesus bore the punishment for blasphemy, not only for the Jewish people alone but for all men' (89). However, where is due weight given to propitiation? See Pannenberg 1994: 421–429. The heading for this section is 'Expiation as Vicarious Penal Suffering'.

[45] Blocher in McCormack 2008: 139. Importantly, he also correctly argues, 'This is not to deny, however, the restorative facet of biblical righteousness/justice . . . Retribution and restoration are not mutually exclusive, and the basis of restoration is in the person of the head and substitute.'

[46] Calvin 2002e: 2.12.3. With regard to Rom. 3:21–26 Calvin understands Christ's death as a propitiation and not simply an expiation, as his comments show; comment on Rom. 3:23–26.

It is worth highlighting that although Calvin is rightly seen as the great advocate of penal substitution, as shown above, his treatment of the cross was not one-dimensional. For Calvin also says:

> In short, since neither as God alone could he feel death, nor as man alone could he overcome it, *he coupled human nature with divine* that to atone for sin he might submit the weakness of the one to death; and that, wrestling with death by the power of the other nature, *he might win victory for us* . . . But we should especially espouse what I have just explained: our common nature with Christ is the pledge of our fellowship with the Son of God; *and clothed with our flesh he vanquished death and sin together that the victory and triumph might be ours.*[47]

In other words, the Christus Victor motif is also strongly thematized by Calvin, but with none of the speculative fantasies of Rufinus of Aquileia. Again, the nexus between incarnation and atonement should be noted. No incarnation, no atonement; but also no atonement, no victory.

The premier contemporary exponent of penal substitution is J. I. Packer, and as we consider his contribution we shall also engage with, as he does, two other key biblical passages adduced as evidence for penal substitution. The doctrine does not rest on Romans 3:21–26 alone. In a seminal article Packer asks the question 'What did the cross achieve?'[48] He then proceeds to unfold the logic of penal substitution. He acknowledges that God's actions are mysterious, as is God himself, by which he means incomprehensible. We do have knowledge of God's actions but not exhaustive knowledge. This is true of the atonement. We must be wary of rationalism that tries to do away with mystery. He is comfortable with the language of models but has a sophisticated understanding of a hierarchy of them. 'Control models' are given in Scripture (e.g. Son of God, kingdom of God etc.). 'Dogmatic models' are those the church 'crystallized out to define and defend the faith' (e.g. Trinity, hypostatic union etc.). The final category consists of 'interpretative models lying between Scripture and defined dogma'. Penal substitution he deems to be an interpretative model 'developed for stating the faith

---

[47] Ibid.; my emphases.
[48] Packer in Packer and Dever 2007: 53–100. This chapter is a reprint of his 1973 Tyndale Biblical Theology Lecture entitled 'What Did the Cross Achieve? The Logic of Penal Substitution'. For the substance of what follows I am indebted *passim*.

to contemporaries'.[49] He briefly looks at historic models of the atonement including exemplarist, Christus Victor and penal substitution. The last of these he argues denies nothing of value in the other two. He vigorously defends as biblical the notions of propitiation (more on this shortly), substitution and satisfaction. Romans 3:21–28 needs to be understood in these terms. He quotes James Denney with approval: 'I do not know any word which conveys the truth of this if "vicarious" or "substitutionary" does not, nor do I know any interpretation of Christ's death which enables us to regard it as a demonstration of love to sinners, if this vicarious or substitutionary character is denied.'[50]

But what kind of substitution? With regard to such a question Packer's answer is unequivocal: penal substitution. Christ bore our punishment before a holy God. The principle of retribution requires that sin be punished, and God did punish sin in Christ for the elect. Packer is a five-point Calvinist. He deals with various objections to penal substitution and reaches all the way back in history to Socinus of the sixteenth century to do so. He closes his argument (with debts to A. M. Hunter) with 'Paul's two *loci classici* on the method of atonement, 2 Corinthians 5:21 and Galatians 3:13'. He quotes Hunter on 2 Corinthians 5:21: 'Paul declares that the crucified Christ, on our behalf, took the whole reality of sin upon himself, like the scapegoat: "For our sake [*hyper hēmōn*, 'on behalf of us'] he made him to be sin who knew no sin, so that in him we might become the righteousness of God."'[51] Packer and Hunter are on firm exegetical ground here. Paul writes of a great exchange in 2 Corinthians 5:21: our sin exchanged for his righteousness.[52] With regard to the

---

[49] Ibid. 63.

[50] Packer (in Packer and Dever 2007: 75, n. 22) is quoting Denney's *The Death of Christ*. Interestingly, Packer does not quote the sentence immediately prior to the Denney quote (1973: 102), which reads, 'The passage in Romans becomes simple as soon as we read it in the light of those we have already examined in 2 Corinthians [5] and Galatians [3].' Denney is right in using the analogy of Scripture (interpreting Scripture by Scripture), for it is in using such a hermeneutic that the substitutionary character of Christ's death in view in Rom. 3:21–26 becomes plain.

[51] Packer in Packer and Dever 2007: 100.

[52] Bridges and Bevington (2007: 14) say, 'The Great Exchange, in which God caused our sin to be traded for Christ's righteousness, is crystallized and summed up in 2 Corinthians 5:21.' N. T. Wright (in McCormack 2006: 252–253) has a very different view of 2 Cor. 5:21. He argues that Paul is not talking soteriologically but vocationally. Paul becomes in Christ an embodiment of the righteousness or covenant faithfulness of God in his apostolic ministry of preaching reconciliation. This is hardly the plain sense. A contemporary theologian who makes much of the idea of 'exchange' in his usual creative way is Vanhoozer (2005: 387–392).

second passage Packer continues to quote Hunter: 'Gal. 3:13 moves in the same realm of ideas: "Christ redeemed us from the curse of the law, having become a curse for us [*hyper hēmōn*, 'on behalf of us'].'"[53] According to Packer, Paul's use of the aorist participle is how he explains the method of redemption. He answers the question of how Christ redeems us in terms of his *'becoming* a curse for us' (original emphasis).[54] Packer clearly agrees with Hunter's conclusion: 'We are not fond nowadays of calling Christ's suffering "penal" or of styling him our "substitute"; but can we avoid using some such words as these to express Paul's view of the atonement?'[55]

Penal substitution has attracted much criticism from the time of Socinus in the sixteenth century to the present day. Some object to the violence they see as inherent in the doctrine. Others object to what they regard as the immorality in the notion. Still others criticize any attempt to make the doctrine central to understanding the atonement. (An attempt is made in the appendix to address some of these objections and criticisms.)

Paul's argument in Romans 3:21–26 is a basis for another historic interpretation of the cross: moral government theory. Twice in Romans 3:21–26 an epistemological aspect comes to the fore. Christ's sacrifice manifests (*endeixin*) God's righteous/justice (vv. 25–26). In other words, in the cross God's righteousness/justice is on public display. But to what end? It shows that God is not indifferent to sin. In his forbearance in the past he had left sins unpunished. Some might take that to mean that God is blasé about sin. Not so! Christ's sacrificial death testifies to the seriousness with which God takes sin. Secondly, it shows that God is not arbitrary in justifying sinners. There is a moral foundation to justification that has to do with Christ's sacrifice. The morality of such a sacrifice we shall consider at greater length in the appendix.

A historic interpretation of the atonement that runs with the idea that the cross is a manifestation of divine righteousness/justice is the governmental theory made famous by Grotius in the seventeenth century and still championed by some Arminian theologians today.[56]

---

[53] Packer in Packer and Dever 2007: 100.

[54] Ibid.

[55] Ibid.

[56] Hugo Grotius (1583–1645) was a follower of Arminius' theology. He was an eminent Dutch jurist, not a theologian per se. He understood the cross as a display of how seriously God takes sin in order to uphold his moral government of the universe. See the account in Olson 2006: 229–230.

A contemporary proponent of a governmental approach is Arminian theologian J. Kenneth Grider.[57] In explaining this interpretation of the cross, Grider argues, 'If, however, we see that the Father could offer forgiveness only because of Christ's crucifixion, we will see the seriousness of sin and will more likely break with it.'[58] He cites Romans 3:23–26 as the biblical basis. Christ dies as our substitute but not as a penal substitute. He suffered for us but did not pay the penalty for our sins. God accepts Christ's suffering as an alternative to punishment.[59] This particular articulation of moral government theory would be more convincing if there were more attention given to key texts such as 2 Corinthians 5:21, Galatians 3:13 and 1 Peter 3:18 that prima facie point in a penal substitution direction.

Satisfaction of divine love through sacrifice

Paul leaves us in no doubt that Christ's love is quintessentially expressed in the cross of Christ: 'For Christ's love compels us, because we are convinced that one died for all, and therefore all died. And he died for all, that those who live should no longer live for themselves but for him who died for them and was raised again' (2 Cor. 5:14–15). Robert Murray McCheyne preached on this text asserting, '*The love of Christ to man constraineth the believer to live a holy life, because that truth takes away all his dread and hatred of God,*' and 'no man was ever frightened into love, and, therefore, no man was ever frightened into holiness'.[60] How right McCheyne is. Dread may frighten us into conformity to the declared will of God and so we do not steal or murder. But only the divine love constraining us will lead to a conformity from the heart and not just the head.

The apostle also makes it patent that the cross is not only the story of Christ's love, because he goes on to argue:

---

[57] Olson (ibid. 224) demonstrates that it is a misconception to identify governmental theory as the Arminian doctrine of the cross. Many Arminian theologians have and do advocate penal substitution, including Arminius himself (228). Moreover, not all Arminian theologians have defended governmental theory (e.g. Thomas Summers, 236).

[58] Grider 1983: 239–240.

[59] Grider argues his case for moral government theory in Grider 1994: 322–335. He rejects penal substitution as unscriptural, unfair to the non-elect, a denial of free moral agency, impugning God's goodness and a denial in effect of actual forgiveness. Grider's work is entitled in part as 'Wesleyan'. Ironically, John Wesley was a proponent of penal substitution and 'there is no hint of the governmental theory in his sermons, letters or essays' (Olson 2006: 231–233).

[60] McCheyne 1961: 5, 10; original emphasis.

All this is from God, who reconciled us to himself through Christ and gave us the ministry of reconciliation: that God was reconciling the world to himself in Christ, not counting men's sins against them. And he has committed to us the message of reconciliation. We are therefore Christ's ambassadors, as though God were making his appeal through us. (2 Cor. 5:18–20)

The atonement is an intratrinitarian event, as Jürgen Moltmann has so forcefully reminded us.[61] He maintains, 'The death of Christ reaches deep into the nature of God and, above all other meanings, is an event that takes place in the innermost nature of God, the Trinity.'[62] Mel Gibson's film *The Passion of the Christ* captures this important biblical truth when at the moment of Christ's death a tear falls from heaven. Hebrews 9:14 rounds out the trinitarian story when it speaks of the Spirit in the context of Christ's sacrifice: 'How much more, then, will the blood of Christ, who through the eternal Spirit offered himself unblemished to God, cleanse our consciences from acts that lead to death, so that we may serve the living God!'[63]

In the cross of Christ the triune God does for us what we could not do for ourselves. This biblical truth needs underlining, as the story of the cross can be told in a way which reinforces that caricature of the atonement which maintains that Christians (often evangelicals in particular are in view) believe that the loving Son bought off the angry Father through his sacrifice. In other words, the loving Son took humanity's part over against a vengeful deity. Some popular acronyms currently used in books, and which figure in some preaching, unfortunately help give the caricature life. For example, GRACE, understood as 'God's Riches At Christ's Expense'.[64] Reality, however, happily is otherwise. The atonement satisfies the divine desire to express transformative love. It is no arbitrary act that says nothing of the character of the agent.[65]

---

[61] Moltmann 1982. For a critique of Moltmann's particular articulation of a trinitarian theology of the cross see Jowers 2001.

[62] Moltmann in Trelstad 2006: 133.

[63] I develop this point in Cole 2007: 165–167. Also see M. Thompson 2004.

[64] An online dictionary defines 'grace' in these terms. See 'Grace', accessed 26 Aug. 2008.

[65] As Campbell (1996: 73) argued so forcefully in the nineteenth century, 'nothing can be clearer to me than that *an arbitrary act cannot reveal character*' (original emphasis). Campbell's alternative proposal that Christ offered a perfect confession of the justice of God's verdict on human sin is speculative at best.

In Christ, God's transformative love creates new creations (2 Cor. 5:17). This is not a love wrung out of reluctant deity. Again, as we saw in an earlier chapter, Augustine reminds us:

> The love, therefore, wherewith God loves, is incomprehensible and immutable. For it was not from the time that we were reconciled unto Him by the blood of His Son that He began to love us; but He did so before the foundation of the world, that we also might be His sons along with His Only-begotten, before as yet we had any existence of our own.[66]

Or, as Clark H. Pinnock rightly argues, divine love does not flow from a decision God made but from the deity he is.[67] Finally, Van Dyk is correct to argue, 'The passion and death of Jesus Christ in some ways satisfied the love of God. In this dramatic divine self-surrender, God's love finds its fullest satisfaction and expression.'[68]

What kind of sacrifice?

There are two kinds of sacrifice that are particularly pertinent to this study of how the atonement in the more narrow sense of Christ's death brings shalom. An *expiatory* sacrifice is directed towards sin. A *propitiatory* sacrifice is directed towards the wrath of God. H.-G. Link solidly captures the conceptual difference: 'In short, propitiation is directed towards the offended person, whereas expiation is concerned with nullifying the offensive act.'[69] But N. T. Wright puts it more colourfully: 'You propitiate a person who is angry; you expiate a sin, crime, or stain on your character.'[70] What do the Scriptures say? Is only one of these ideas to be found in the key texts, or can both be found? On that question there is much debate.

An examination of the commentaries on four disputed texts is a useful way into the issues. The first of these texts is Romans 3:25: 'God presented him as a sacrifice of atonement, through faith in his blood.' The crucial term is the noun *hilastērion*, and three popular translations show the challenge that it poses the translator. Both the NRSV and NIV render the term as 'a sacrifice of atonement'. These

---

[66] Augustine 2007: tractate 110. Augustine is probably drawing on Eph. 1:4–6.

[67] Pinnock 2006: 384.

[68] Van Dyk in Placher 2003: 217. I am not sure that she would be happy with my including divine righteousness and holiness in the mix.

[69] Link and Brown 2006.

[70] N. T. Wright 2002, 10: 476.

translations beg the question 'A sacrifice of atonement in what sense exactly?' The ESV decides the question with its far more specific 'a propitiation'. Leon Morris has no doubts as to the preferred translation. He is adamant only 'propitiation' fits the context. He draws attention to the prominence of the wrath theme in Romans 1 – 4. He cites as evidence Romans 1:18, 2:5, 8, 3:5 and 4:15, and maintains, 'But unless *hilastērion* means "propitiation", Paul has put men under the wrath of God and left them there.'[71] Morris will have none of 'expiation' or even 'mercy seat' as the translation. He concludes, 'The plain fact is that *hilastērion* signifies "the means of averting wrath" and the new translations miss this.'[72] J. D. G. Dunn thinks the debate about whether the term should be rendered 'propitiation' (as Morris famously did) or 'expiation' (as C. H. Dodd famously did) is 'an unnecessary polarizing of alternatives'.[73] Yet in his commentary on Romans, after having rightly acknowledged the wrath motif in Romans 1 – 3, he consistently uses the language of expiation rather than propitiation. For example, he writes of 'Christ as the "means of expiation"', and sums up the central point of the passage as God's 'provision of Christ as a ransom and expiatory sacrifice',[74] an idea he repeats twice in his summation.

However, there is a third possibility. In Old Testament Greek *hilastērion* refers to the mercy seat that provides the cover to the ark and features in the Day of Atonement ritual. In fact, there are twenty-seven instances of its use in the Septuagint. Of these, twenty-one refer to the mercy seat. There is only one New Testament use of the term in this context: in Hebrews 9:5 it clearly means 'mercy seat'.[75] The mercy seat was the place where sin was expiated and God propitiated, as Doug Moo argues:

> Since in its only other NT occurrence (Heb. 9:5) *hilastērion* refers to this mercy seat, it seems likely that Paul uses the word with this meaning. His point, then, would be that Jesus

[71] L. Morris 1983: 169. N. T. Wright (2002, 10: 476) concurs: 'Paul's context here demands that the word not only retain its sacrificial overtones (the place and means of atonement), but that it carry the note of propitiation of divine wrath – with, of course, the corollary that sins are expiated.'

[72] L. Morris 1983: 169.

[73] Dunn 2004a, comment on Rom. 3:21–26. The famous theological disagreements between Dodd and Morris over exegesis and translation are treated in many places. See e.g. Letham 1993: 140–141; Stott 1996: 170–172; and for the linguistics as well Link and Brown 2006.

[74] Dunn 2004a, comment on Rom. 3:21–26.

[75] I am indebted to Carson (in Hill and James 2004: 129) for these statistics.

Christ is the NT counterpart to the OT 'mercy seat'. As this 'mercy seat' was the place where God took care of his people's sin, so now Jesus Christ has been *presented* (publicly displayed for all to see) as the 'place' where God now deals, finally and forever, with his people's sin. Atonement now takes place in him and this atonement, as in the OT, includes both the forgiving of sins – expiation – and the turning away of God's wrath – propitiation.[76]

D. A. Carson likewise states, 'Paul is presenting Christ as the ultimate "mercy seat," the ultimate place of atonement, and, derivatively, the ultimate sacrifice.'[77] Indeed, the wiping away of sin removes the offence and averts the divine wrath.

Our second passage is Hebrews 2:17, 'For this reason he had to be made like his brothers in every way, in order that he might become a merciful and faithful high priest in service to God, and that he might make atonement for the sins of the people.' In this text we are dealing with a cognate of *hilastērion*. The key term is the verb *hilaskomai*. Again translations differ. The NRSV has 'to make a sacrifice of atonement'. The NIV renders it 'make atonement'. The ESV is rightly or wrongly more precise when it renders *hilaskesthai* 'to make propitiation'. Once again commentators disagree. According to F. B. Craddock:

> In the LXX, the primary uses express the mercy of God in the provisions for the removal of human sin in order to restore divine–human relations. This removal or covering of sin, usually by blood sacrifice, is often called 'expiation,' a term no longer familiar to most believers. *Neither in the LXX nor in the NT does the word mean 'propitiate' in the sense of placating or appeasing God, since it is not human but divine initiative that effects mercy and atonement.*[78]

By way of contrast, according to W. L. Lane:

> The proper translation of *hilaskesthai* has been a matter of academic debate. *In a full and balanced treatment of the subject Morris has demonstrated That 'to make propitiation' is*

[76] Moo 2001, comment on Rom. 3:25.
[77] Carson in Hill and James 2004: 129.
[78] Craddock 2002: 42; my emphasis.

to be preferred rather than 'to make expiation,' because this is the usual meaning of the verb and its cognates not only in secular usage but in the LXX (Apostolic Preaching, 125–60). Moreover, the accusative of respect in the expression *hilaskesthai tas hamartias,* 'to make propitiation with respect to sin,' is an unusual Greek construction, but in the few examples where it is preserved it 'seems generally to imply the thought of propitiation.' . . . The making of propitiation for sins exhibits the primary concern of the high priestly office with the reconciliation of the people to God. The concept implies sacrifice, and in this context the propitiatory work of the Son consisted in the laying down of his life for others (cf. vv 10, 14, 18).[79]

Craddock and Lane cannot both be right about the evidence of the LXX. Moreover, Craddock's sweeping statement 'Neither in the LXX nor in the NT does the word mean "propitiate"' simply does not hold up in the light of our treatment of Romans 3:25 and Morris's scholarship.[80]

Once again the exegete is not shut up to a disjunctive either/or.[81] As Simon Kistemaker argues, *hilaskomai* 'can communicate the sense of both propitiation and expiation and thus express a double meaning'.[82] With regard to Hebrews 2:17, the argument in Hebrews at this point is about how Jesus helps Abraham's descendants. He does so as the merciful and faithful high priest who deals with the problem of sin. That role had been telegraphed at the very beginning of the letter when Jesus was presented implicitly as a priest: 'he had made purification [*katharismon*] for sins' (Heb. 1:3; NRSV is preferred to NIV here).[83] According to W. L. Lane, 'The purification of the people was similarly achieved by blood *in an act of expiation* (cf. Lev 16:30)' (my emphasis).[84] So Jesus, according to Hebrews 2:17, helps Abraham's children specifically by making a sacrifice. But the

---

[79] Lane 2004a, comment on Heb. 2:17; my emphasis.

[80] With regard to the LXX see Kistemaker in Hill and James 2004: 166.

[81] L. Morris (1983: 171) argues for an either/or. He unconvincingly draws on Sirach 5.6 as evidence of a nexus between the verb *hilaskomai* and assuaging divine wrath. To him only propitiation will do. In my view this is too strong.

[82] Kistemaker (in Hill and James 2004: 166) with regard to the LXX.

[83] The NIV translates *poiēsamenos* (lit. 'having made', aorist participle) as 'had provided', which is too vague. Such provision could have been made by another at the Son's behest. The NIV leaves that possibility open – albeit unintentionally.

[84] W. L. Lane 2004a, comment on Heb. 1:3.

question is how so? Expiation makes sense here, as John Stott acknowledges.[85] Sins are in view both in Hebrews 1:3 and 2:17. Even so, in my view that answer regarding Hebrews 2:17 will lead theologically to considering propitiation by way of implication, especially considering the motif of judgment prominent at a later stage in the letter (e.g. Heb. 9:26–28; 10:26–27). As Robert Letham says, 'Again, the question of propitiation is raised, when it is asked who requires expiation for our sins.'[86]

Our third and fourth passages are both found in 1 John. In 1 John 2:1–2 Jesus is presented as our advocate (*paraklēton*) with the Father and as the *hilasmos* for our sins: 'But if anybody does sin, we have one who speaks to the Father in our defence – Jesus Christ, the Righteous One. He is the atoning sacrifice for our sins, and not only for ours but also for the sins of the whole world.' Both the NRSV and NIV render the noun *hilasmos* as 'atoning sacrifice'. The ESV once more has 'propitiation'. J. Ramsey Michaels argues, 'The image of Jesus as "Advocate" with the Father makes God the *object*, not the subject, of the reconciliation said to be taking place, and to that extent supports "propitiation" as the meaning of [*hilasmos*].'[87] C. Clifton Black takes an opposite tack: 'Whereas Hebrews develops dual understandings of Jesus as both the superlative high priest (Heb. 4:14–5:10; 7:1–28) and superior sacrifice (Heb. 9:11–10:18), 1 John zeros in on the second of these claims by characterizing Jesus as an *expiation*.'[88] He further argues, 'It is not God's anger with us that must be turned away, but our rebellion against God. Accordingly *expiation* is not a human

---

[85] Stott 1996: 172. Averbeck (1996) argues, 'In sum, if the issues that would cause God's wrath to be turned against us are wiped away, expiation, then there is no reason for God to be angry anymore – he is "propitiated" . . . In light of the above, the debated passages can include a combination of both expiation and propitiation, even though the underlying rationale is expiation. This is the case, e.g. in Heb 2:17, where it is argued that Jesus became "a merciful and faithful high priest in service to God . . . that he might make atonement for the sins of the people."' P. T. O'Brien ('Hebrews 2', unpublished MS, 38, n. 209) likewise maintains with regard to Heb. 2:17, 'This is not to deny that sin is expiated, indeed must be expiated. It simply means that [*hilaskomai*] includes the notion of propitiation.'

[86] Letham 1993: 141. I suspect the question would be raised by the references to divine wrath that follow so soon after in the argument of Hebrews (*orgē*, Heb. 3:11; 4:3). The case for propitiation in Heb. 2:17 is strengthened if God is regarded as the direct object of *hilaskesthai*, and *tas hamartias* is understood as an accusative of respect, as in Peterson 2001a: 48, n. 50. The text does not demand this construal, however.

[87] Michaels in Hill and James 2004: 114; original emphasis.

[88] Black 2002: 388; my emphasis.

maneuver that changes God from furious to loving; expiation is an expression of God's love, which removes sin from the sinner.'[89] Michaels has the better of the argument since Black does no justice to the notion of Jesus as our advocate and with the Father as the object of his advocacy. This does not deny that expiation is a corollary in this context.

The last text to consider is 1 John 4:10. Again *hilasmos* is the key term. Both the NRSV and NIV use 'atoning sacrifice' to translate it. The ESV has 'propitiation'. The letter encapsulates the gospel in our text: 'This is love: not that we loved God, but that he loved us and sent his Son as an atoning sacrifice for our sins.' Michaels observes that God is not the object of the action in this verse but the subject. God provides the *hilasmos*. He argues, 'But here the initiative rests with God the Father, not with Jesus acting as Advocate in our behalf, and the accent is not placating God so much as on removing the guilt of "our sins."'[90] He concludes cautiously that the usage here 'supports "expiation"'. Black agrees: 'he [Jesus] unquestionably came into this world for the purpose of *expunging* [clearly expiatory] human sin'.[91] Even Leon Morris concedes that in the case of 1 John 4:10 the case for 'propitiation' is not compelling. He commends it though, since 'expiation' is 'less colourful'.[92] Hardly a strong argument! When considered together, the two references to *hilasmos* in 1 John present Christ's sacrifice as both propitiatory and expiatory. Michaels forcefully captures the significance: 'at the heart of the Christian gospel, defying all our attempts at rationalization: God placates God!'[93]

Thus 'mercy seat' or 'propitiation' would be appropriate translations of *hilastērion* in Romans 3:25; 'to make expiation' is defensible for *hilaskomai* in Hebrews 2:17 but with the idea of propitiation as a corollary; 'propitiation' makes sense as a translation for *hilasmos* in 1 John 2:2, with expiation as a corollary, and finally, 'expiation' is a suitable translation for *hilasmos* in 1 John 4:10. The wisdom of the NRSV and NIV translations is to leave more open to the reader the exact nature of the sacrifice of God's faithful Son.

In sum, Christ's death on the cross was both expiatory and propitiatory.

[89] Ibid.; my emphasis.
[90] Michaels in Hill and James 2004: 115.
[91] Black 2002: 430; my emphasis.
[92] L. Morris 1983: 172.
[93] Michaels in Hill and James 2004: 116.

Covenant-making through sacrifice

The theological importance of the Lord's Supper, also known as the Mass, the Eucharist and Holy Communion in some churches, has been a matter of great debate in church history. As I have written in another place:

> A relatively few clear biblical references to the Supper have provided a platform for a large amount of varied theological superstructure. For example, a difference in understanding the Supper was one of the sticking points between the reformers of the sixteenth century and their catholic counterparts and even amongst themselves. The 'Supper strife' between Luther and Zwingli over *hoc est corpus meum* comes to mind.[94]

One debate centres on the nature of Christ's presence when believers gather to obey his command to eat and drink in remembrance of him.[95] Another debate revolves around the idea of the Lord's Supper as a sacrifice.[96] Our interest, however, lies elsewhere.

Matthew, Mark and Luke contain a Last Supper narrative (Matt. 26:17–30, Mark 14:12–25 and Luke 22:7–23). According to the Lucan account, during the Passover festival in the upper room we read of Jesus that

> he took bread, gave thanks and broke it, and gave it to them, saying, 'This is my body given for you; do this in remembrance of me.' In the same way, after the supper he took the cup, saying, 'This cup is *the new covenant in my blood*, which is poured out for you.' (Luke 22:19–20; my emphasis)

---

[94] Cole 2005b: 464.

[95] The risen Christ is not absent from the Supper. Now at the right hand of the Father, he relates to us by way of sign (sacrament) to be met with faith on our part. Over time the discussion of Christ's words of institution – 'this is my body' and 'this is my blood' – has generated many sophisticated ideas of Christ's presence, such as the miracle of transubstantiation (as in Aquinas), consubstantiation (as in Luther), transvaluation (as in Spens) and transignification (as in Schillebeeckx). None of these ideas is obvious in the scriptural record (Cole 2005b: 465).

[96] As I have written elsewhere, 'The content of the biblical testimonies makes it hard to see any justification for the idea of the mass as a propitiatory sacrifice (a repetition or representation of Calvary) or notions of Eucharistic sacrifice (our sacrifice of praise becomes a part of Christ's eternal offering of praise to the Father or the rite is a pleading of his sacrifice before the Father). Instead, the biblical accents fall on what God in Christ's death has done for us rather than on what we do – except by way of remembrance' (Cole 2005b: 465).

Matthew's version adds this important nuance: 'poured out for many for the forgiveness of sins' (Matt. 26:29). As J. I. Packer suggests, 'Christ's atoning death ratified the inauguration of the new covenant, in which access to God under all circumstances is guaranteed by Christ's one sacrifice that covers all transgressions (Matt. 26:27–28; 1 Cor. 11:25; Heb. 9:15; 10:12–18).'[97] Packer is right to cite Paul. For in his first letter to the Corinthians the apostle explicitly sounds the new-covenant note, quoting Jesus: 'This cup is the new covenant in my blood; do this, whenever you drink it, in remembrance of me' (1 Cor. 11:25).

Robert Letham helpfully points out that the Old Testament background to both Jesus' words and Paul's quote

> is not the Passover but . . . the covenant meal eaten by Moses and Aaron, Nadab and Abihu, and the seventy elders of Israel on the top of Mount Sinai (Exod. 24:1–11). Moses offered burnt and fellowship offerings. Some of the blood he sprinkled on the altar. The rest went into bowls. He read the Book of the Covenant then sprinkled the blood that remained on the people uttering: 'This is the blood of the covenant.' A covenantal fellowship meal is the backdrop to Jesus' last supper.[98]

Even so, that is not the whole story. The meal is 'Passover-like', to quote Scot McKnight. Jesus' words 'storify' 'his own death by setting that death in the context of Passover and exodus'.[99] McKnight draws out the theological implications of Jesus' choice of the Passover festival rather than that of the Day of Atonement:

> By choosing Passover instead of Yom Kippur to explain his death, Jesus chooses the images of divine protection and liberation. He offers himself – in death – to absorb the judgment of God on behalf of his followers so he can save his people from their sins. His is the blood of the lamb that will secure his followers for the kingdom of God.[100]

---

[97] Packer 1993: 136.

[98] For much of this paragraph I am indebted to Letham (2001: 4–5).

[99] McKnight 2007: 83. McKnight argues that the meal is Passover-like because of the absence of any reference to a lamb. Interestingly, Paul describes Christ as 'our Passover lamb' in the context of church discipline. However, in discussing the Lord's Supper in the same letter does not return to the idea (cf. 1 Cor. 5:7; 10:14–22; 11:17–34).

[100] Ibid. 86.

Finely said.

Through his sacrificial death Jesus establishes a new relationship (covenant) between God and his people. The ongoing celebration of the Lord's Supper assumes that this relationship is in place. I shall leave open the question of whether in the death of Christ the atonement was intended only for the elect (his people) or for all or whether there was a double intention in the cross; namely, to provide an atonement sufficient for all without exception but effective for the elect without distinction.[101]

Significantly then, Jesus left his disciples a message and a meal. Both the message and the meal point to his sacrifice (cf. 1 Cor. 2:2; 11:26).

The vindication of the faithful Son

The apostle Paul was a realist and no fool. He could see the implications if Christ's death had been the end. His first letter to the Corinthians provides the evidence, as his argument in chapter 15 for the resurrection of Christ shows. Impressively, he could think through the logic of the alternative to his core convictions using a series of hypothetical syllogisms to do so (1 Cor. 15:12–19).[102] In other words, in Socratic fashion he could follow the argument to wherever it might lead. No resurrection, no hope. Even worse, no resurrection meant that his claiming a resurrection was actually misrepresenting God, saying that God had done what he had not. The consequences of no resurrection of Christ include (1) the apostolic preaching is useless and (2) so is faith, (3) there is no answer to sin, and (4) there is no hope for those who have died as believers. As

---

[101] The classic defence of an atonement intended only for the elect is found in John Owen's *The Death of Death in the Death of Christ*. For an account of Owen's position see Packer in Packer and Dever 2007: 111–144. John Wesley defended general atonement. For an account of Wesley's stance see Olson 2006: 221–225, 231–233. Knox (in Payne 2000: 260–266) defends an atonement sufficient for any sinner, but effective only for the elect (the Amyraldian position to which I incline). For a fine discussion of the history of discussion and a judicious treatment of the issues see Demarest 1997: ch. 4, *passim*; and Boersma 2004: 53–73. For a contrary view that critiques Knox see Jeffery, Ovey and Sach 2007: 276–278. Jeffrey, Ovey and Sach fail to reckon with the idea that God may have had more than one design with regard to the cross. Caution is needed with regard to this subject since the desire for logical completeness may trump the degree of exegetical warrant provided by Scripture.

[102] A hypothetical syllogism has an 'if . . . then . . .' form. A step-hypothetical syllogism has a form where the conclusion of a prior hypothetical syllogism forms the first part of the next, etc.

Hans Urs von Balthasar suggests, 'Without the resurrection the whole Trinitarian salvific plan would be incomprehensible, and the work begun in the life of Jesus would remain incomprehensible.'[103] All this is very grim but honest and, if true, tragic.

Hendrikus Berkhof draws out some further implications if Christ was not raised from the dead. He asks:

> Why should we ascribe redemptive significance to *one* of the innumerable Roman executions in an occupied territory? Without the resurrection all we have left is the late Jesus of Nazareth, one of the many martyrs who died for a conviction. Then he can only be a teacher and example to us. In fact not even that, because in that case he failed in both respects: he was too much mistaken in his own role to be our teacher, and he put his own person too much in the foreground and covered it too much with divine authority to be an example. Therefore the Christian faith stands and falls with the resurrection.[104]

As already suggested above, the apostle Paul drew the same conclusion from his reflection on the implications of no resurrection of Christ: 'If only for this life we have hope in Christ, we are to be pitied more than all men' (1 Cor. 15:19).

I would add a further implication. If Christ did not rise from the dead, then theodicy or defence in the face of evil becomes even more difficult as an enterprise. For if Christ did not rise, then his death was the end, and shows that such goodness and such faithfulness have no real future in our universe. In other words, death has the final say and Bertrand Russell was justified in writing in his famous essay *A Free Man's Worship*:

> Such, in outline, but even more purposeless, more void of meaning, is the world which Science presents for my belief. Amid such, if anywhere, our ideals henceforward must find a home. That man is the product of causes which had no

---

[103] Balthasar in Kehl and Löser 1982: 154.

[104] H. Berkhof 1979: 307; original emphasis. Crucifixions were common in Jesus' world. E.g. in 4 BC the Roman general Varus pacified the country around Galilee after revolts took place by some of the Jews upon the death of Herod the Great. In one case he had two thousand people crucified, according to Josephus, *Ant.* 17.10.

prevision of the end they were achieving; that his origins, his growth, his hopes and fears, his loves and beliefs, are but the outcome of accidental collocations of atoms; that no fire, no heroism, no intensity of thought and feeling, can preserve an individual life beyond the grave; that all the labour of the ages, all the devotion, all the inspiration, all the noonday brightness of human genius, are destined to extinction in the vast death of the solar system, and that the whole temple of Man's achievement must inevitably be buried beneath the debris of a universe in ruins – all these things, if not quite beyond dispute, are yet so nearly certain, that no philosophy which rejects them can hope to stand. *Only within the scaffolding of these truths, only on the firm foundation of unyielding despair, can the soul's habitation henceforth be safely built.*[105]

However, the New Testament will not leave us in such despair. Paul writes, 'But Christ has indeed been raised from the dead, the firstfruits of those who have fallen asleep' (1 Cor. 15:20). These are the words of someone who knew Old Testament expectations, had met eyewitnesses of the risen Christ and had seen the risen Christ himself.[106]

The New Testament writers draw out the positive theological significance of Christ's resurrection in more than one way. The apostle Peter preached at Pentecost, 'Therefore let all Israel be assured of this: God has made this Jesus, whom you crucified, both Lord and Christ' (Acts 2:36). Jesus is vindicated; he is enthroned and in session (cf. Acts 2:36 and 7:56).[107] In Pauline idiom the enthroned Christ must reign until all his enemies are under his feet (1 Cor. 15:20–28). We are in the *regnum Christi*, as Oscar Cullmann suggests.[108] When opposition is no more, the *regnum Christi* will give way to the *regnum*

---

[105] Russell, accessed 4 Sept. 2007; my emphasis.

[106] For a magisterial study of the resurrection of Christ, its historicity and meaning see N. T. Wright 2003. Also see Pannenberg 1982: 96–115 for a fine, albeit brief, treatment of the resurrection and its meaning.

[107] The *regnum Christi* and the claim that Christ is king now can be understood in ways consistent with amillennialism (e.g. J. I. Packer), historic premillennialism (e.g. E. Ladd) and progressive dispensationalism (e.g. D. L. Bock) but not classic dispensationalism. See the discussion in Ryrie 1995: 161–1810. Ryrie writes from a classic dispensationalist position and thus would reject the interpretation of Pentecost advocated in this book.

[108] Cullmann 1956: 109–120. Letham (1993: 208) describes the period from the resurrection to the parousia as that of 'the mediatorial kingship of Christ'.

Dei. The Son's messianic subordination will end (1 Cor. 15:28).[109]
Or, to use the language of Hebrews, Christ is now sat down at the
right hand of God (Heb. 1:3). His sacrifice has done its work. He
now ever lives to intercede for us as our merciful high priest (Heb.
7:25). The early church knew this well. In the words of Nicetas of
Remesiana (d. 414), known in liturgical churches as the Te Deum:

> You [Christ] overcame the sting of death:
> and opened the kingdom of heaven to all believers.
> You are seated at God's right hand in glory:
> We believe that you will come to be our judge.
> Come then, Lord, and help your people,
> Bought with the price of your own blood:
> And bring us with your saints to glory everlasting.[110]

A dead Christ cannot open the kingdom to anyone.[111] A dead Christ
helps no one. Wayne Grudem, ably expresses the theological entailments of Christ's vindication with respect to the atonement, but in
more prosaic terms: 'There is no penalty left to pay for sin, no more
wrath of God to bear, no more guilt or liability to punishment – all
had been completely paid for, and no guilt remained.' He adds, 'In
the resurrection, God was saying to Christ, "I approve of what you
have done, and you find favor in my sight."'[112] Christ's sacrifice
stands vindicated.

---

[109] The view that the sonship in view in 1 Cor. 15:20–28 is messianic can be
understood in ways consistent both with the position of those who affirm the eternal
subordination of the Son and that of those who do not.

[110] *A Prayer Book for Australia* 1999: 8; and for Nicetas see Broderick 1987: 572–
573.

[111] Pelikan (1971: 149) points out that a modern Western Christian would be sur-
prised to find the extent to which the Fathers of the second and third centuries high-
lighted the resurrection in their understanding of salvation in contrast to accenting
Christ as teacher or example or vicarious atoner. From the perspective of Eastern
Orthodoxy one of the great weaknesses in Mel Gibson's film *The Passion of the Christ*
is its violent lack of restraint (compared to the Gospels) in presenting the passion of
Christ and its lack of an emphatic and victorious resurrection. See Hopko (Dean
Emeritus of St. Vladimir's Orthodox Seminary in New York), accessed 28 Aug. 2008;
and Bell, accessed 29 Aug. 2008. Bell points to the very Western emphasis on the
passion of Christ in Gibson's film in contrast to the Eastern Christian emphasis on the
resurrection. From an Eastern perspective this book is clearly an exercise in Western
theology, as much of this chapter has focused on the cross. However, Martin Kähler
was right to observe with reference to Mark's Gospel, 'a passion narrative with an
extended introduction' (quoted in Carson and Moo 2005: 185). Mark, for example, is
not a *resurrection* narrative with an extended introduction.

[112] Grudem 1994: 615.

Conclusion

There is no shalom without sacrifice. As Paul contends, peace is made through the blood of the cross. The sacrifice of the faithful Son on that cross satisfies the divine holiness and righteousness, and has its source in the gracious love of the triune God. Christ bears our sins on the cross and endured the penalty of sin. He suffered the judgment we deserve and in our place. He is the faithful servant of Isaianic promise. Moreover, the blood shed at the cross establishes the new covenant of Old Testament hope. In addition, Christ's cross and what was achieved there are integral to victory over the devil and evil. However, none of the foregoing stands if Christ is not raised. If Christ is not raised, then evil has the final word. No resurrection means that supreme goodness, as exemplified by Christ, has no future beyond the grave. No vindication means that the inscription found on a first-century tomb is chillingly right: 'Charidas, what is below? Deep darkness. But what of the paths upward? All a lie . . . *Then we are lost.*'[113] The great new of the gospel is that the faithful Son is vindicated, and his sacrifice divinely validated.

---

[113] Quoted in Green 1974: 139; my emphasis. I have modernized the English.

Chapter Seven

The 'peace dividend'

A good test of any doctrine is to ask what is lost if the doctrine were abandoned. For example, if Christ is not God incarnate but merely human, then God does not know what it is to weep a human tear. This has implications for addressing the problem of evil and the question of divine impassibility. So what is lost if the atonement is removed from theological view? How would the divine project to set free the created order be affected, the project that Robert Murray McCheyne described as God's 'restorative scheme'?[1] The New Testament answer would be stark: no union with Christ, no forgiveness of sins, no cleansing, no justification before God, no redemption from sin, no adoption, and no reconciliation with God. In short, no peace with God, no gospel. And the loss would not only be at the personal level. In New Testament perspective there would be deleterious consequences at both the corporate and cosmic levels as well.

In this chapter we shall examine each of these levels and in doing so are shifting our focus from the atonement in the narrow sense of what Christ accomplished in his faithful life and death to the great benefits that flow from his achievement and vindication.[2] His sacrifice brings shalom. It is a peace that brings restoration for some and pacification to others, as we shall see. Importantly, the peace that is to be explored in this chapter is an objective reality. It is relational ('peace with', 'peace between') rather than psychological ('peace within'). In other words, generally speaking I am not discussing feeling at peace, although such peace within may be a result of peace with God and between one another.

---

[1] McCheyne (1961: 9) says, 'the Gospel is a restorative scheme; it brings us back to the same state of friendship with God which Adam enjoyed'.

[2] Schmiechen (2005: vii–viii) posits ten theories of the atonement: sacrifice, justification, penal substitution, liberation, renewal of creation, restoration of creation, Christ the goal of creation, Christ the way to the knowledge of God, Christ the reconciler and the love of God. How many of these are strictly atonement theories or rather consequences of atonement? E.g. penal substitution is clearly an atonement theory, but surely justification is a consequence of atonement. There is category confusion in his approach.

Peace with God for the individual

Our attention now turns to the personal benefits that flow from of the atonement. These include union with Christ, the forgiveness of sins, cleansing from sin, justification, redemption, adoption and reconciliation. This list accents the divine initiative in salvation.

Union with Christ

One of Calvin's great insights is that unless we are united to Christ in some real way, the benefits of his faithfulness are lost to us. But if the Spirit unites us to Christ, then all he brings to the table is ours. He famously wrote:

> We must examine this question. How do we receive these benefits which the Father bestowed on his only-begotten Son – not for Christ's own private use but that he might enrich poor and needy men? First, we must understand that as long as Christ remains outside of us, and we are separated from him, all that he has suffered and done for the salvation of the human race remains useless and of no value for us. . . . all that he possesses is nothing to us until we grow into one body with him. . . . To sum up, the Holy Spirit is the bond by which Christ effectually unites us to himself.[3]

More recently, and in Calvin's wake, Robert Letham contends, 'Union with Christ is, in fact, the foundation of all the blessings of salvation. Justification, sanctification, adoption and glorification are all received through our being united to Christ.'[4]

The Paulines provide exegetical warrant for Calvin's and Letham's

---

[3] Calvin 2002e: 3.1.1. Calvin's heading for ch. 1 is, 'The Things Spoken Concerning Christ Profit us by the Secret Working of the Spirit', and that of the first section is, 'The Holy Spirit as the Bond that Unites us to Christ'. Other Reformers likewise saw the need for union with Christ. Luther drew an analogy between marriage, and Christ and the believer. Becoming one flesh in marriage leads to a great exchange. The riches of the one become those of the other. See Martin Luther, 'Freedom of the Christian Man', in Dillenberger 1961: 52–85. Pinnock (1996: 155) with his usual verve maintains, 'Union with God was not the central category for the Reformers.' His example is Luther and there is some merit in his contention, but he does not refer to Calvin, which is a significant weakness. Pinnock's (149–183) strength though lies in his appreciating the significance of the Spirit's role in the believer's union with Christ. The 'New Finnish Interpretation of Luther' or the so-called Mannermaa School makes much of Luther's idea of participation in Christ and its similarities with Eastern views of theosis. See the discussion by Kärkkäinen 2006.

[4] Letham 1993: 80. His debt to Calvin is evident on the next page.

claims.[5] The apostle Paul helps us understand both the importance of union with Christ and the role of the Spirit in securing that union. In his theology of the body of Christ, Paul states, 'For in one Spirit [*en heni pneumati*] we were all baptized into one body – Jews or Greeks, slaves or free – and all were made to drink of one Spirit' (1 Cor. 12:13 ESV). The NIV translation has the Spirit as the baptizer ('baptized by one Spirit') but I think this is unlikely. As I have written elsewhere, 'More likely this Pauline statement is all of piece with those in the Gospels and Acts that it is Christ who is the baptizer – as has been argued in previous chapters – and that the Spirit is the medium.'[6] Put another way, the same Spirit who animated Christ's humanity animates that of the believer's own. Thus the gap between the one and many is bridged, and that between past and present. Pneumatology is the key to understanding a realistic view of the believer's union with Christ and participation in the benefits of his faithful life, death and his vindication.[7]

Again Paul argues in his letter to the Ephesians that believers have been blessed 'in Christ [*en Christō*] with every spiritual blessing in the heavenly places' (Eph. 1:3 ESV). Importantly, Paul locates the blessings of salvation such as redemption and the forgiveness of sins 'in him [Christ]' (Eph. 1:7–10). In fact, the phrases 'in Christ', 'in him' and 'in the Lord' are found 164 times in the Paulines.[8] This is the language of union, not merely in a moral sense of identifying with Christ but meaning something real and organic.[9] Indeed, Paul is

[5] There are anticipations of Calvin's position on union in Aquinas, *Summa Theologica*, NA 3.49.1: 'For since He is our head, then, by the Passion which He endured from love and obedience, He delivered us as His members from our sins, as by the price of His Passion: in the same way as if a man by the good industry of his hands were to redeem himself from a sin committed with his feet. For, just as the natural body is one though made up of diverse members, so the whole Church, Christ's mystic body, is reckoned as one person with its head, which is Christ.' However, Calvin as the great theologian of the Holy Spirit sees the pneumatological dimension to union with Christ.

[6] Cole 2007: 217.

[7] This pneumatological and Calvinian approach to union with Christ turns the flank of Rashdall's (1919: 353, 424) criticism of realist language as 'the old bastard Platonism'.

[8] Stott 1979: 56.

[9] For a contrary view see Denney 1973: 197, 'The New Testament has much to say about union with Christ, but, as we have already noticed, it has no such expression as mystical union. The only union it knows is a moral union, a union due to the moral power of Christ's death, operating morally as a constraining motive on the human will and begetting in believers the mind of Christ in relation to sin.' Does this do justice to 'in Christ' is the question? For the use of the term 'organic' see Stott 1979: 54.

bold enough to assert, 'But anyone united [*kollōmenos*, taken as passive rather than middle contra the NIV] to the Lord becomes one spirit with him' (1 Cor. 6:17 NRSV). For Paul (in a context in which he discusses immorality) marital one-flesh union is an analogue of the divine–human one.

In sum, the rule of real estate applies to the soteriology: 'Location, location, location!' The question Paul poses is whether we are located in Adam or in Christ. The second-century letter to Diognetus puts it well: 'O sweet exchange! O unsearchable working! O benefits unhoped for – that the wickedness of the multitudes *should thus be hidden in the One holy,* and the holiness of One should sanctify the countless wicked!'[10]

Forgiveness of sins

According to Leon Morris, 'The central emphasis in the NT is on the wonder of forgiveness. In this sense, none of the NT writers dwells on guilt. It is forgiveness and not sin that is at the centre of their interest.'[11] Early Christianity seems to have adopted a similar view, as can be seen in the Apostles' Creed.[12] The great benefit Christ brings is 'the forgiveness of sins'. Reading some contemporary systematic theologies one would not learn this. The forgiveness of sins surprisingly is treated in a peremptory way.[13] Who is right? Has Morris exaggerated the importance of the forgiveness of sins? Further, if Morris is correct, how does the forgiveness of sins emanate from the cross? But first we ask, 'What does the forgiveness of sins look like, and then is such forgiveness linked to the atonement?'

The vocabulary for forgiveness is rich and varied. For example, the LXX uses twenty different Greek terms to translate the Hebrew.[14] However, there is an Old Testament story, a New Testament one and a Gospel parable that narratively illustrate the key aspects of the forgiveness of sins. The story of Joseph and his brothers found in

[10] In Staniforth 1972: 180–181; my emphasis.

[11] L. Morris 2001a.

[12] Grudem 1994: 1169.

[13] For examples and to look no further than evangelical theologies, Erickson (1993: 296–297, 963, 684–685) has five references but only one (693) has to do with the forgiveness of sins as a gospel benefit, and then as a subset of adoption. Grudem (1994: 386 twice, 695, 740) has four isolated references. Happily, there are exceptions. McGrath (2007a: 337–343) e.g. has a more sustained study as part of his discussion of salvation in Christ.

[14] For the linguistics and statistics see Yarbrough 2001b. Also see the more comprehensive discussion in Vorländer 2006.

Genesis 50:15–21 provides the Old Testament example. The patriarch Jacob is dead and the brothers fear that it is now payback time. Bearing Jacob's last request they come to Joseph, whom they have sold into slavery: 'I ask you to forgive [*aphiēmi*, Gr.] your brothers the sins and the wrongs they committed in treating you so badly' (Gen. 50:17). What does Joseph do? He forgives them. With regard to action, that meant he did not take revenge upon them. He did not treat them as they had mistreated him. He did not hold their sin against him against them. Moreover, he promised and did them good: 'I will provide for you and your children' (Gen. 50:21). The New Testament parable presents the story of a merciless servant (Matt. 18:21–35). The parable shows the need for the forgiven to forgive in turn. The king's servant owed a vast sum, which meant prison. However, the king took pity on the servant who had implored mercy, and the debt was cancelled: 'The servant's master took pity on him, cancelled the debt [*aphiēmi*] and let him go' (Matt. 18:27). The term *aphiēmi* is the one most commonly used in the New Testament that is translated 'forgive'.[15] This is especially so in the Gospels, as we see in the next story. In Luke's Gospel a woman with a dubious reputation ('a sinner') anoints Jesus with perfume at the house of Simon the Pharisee (Luke 7:36–50). But Simon has a problem with this woman and her behaviour. In response, Jesus tells a parable about two servants. One has a huge debt cancelled (*charizomai*); the other, a small one (Luke 7:41–42). Who will love more the one who forgave them is the question. Clearly, it ought to be the servant who owed so much. The point Jesus makes is that the woman is in an analogous situation. She has been forgiven (*aphiēmi*) so much; hence her devotion (Luke 7:47–48). Jesus says to the woman, 'Your faith has saved you; go in peace' (Luke 7:50). J. Nolland comments on the concept of peace (*eirēnē*) in this context, '"Go in peace" is a common farewell formula in Judaism . . . which here takes on deeper significance in the context of the coming of eschatological salvation.'[16] Put another way, eschatological shalom is implied in Jesus' words (cf. Luke 1:79; 2:14: 7:50; Acts 10:36).

In sum, forgiveness does not pay back as deserved. Forgiveness shows itself in doing good to the other. Forgiveness is having one's debt of X or Y cancelled. The cancellation leads to freedom and peace.

---

[15] Yarbrough 2001b.
[16] Nolland 2004, comment on Luke 7:50.

The question we next consider is whether Jesus and New Testament writers link the forgiveness of sins to the atonement. Recall that in the Matthean account of the Lord's Supper, Jesus pronounces, 'This is my blood of the covenant, which is poured out for many for the forgiveness [*aphesis*] of sins' (Matt. 26:28). Paul, in Ephesians, affirms the connection: 'In him we have redemption through his blood, the forgiveness [*aphesis*] of sins, in accordance with the riches of God's grace that he lavished on us with all wisdom and understanding' (Eph. 1:7–8). The phrases 'Redemption through his blood' and 'the forgiveness of sins' are in apposition. The letter to the Hebrews adds to the picture. When speaking of Jesus' priestly ministry, the letter says:

> When Christ came as high priest of the good things that are already here, he went through the greater and more perfect tabernacle that is not man-made, that is to say, not a part of this creation. He did not enter by means of the blood of goats and calves; but he entered the Most Holy Place once for all by his own blood, having obtained eternal redemption. (Heb. 9:12)

P. T. O'Brien comments, 'At the heart of this *eternal redemption* which is perfect in nature and eternal in its effects is the once-for-all and climactic offer of forgiveness of sins promised under the new covenant of Jeremiah 31:34 (Heb. 8:12; 10:17–18).'[17] The writer to the Hebrews continues the argument:

> In the same way, he sprinkled with the blood both the tabernacle and everything used in its ceremonies. In fact, the law requires that nearly everything be cleansed with blood, and without the shedding of blood there is no forgiveness [*ou ginetai aphesis*]. (Heb. 9:21–22)

What stands out in these references is the linkage between forgiveness and the shed blood of Christ.

We have examined what the forgiveness of sins looks like and have found exegetical warrant for linking forgiveness of sins to the cross. Now we return to our primary question, 'Is the forgiveness of sins as important as Leon Morris argues?' Morris's claim has firm

---

[17] P. T. O'Brien, 'Hebrews 9', unpublished MS; original emphasis.

backing in the testimony of Luke-Acts. Luke and Acts when viewed as one work in two volumes constitutes over a quarter of the New Testament.[18] The importance of the forgiveness of sins is signalled right at the start of Luke's account. The theme is to be prominent in the ministry of John the Baptist, as Zechariah's song shows:

> to give his people the knowledge of salvation
> through the forgiveness [*aphesis*] of their sins.
>
> (Luke 1:77)

Salvation in the New Testament is multifaceted, but the forgiveness of sins is a key element. The Baptist's practice fulfilled Zechariah's prediction: 'He went into all the country around the Jordan, preaching a baptism of repentance for the forgiveness [*aphesis*] of sins' (Luke 3:3). One of Christ's seven words spoken from the cross is the word of forgiveness: 'Father, forgive [*aphes*] them, for they do not know what they are doing' (Luke 23:34).[19] The prayer most probably is on behalf of all those complicit in his death, as R. Alan Culpepper suggests.[20] The Lucan Great Commission is all of a piece with the Baptist's ministry and Jesus' prayer from the cross. The risen Christ informs his disciples, 'repentance and forgiveness [*aphesis*] of sins will be preached in his name to all nations, beginning at Jerusalem' (Luke 24:47). The Acts tells the same story. Peter preaches to the anxious crowd on Pentecost that the forgiveness (*aphesis*) of sins in Jesus Christ's name is held out even to those responsible for the crucifixion of Jesus (cf. Acts 2:36, 'whom you crucified', and 2:38). Individuals need to hear this message. He has the same proclamation for the Sanhedrin, that the enthroned Christ gives the forgiveness (*aphesis*) of sins to Israel (Acts 5:31). The nation needs to hear this message. This great benefit is not only offered to Israel and Jews. Peter informs the Gentile Cornelius at Antioch that 'everyone who believes in him [Jesus] receives forgiveness [*aphesis*] of sins through his name' (Acts

---

[18] An argument can be made that the New Testament canon could be ordered differently. Matthew as the first book has the merit of connecting the New Testament with the Old Testament, beginning as it does with a genealogy going back to Abraham (Matt. 1:2–17). However, our present order unfortunately splits Luke from Acts. A useful alternative would be to start with John (John 1:1–2, beginning with eternity as it were), then follow with Matthew, Mark, Luke-Acts, Romans etc.

[19] Nolland 2004. He notes (in his comment on Luke 23:33–38) that this prayer is missing 'from P[75] א[1] B D W Θ 070 579 A, d. syrs sa bopt etc'. However, he argues, 'the best explanation of its presence in many MSS is that Luke put it there'.

[20] Culpepper 2002: 455. He, like Nolland, believes the prayer to be authentically Lucan.

10:43). In the second half of the Acts account of the early church Paul rises to prominence, and with him the Gentile mission. The message, however, remains the same. The benefit of the gospel offered to the Jews is the forgiveness (*aphesis*) of sins, as his sermon in the synagogue in Psidian Antioch reveals (Acts 13:38). Ironically, the offer is rejected by these Jews but embraced by the Gentiles to whom Paul turns (Acts 13:46–48). In fact, Paul understood his commission from the risen Christ to include the forgiveness (*aphesis*) of sins as a gospel benefit for the Gentiles (Acts 26:18). Thus, according to Luke-Acts, the forgiveness of sins is not a minor benefit of the gospel. Morris is certainly right to claim, 'The central emphasis in the NT is on the wonder of forgiveness' so far as Luke-Acts is concerned.[21]

The forgiveness of sins by definition presupposes the fact of sin; and unless sin is dealt with, the individual faces the prospect of divine judgment. Given that such forgiveness is the great benefit held out by the risen Christ in his Lucan Great Commission, the importance of the forgiveness of sins cannot be gainsaid by any who value the scriptural testimony. In this light the lament of William Willimon is to be taken seriously:

> It would take a mainline liberal Protestant type like me to say this, but I find contemporary evangelicalism disillusioning in some of its aspects and it's as if moralistic therapeutic deism has got all of us. I remember listening on TV – it's the only place I can hear evangelicals preach – and he's up there saying, 'You're good and you mean well and God loves you and you need to work harder and believe more in your self.[22]

To adapt Paul, if righteousness comes through niceness, Christ died for nothing (cf. Gal. 2:21).

Cleansing

There is a close connection in a number of biblical contexts between the atonement, forgiveness and cleansing. The first letter of John

---

[21] L. Morris 2001a. This illustrates the need for systematic theology to be informed by biblical theology in order to preserve the accents of revelation rather than flatten them out for comprehensiveness' sake.

[22] Willimon 2008: 42. Willimon is a bishop in the United Methodist Church. Yarbrough (2001b) says, 'Only where Christ's death for sin is taken with apostolic seriousness can the rains of divine restoration wash human hate away and moisten seeds of love. The prospects for real and lasting forgiveness in the many trouble spots of the postmodern world depend on the grace God grants as the gospel of his reconciling Son is proclaimed, believed and applied.'

advocates realism about sin in the life of the Christian and the Christian community over against a schismatic community that thought it had moved beyond sin (cf. 1 John 1:5–10 and 2:19). Those who remained needed assurance that they were in the right community of faith. To enjoy fellowship (*koinōnia*) with the Father and the Son as well as with one another is to walk in the light (1 John 1:3–7). Any darkness needs to be addressed and the blood of Christ does so. Sin needs cleansing (*katharizō*) and the blood of Christ is the means of it (1 John 1:7). The good news is that if the believer sins, the God who is light is also faithful and just. If sin is confessed to this God, he will forgive and cleanse (1 John 1:8–9). G. M. Burge comments:

> Two consequences necessarily follow [such confession]: forgiveness and purification. To forgive (Gk. *aphiēmi*) really means 'to let go' (as a debt, cf. Luke 7:43), and so John indicates that our sins are removed from God's accounting. To purify (cf. 1:7) carries a different nuance and suggests the removal of the residual effects of sin, consequences that linger (such as a stain).[23]

John's first letter excludes any theology of sinless perfectionism at the level of the individual, and ecclesial perfectionism at the level of the group.

The letter to the Hebrews adds a different perspective when it describes Jesus' priestly ministry. Drawing on the Old Testament presentation of the Day of Atonement, the writer argues that definitive cleansing from sin is provided through the sacrifice of Christ. The writer mounts an a fortiori or, in rabbinic terms, a 'light and heavy' argument ('by how much more', *posō mallon*). Under the old covenant the shed blood of bulls and goats could provide outward cleansing (Heb. 9:13). How much more under the new covenant can the blood of Christ cleanse the conscience, enabling the service to God (Heb. 9:14)? This cleansing is not merely outward but inward. There is a further benefit. The writer concludes the long argument begun in Hebrews 4:14 with the claim that the blood of Christ opens access into God's most holy place and to God himself for believers, who have had '[their] hearts sprinkled [by that blood implied] to cleanse [them] from a guilty conscience' (Heb. 10:22). With regard to

---

[23] Burge 1996: 83.

conscience, William L. Lane explains, 'Conscience' [*syneidēsis*] is the human organ of the religious life embracing the whole person in relationship to God. . . . It is the point at which a person confronts God's holiness.'[24] The sacrificial death of Christ enables believers to approach the holy God with boldness (*parrēsian*) and without guilt (cf. Heb. 9:14; 10:19).

In brief, the atonement enables fellowship, service to God and access to God.

Justification

Another important benefit that stems from the cross is justification. The meaning of this term is greatly disputed at present with the rise of the New Perspective on Paul and its chief advocates: E. P. Sanders, J. D. G. Dunn and N. T. Wright. The phrase 'New Perspective on Paul' was coined by J. D. G. Dunn in 1992.[25] Perhaps 'New Perspectives on Paul' is a more accurate phrase since the chief exponents disagree on many details.[26] I shall discuss this controversy where relevant but it is not the main concern of this book. In this section I shall ask what the term 'justification' means and how justification is related to the atonement.

Scot McKnight describes the question of the meaning of 'justification' as 'the ten million dollar question today'.[27] The Protestant scholastics had a precise answer. Justification (*iustificatio*) is an act of divine grace that in negative terms is the forgiveness of sin and in positive terms is the imputation or reckoning of Christ's righteousness to the sinner. It is a legal declaration. The term does not mean to make righteous (in their view, the Roman Catholic error) but to declare someone righteous.[28] N. T. Wright, an eminent proponent of the New Perspective on Paul, endorses some of these scholastic notes in the following definition but with important differences when teased out in the light of his other works:

> JUSTIFICATION denotes, primarily, that *action in the lawcourt* whereby a judge upholds the case of one party in dispute before him (in the Hebrew lawcourt, where the image originates, all cases consist of an accuser and a defendant, there

[24] W. L. Lane 2004a, comment on Heb. 9:14.

[25] N. T. Wright in McCormack 2006: 244–245.

[26] The literature on this debate is voluminous. Useful summaries are to be found in Gathercole 2007, M. B. Thompson 2005 and N. T. Wright in McCormack 2006.

[27] McKnight 2007: 66.

[28] Muller 1986: 162.

being no public prosecutor). Having heard the case, the judge finds in favour of one party, and thereby 'justifies' him: if he finds for the defendant, *this action has the force of 'acquittal'*. The person justified is described as 'just', 'righteous' . . . not as a description of moral character but as *a statement of his status before the court* (which will, ideally, be matched by character, but that is not the point).[29]

N. T. Wright rightly grasps the forensic and declarative nature of justification. The definition would be stronger if the polar opposite to 'justification' were thematized. As A. N. S. Lane writes, 'The Greek word for "justify," like the Hebrew word in the OT, means primarily "to acquit" or "to declare righteous," the opposite of "to condemn."'[30] Lane is right. In Israel the role of the judge was to acquit the innocent and condemn the guilty (e.g. Deut. 25:1). Condemnation then is the verdict of the court when someone is found to be in the wrong. Unrighteous is their status before the court. It is hard to do justice to the Pauline doctrine of justification if the condemnation theme (*katakrima*) is not given its due weight (cf. Deut. 25:1; Prov. 17:15; Rom. 5:16, 18; 8:1, 33–34).[31] This is an important omission and therefore weakness in N. T. Wright's account.

N. T. Wright argues in other places that 'justification' as found in Paul also means covenant membership. According to Wright, justification is a single idea for Paul involving notions of both forgiveness and covenant membership.[32] I am comfortable, exegetically speaking, with 'justification' meaning 'acquittal' or 'forgiveness' as a dictionary definition but am not convinced about 'covenant membership'. I argue this because of the themes of wrath and condemnation in Romans. However, I am more than comfortable in seeing covenant membership as a benefit of justification. Furthermore, N. T. Wright contends that the righteousness imputed to the believer is not that of Christ's flowing from his obedience (both active and passive) but a

[29] N. T. Wright 2001; my emphases.
[30] A. N. S. Lane 2005: 416.
[31] There is an excellent definition of 'justification' in an early work of N. T. Wright (in G. Reid 1980: 14), which reads, 'Justification is the judge's verdict that someone is in the right. Righteousness is the status before the court which results from that declaration.' This definition needs though the antithesis stated to provide balance: 'Condemnation is the judge's verdict that someone is in the wrong. Unrighteousness is the status before the court which results from that declaration.'
[32] N. T. Wright in McCormack 2006: 258.

status granted by God of 'covenant member' 'and/or justified sinner'.[33] However, Paul argues in his letter to the Galatians that 'You are all sons of God through faith in Christ Jesus, for all of you who were baptized into Christ have clothed yourselves with Christ' (Gal. 3:26–27). 'Clothed with Christ' makes best sense if explained in terms of the imputation of Christ's righteousness.

Justification is a legal declaration, the end-time verdict now.[34] But it is not a legal fiction, not that N. T. Wright argues this, but others do. On the contrary, as D. A. Carson correctly and forcefully asserts, 'I cannot too strongly emphasize how often Paul's justification language is tied to "in Christ" or "in him" language . . . justification is, in Paul, irrefragably tied to our incorporation into Christ, to our union with Christ.'[35] Union with Christ is the basis of imputation of Christ's righteousness, as Calvin knew. Calvin wrote:

> We do not, therefore, contemplate him outside ourselves from afar in order that his righteousness may be imputed to us but because we put on Christ and are engrafted into his body – in short, because he deigns to make us one with him. For this reason, we glory that we have fellowship of righteousness with him.[36]

Our question now becomes whether Scripture links our justification to the cross. There are three main passages in the New Testament that speak of justification per se. Two are Pauline (Rom. 1:16 – 5:21; Gal. 2:16 – 3:24) and one is found in James (Jas 2:21–25).[37] The key text is Romans 5:9: 'Since we have now been justified [*dikaiōthentes*] by his blood, how much more shall we be saved from God's wrath through him!' Here is another example of a New Testament a

---

[33] Ibid. 252.

[34] N. T. Wright (2004: 169) agrees with the eschatological note but introduces the idea of a 'final' justification 'on the basis of an entire life'. It seems to me that Wright has turned New Testament salvation into probation. If so, personal assurance of salvation becomes highly problematical. The questions and criticisms raised in this section should not mask the genuine appreciation I have for Wright's many fine contributions to New Testament scholarship, especially on the resurrection.

[35] Quoted to good effect in McKnight 2007: 59. It is worth observing that only the righteousness of a sinless Christ could effectively be put to our account. Another sinful person may represent us but not substitute definitively for us.

[36] Calvin 2002e: 3.11.10.

[37] A. N. S. Lane 2005: 416. James is not relevant to this discussion, as the letter does not link its discussion of justification to the cross. It has a different pastoral point to make, as N. T. Wright (2001) helpfully shows.

fortiori or 'light and heavy' argument (*pollō oun mallon,* 'by much therefore rather'). The term 'blood' refers as is typical in the New Testament to the sacrificial death of Jesus on the cross and unpacks an implication of the text's presenting Christ's death as a propitiatory sacrifice (earlier argued by Paul in Rom. 3:21–26[38]). The statement comes immediately after Paul's affirmation of the love of God demonstrated in the cross (Rom. 5:6–8). Justification addresses the problem of human condemnation in the face of divine wrath. John Murray is forceful when speaking of justification: 'If we are to appreciate that which is central in the gospel, if the jubilee trumpet is to find its echo again in our hearts, our thinking must be revolutionized by the realism of the wrath of God, of the reality and gravity of our guilt, and of the divine condemnation.'[39] Paul develops the argument positively in succeeding verses in terms of reconciliation (Rom. 5:10–11). Reconciliation is a theme we shall soon consider in its own right.

Redemption

The paradigmatic story of redemption in the Old Testament is Yahweh's rescue of his people from Egyptian slavery (Exod. 6:6; Deut. 7:8). As John Murray says, 'it is the exodus from Egypt that constitutes *par excellence* the Old Testament redemption'.[40] To be redeemed also, in other Old Testament contexts, is to be set free after a price has been paid. For example, in Israel the nearest male relative was obligated to buy a relative out of slavery (Lev. 25:47–52). Kinsman redemption is the most common kind in the Old Testament. Indeed, in redeeming Israel, Yahweh redeemed his 'first born son' as kinsman redeemer (Exod. 4:22). Unsurprisingly then, God became known as the redeemer (*gō'ēl*) of Israel (Isa. 49:7), and Isaiah, for example, looked to Yahweh to redeem the exiles similarly from bondage in Babylon (Isa. 48:20). The ideas of rescue and release from bondage through the payment of a price have their resonances in the New Testament, as do contemporary Greco-Roman practices of the manumission of slaves, as we shall soon see. However, as I. H.

[38] See N. T. Wright 2002, 10: 519.

[39] J. Murray 1961: 118.

[40] J. Murray 1976: 23. Liberation theologians make much of the exodus paradigm as indicative of God's preferential option for the poor and of what God seeks to do in any context of oppression and injustice. However, this approach too often fails to locate the exodus deliverance within the Abrahamic promise framework and thus misses the unique elements in the story (cf. 2:23–25; 4:22). For a liberation approach see Boff and Boff 1989: 43–65.

Marshall observes, 'The controlling background lies in the OT.'[41] With regard to the New Testament per se it is worth observing that most references to the idea of redemption are found in the Paulines and in the book of Revelation.[42]

As we saw in chapter 6, Jesus, drawing on Isaiah 53, understood his mission in ransom categories.[43] As Mark's Gospel has it, 'For even the Son of Man did not come to be served, but to serve, and to give his life as a ransom [*lytron*] for many' (Mark 10:45). S. Page rightly recognizes the importance of this dominical statement: 'It is extremely important because it purports to show the significance Jesus attached to his death . . . Any attempt to determine how Jesus understood his mission or to trace the development of the christology of the early church must take his saying into account.'[44] The cross is an expression of other person-centred service that brings about a new exodus for the many (*anti pollōn*).[45] The squabbling disciples needed to hear that as they disputed about which of them would be the more eminent in the kingdom (Mark 10:35–45). There is a cost to setting people free: a cup drunk and a baptism undergone. Again Page is helpful: 'In extrabiblical sources *lytron* denotes the price paid to free slaves, and it is likely that it has this meaning here, though obviously it is used in a metaphorical sense . . . It specifically designates the means of deliverance and always seems to include the notion of cost.'[46]

The ideas of redemption and ransom also feature in Paul's letters. In several places redemption as a benefit of the cross deals with sin. In Ephesians 1 redemption (*apolytrōsin*) is gracious act on God's part and is found in Christ (*en hō*, 'in whom'). In fact, it expresses the wealth of that grace and is lavished upon those in Christ (Eph. 1:8).

---

[41] Marshall 2001.

[42] For the substance of this paragraph I am indebted both to Hubbard (2001), and Marshall (2001). Hubbard usefully sums up the linguistics: 'The language of redemption involves the Hebrew roots *pādâ* ("to redeem, ransom") and *gā'āl* ("to redeem, serve as redeemer") and the Greek *lytroō* ("to redeem, ransom") and *agorazō* ("to buy"), often with the prepositions "from" or "in place of".'

[43] The Isaianic debts are ably argued for by R. E. Watts (2007: 203–204). Also see Page 2001, who points out the conceptual, even if not linguistic, parallels with Isaiah. For a contrary view see Tuckett 2000: 908, who sees no allusion to Isa. 53, no substitutionary element and no suggestion of a cost. He does, however, believe that there may be an underlying debt to the Old Testament story of the exodus.

[44] Page 2001.

[45] Page (ibid.) argues persuasively for the substitutionary accent represented by *anti*.

[46] Ibid.

Significantly, redemption is in apposition to the forgiveness of sins and comes through the blood of Christ (Eph. 1:7). There is a very similar statement in Colossians 1:14. Redemption is in apposition to the forgiveness of sins, but without the reference to blood. That is what redemption looks like in these contexts. It is linked with the forgiveness of sins. John Murray expresses it more strongly: 'redemption through Jesus' blood is *defined* as "the forgiveness of sins"'.[47] Paul sees a clear connection between the death of Christ and redemption (also see 1 Tim. 2:5). According to Titus 2:14, Christ gave (*edōken*) himself for us to redeem (*lytrōsētai*) us from all lawlessness with a view to the formation of a people zealous to do what is beautifully good. The same corporate note is struck in 1 Timothy 2:6. Christ gave himself as 'a ransom [*antilytron*] for all [*pantōn*; my tr.]'. Leon Morris comments:

> Paul does not use the customary word for ransom (*lytron*), but he does employ a stronger term to denote the price (*antilytron*, 1 Tim 2:6). There is perhaps no great difference in meaning, but the compound strengthens the idea of substitution. Christ took the place of humans, undergoing death to set them free.[48]

Of course, Paul's focus on the group does not mean that he thought only of Christ's self-giving on the cross in relation to the group, as a comparison between Galatians 2:20 ('the Son of God, who loved me and gave [*paradontos*] himself for me') and Ephesians 5:25 ('Christ loved the church and gave [*paredōken*] himself up for her') shows. Paul's robust ecclesiology never eclipsed the individual before God, nor did his sense of the individual mask the church. (More on this in the next section.)

In Paul's letters the believer is not only redeemed from sin and lawlessness but also from the curse of the law. Paul writes to the Galatians, 'The law is not based on faith; on the contrary, "The man who does these things will live by them"' (Gal. 3:12). The Galatians needed to realize that by heeding the Judaizers they too would come under the law and its curse. Because who can keep it? The law in itself is not the problem (e.g. Rom. 7:12). Rather, it is the inability of fallen humanity, including Israel, to keep the law that constitutes the

---

[47] J. Murray 1976: 22; my emphasis.
[48] L. Morris 2001c.

problem. However, God has acted in Christ to address the human predicament at this point. The divine move is astounding, for a great exchange has taken place.[49] As Jeffery, Ovey and Sach suggest, 'It is hard to imagine a plainer statement of the doctrine of penal substitution.'[50] Paul draws on both commercial (redeem) and cultic language (curse) to articulate it.[51] The apostle asserts, 'Christ redeemed us from the curse of the law by becoming a curse for us, for it is written: "Cursed is everyone who is hung on a tree" (Gal. 3:13). Christ ends the exile by taking Israel's curse upon himself.[52] Paul has the cross in mind, and then states its purpose: 'He redeemed [*exēgorasen*, aorist aspect with a specific event in mind] us [Jews like Paul] in order that the blessing given to Abraham might come to the Gentiles through Christ Jesus, so that by faith we [Jews and Gentiles] might receive the promise of the Spirit' (Gal. 3:14).[53] Paul is drawing on the language of the marketplace. A price is paid to set a slave free and the price of this redemption is unfathomable, as John Murray notes.[54] We shall return to this idea when we consider adoption as found in Galatians 4:5.

Outside the Paulines the letter to the Hebrews affirms that Christ, as we saw in an earlier discussion, secured an eternal redemption (*lytrōsin*) through his blood (Heb. 9:12). That same cultic note is struck in 1 Peter. Peter writes:

> For you know that it was not with perishable things such as silver or gold that you were redeemed [*elytrōthēte*] from the empty way of life handed down to you from your forefathers, but with the precious blood of Christ, a lamb without blemish or defect. (1 Pet. 1:18–19)

I. H. Marshall observes, 'Here the deliverance is not so much from a master as from a way of life that was godless, sinful and leading

---

[49] Hays 2002: 260. In Jesus' death a mysterious pattern of exchange was enacted, so that for our sake he took upon himself all the consequences of the world's sin. True, but is it strong enough? Is not Paul arguing that Christ took our place?

[50] Jeffery, Ovey and Sach 2007: 89.

[51] Finely discussed by Longenecker (2004, comment on Gal. 3:14).

[52] I am following Jeffery, Ovey and Sach (2007: 93–95) on this point. The ending of the exile approach (N. T. Wright) is consistent with the text, although it must be noted that it is not demanded by the text. For a contrary view concerning the sense of exile in first-century Judaism see P. T. O'Brien, 'Was Paul a Covenantal Nomist?' (in Carson, O'Brien and Seifrid 2004: 285–286).

[53] I am following Hays (2002: 262) here.

[54] J. Murray 1976: 25.

nowhere.'[55] Paganism was a dead end as a way of life, let alone as a belief system.[56] Both cultic and commercial motifs are present in the text. Sacrificial blood was shed. That payment far outvalues that of any monetary payment, even if of silver or gold. Again, Marshall comments helpfully, 'The comparison with a monetary payment suggests that a parallel is being drawn with the state of slavery, from which people could be released by a ransom.'[57] The reference to 'a lamb without blemish or defect' resonates with Leviticus and Old Testament cultic protocols. D. L. Bartlett comments, 'The reference to the unblemished lamb probably recalls Lev 22:21. The perfection of the lamb may be another reminder from Leviticus: Now just as Christ is holy, so also Christians are to be holy (see v. 16).'[58] Another important non-Pauline text for our purposes is found in the last book in the canon. The seer sees the throne of God. He also hears the songs of heaven that celebrate God as the Creator and the Lamb. The song addressed to the Lamb is a new one indicating that something significant has taken place in salvation history.[59] John hears:

> You are worthy to take the scroll
>   and to open its seals,
> because you were slain,
>   and with your blood you purchased [ēgorasas] men for God
>   from every tribe and language and people and nation.
>
> (Rev. 5:9)

C. C. Rowland notes and suggests:

> There has been much debate over the background to the imagery. The juxtaposition of buying/redeeming/loosing, blood, and a lamb suggests a Passover context, in which deliverance is effected for the children of Israel by the blood of a lamb, bringing deliverance from the angel of death and facilitating the process of liberation from Egypt (Exod. 12:22–23, 31).[60]

Although the text does not state what men and women have been redeemed from, a comparison with Revelation 1:5 suggests that it is

---

[55] Marshall 2001.
[56] Michaels 2004, comment on 1 Pet. 1:18–19.
[57] Marshall 2001. There is a similar mix of the commercial and cultic in Rev. 1:5.
[58] D. L. Bartlett 2002: 258.
[59] Rowland 2002: 604.
[60] Ibid. 602.

from sins. What is striking about the song though is the positive aspect of redemption it features. Men and woman are purchased *for* God (*tō theō*) through the sacrificial blood of Christ, the 'Lamb, who was slain' (Rev. 5:12). In fact, 'lamb' is a prominent title of Christ's in the Apocalypse, appearing some twenty-six times.[61] Once again the cultic and commercial provide the conceptual pools from which John draws.

According to John Murray, 'No category is inscribed more deeply upon the consciousness of the church of Christ than that of redemption.'[62] And, as we have seen, this redemption flows from the atoning death of Christ. With this redemption comes freedom from bondage and sets God's people singing (Rev. 5:9). Moreover, it purchases men and women for God. 'But with what status?' is the question. Is it a mere change of ownership? Or is something more extraordinary in view in New Testament perspective?

Adoption

When we consider the idea of adoption in Paul, we see the most positive aspect of redemption.[63] In fact, Paul is the only New Testament writer to employ the concept (*huiothesia*) in any explicit way. He does so with an Old Testament background in mind, that of Israel's adoption by Yahweh (Rom. 9:3–4) and probably that of Israel's Davidic king (Rom. 1:4).[64] Importantly, the term *huiothesia* is probably better translated as 'adoption' rather than 'sonship' (as in the NRSV and ESV, contra the NIV's 'the full rights of sons', which is somewhat strained).[65] The crucial passage is Galatians 4:4–7:

> But when the time had fully come, God sent his Son, born of a woman, born under law, to redeem [*exagorasē*] those under law, that we might receive the full rights of sons [better, 'the adoption']. Because you are sons, God sent the Spirit of his Son into our hearts, the Spirit who calls out, '*Abba*, Father.' So you are no longer a slave, but a son; and since you are a son, God has made you also an heir.

---

[61] Grogan in Tidball, Hilborn and Thacker 2008: 94.

[62] J. Murray 1976: 21.

[63] For a recent study of this Pauline metaphor see Burke 2006.

[64] See the discussions in Ciampa 2001 and Scott 2001.

[65] Scott asserts strongly, 'any attempt to translate the term more generally as "sonship" sets the study of the background [of Gal. 4:5] off on the wrong foot from the start'. See his argument in Scott 2001. Note, however, that others are more comfortable with 'sonship'. E.g. see Longenecker 2004, comment on Gal. 4:1–7.

This rich passage is replete with important ideas. The Son was sent and a chain of events ensued. After the incarnation comes the cross. The reference to the death of Christ is seemingly hidden from sight; but once Galatians 3:13–14 is recalled, the connection between the redemptive mission of the Son and the cross comes into view, as Richard Hays points out. Hays comments, 'Although the cross is not explicitly mentioned in v. 5, it would be misleading to suppose that Paul here thinks of a redemption achieved solely through the incarnation of the Son as opposed to through his death.'[66] The redemption referred to in Galatians 4:5 most probably echoes the great deliverance of Israel from slavery in Egypt rather than a first-century Greco-Roman marketplace.[67] After the cross comes the sending of the Spirit. The framework is salvation history and the events that make it up go back to Abraham rather than a framework that merely has the individual in view (Gal. 3:29). There are no grounds for a second blessing theology here, as though the individual receives adoption first and subsequently the Spirit.[68] The gift of the Spirit enables Jew and Gentile to enter into the very prayer life of the Son (*abba*; cf. Gal. 4:6; Rom. 8:15; Mark 14:36). This is astounding! After all, the believer is no longer a slave (*doulos*) but God's adopted child (lit. 'son') and as such now a fellow heir with the unique Son ('his Son') of the eschatological inheritance.[69]

As John Murray affirms, 'This is the apex of privilege and blessing secured by Christ's redemption – we receive the adoption.'[70] J. I. Packer similarly describes adoption as 'the crowning blessing'.[71] Indeed, he argues persuasively that, although justification is 'the *fundamental* blessing' of the gospel, 'Adoption is higher'.[72] No cross, no redemption; no redemption, no adoption.

---

[66] Hays 2002: 284.

[67] Scott 2001.

[68] Hays (2002: 285) is excellent on this point.

[69] There are many exegetical cruxes in Gal. 4:1–7 that are beyond the scope of the present work. For instance, what is the relation of 'under the basic principles of the world' (*ta stoicheia tou kosmou*) to 'under law' (*hypo nomon*, anarthrous)? Again to what does 'basic principles' or, as in the NSRV, 'elemental spirits' refer? Hays (2002: 283) rightly contends, 'In any case, Paul portrays all humanity as existing in a condition of slavery prior to God's dramatic intervention. That intervention is the theme of vv. 4–7.'

[70] J. Murray 1976: 26.

[71] Packer 1993: 167.

[72] Packer 1973: 187; original emphasis.

Reconciliation

From Genesis 3 to Revelation 22, the Scripture unfolds a story of estrangement and reconciliation. According to D. A. Carson:

> The heart of the issue may be put this way: if the human plight is our sin and its effects, not the least the fact that *we stand alienated from God* and rightly under his wrath, then, granted the place of the cross in the Bible's story line, *whatever else the cross accomplishes, it must reconcile us to God*, it must remove the ground of our alienation, it must set aside God's wrath – or it does not meet the plight that the Scriptures themselves set forth.[73]

Murray has firm exegetical warrant for this claim, as Paul's letter to the Romans shows. The key passage for our purposes is Romans 5:1–11, especially verse 10.

Romans 5:1–11 is a singularly important passage in the argument of the letter to the Romans. W. J. Dumbrell captures its structural importance: 'Romans 5 is the pivot on which the argument of Romans 1–8 turns. It is frequently noted that 5:1–11 anticipates the conclusion of the whole section, 8:31–30 [*sic*], while it also summarizes the whole argument to this point.'[74] The idea of reconciliation suffuses the passage, as Paul's use of three significant terms shows (*eirēnē, katallassein, katallagē*). I quote *in extenso*:

> Therefore, since we have been justified through faith, *we have peace [eirēnē] with God* through our Lord Jesus Christ, through whom we have gained access by faith into this grace in which we now stand. And we rejoice in the hope of the glory of God. Not only so, but we also rejoice in our sufferings, because we know that suffering produces perseverance; perseverance, character; and character, hope. And hope does not disappoint us, because God has poured out his love into our hearts by the Holy Spirit, whom he has given us. You see, at just the right time, when we were still powerless, *Christ died for the ungodly*. Very rarely will anyone die for a righteous man, though for a good man someone might possibly dare to die. But God demonstrates his own love for us in this: *While*

[73] Carson 2008: 56; my emphases.
[74] Dumbrell 2005: 59.

we were still sinners, Christ died for us. Since we have now
been justified *by his blood,* how much more shall we be saved
from God's wrath through him! For if, when we were God's
enemies, *we were reconciled* [*katēllagēmen*] *to him* through the
death of his Son, how much more, *having been reconciled*
[*katallagentes*], shall we be saved through his life! Not only is
this so, but we also rejoice in God through our Lord Jesus
Christ, through whom we have now received *reconciliation*
[*katallagēn*]. (My emphases)

To explore all the exegetical and theological riches of this passage is
beyond my brief. However, we need to observe the inclusio (cf. vv. 1,
11). The inclusio is conceptual. In both verses peace with God is the
idea.

What is the peace in view in the passage? What is the reconciliation? How are peace and reconciliation achieved? The peace in view
most likely has the rich Old Testament background of shalom.
Again Dumbrell is illuminating:

Peace (Greek *eirēnē*, 5:1) is the absence of conflict and this fits
here, but the notion of Heb. Shalom, for which Gk. *eirēnē* is
used in the OT – indicating wholeness of being, at one with
God's plan for the world – fits even better . . . The call to
believers is now to appropriate the blessings of access previously associated with Israel's temple worship. They are now
to hope in the glory of God (which Adam lost 3:23), which is
to be restored in Christ (8:18–30).[75]

As for reconciliation, it has to do with an objective change in relations. According to Leon Morris, 'Christ died to put away our sin.
In this way he dealt with the enmity between man and God. He put
it out of the way. He made the way wide open for men to come back

---

[75] Ibid. 60. Likewise, see L. Morris 1983: 141–142. For a contrary view see Porter
2001b, who argues for a Greek rather than Hebrew background. He contends,
'Although many scholars believe that the sense of "peace" (*eirēnē*) depends upon the
OT sense of external or material well-being, the Greek sense denoting a time or state
without hostility or war fits the context better' (696). My guess is that both back-
grounds are probably in play in some way. Expressed in Polanyian terms, the Old
Testament one was more Paul's focal awareness and the Greek one his subsidiary
awareness. When I write 'apple', most probably your focus (focal awareness) is on
meaning (a fruit). Your subsidiary awareness is on the *letters of the alphabet* sequenced
a certain way ('a–p–p–l–e'). Both kinds of awareness are in play.

to God. It is this which is described by the term "reconciliation".'[76] Enmity gives way to embrace. Reconciliation is a cause for celebration (lit. 'boasting', *kauchōmenoi*) on the part of all who have been caught up in it, as N. T. Wright observes.[77] The extraordinary claim is that God took the initiative while humanity was in rebellion, and the means of overcoming his wrath towards ungodly humanity is the death of Christ (v. 10). The reference to blood in verse 9 should be understood in cultic rather than martyr terms. As Dumbrell argues, 'Perhaps that view provides a glimmer of truth, but Jesus did not die a "national martyr."'[78]

Elsewhere in Paul's writings we find that reconciliation was the gravamen of his apostolic preaching. He informs the Corinthians, 'And he [God] has committed to us the message [*ton logon*] of reconciliation [*katallagēs*]' (2 Cor. 5:19). This reconciliation is effected through Christ's death, as following the logic of 2 Corinthians 5:11–19 reveals. Indeed, it is this message that provides him with his ambassadorial brief on behalf of Christ his king (2 Cor. 5:20). And, as we have seen, in Romans 5:1–11 that reconciliation is predicated on the atoning sacrifice of Christ. However, this reconciliation provided from the Godward side requires embrace from our own. Hence Paul implores the Corinthians, 'Be reconciled to God! (2 Cor. 5:20).'[79]

Peace between Jew and Gentile: the one new man

In the previous material we explored the peace dividend for the individual and its relation to the atonement. At the existential level, for the individual the benefits of atonement and the loving divine motivation behind them are of central importance. As Paul expresses it, 'the Son of God, who loved me and gave himself for me' (Gal. 2:20). I have been died for. Christ died in my place. The peace dividend, however, does not end there. For this same Paul writes, 'Christ loved the church and gave himself up for her' (Eph. 5:25). We have been died for. Christ died in our place. An earlier generation of

[76] L. Morris 2001b.

[77] N. T. Wright 2004: 88.

[78] Dumbrell 2005: 63. Those who argue for echoes of Jewish martyr theology usually draw on 4 Maccabees 6.28–29; 17.20–22.

[79] How an individual appropriates the peace dividend is an important subject, but it is not the focus of this book. Such a discussion would need to cover the story of divine initiative in effectual call and regeneration, and the human story of repentance and faith. For a fine treatment of these matters and their relation to the cross see Demarest 1997 and Calvin 2002e, esp. bk. 3.

Bible-believing Christians understood this. As church historian Mark Noll observes, 'Up to the early 1700s, British Protestants preached on God's plan *for the church*. From the mid-1700s, however, evangelicals emphasized God's plans *for the individual*.'[80] Furthermore, if Colin E. Gunton is right, 'Reconciliation with God, that is to say, is the necessary condition for reconciliation between people and peace with the environment.'[81] With a broader understanding of the peace dividend in mind we turn our attention in this section to peace between people in general, and between Jew and Gentile in particular, and how the atonement is integral to it. In the next section we shall consider the peace dividend and the cosmos.

The church presented in the New Testament is made up of both Jews and Gentiles who believe in Jesus and acknowledge him as Lord. However, the book of Acts testifies to the difficulty such an assembly constituted in the earliest days of Christianity. As we saw in chapter 3, the story of Peter's reluctance to go to the house of the Gentile Cornelius and the subsequent negative reaction to his evangelizing Cornelius on the part of some in Jerusalem exemplify the problem in a world where there was an inscription in the temple in Jerusalem that read, 'No foreigner may enter within the balustrade and enclosure around the Sanctuary. Whoever is caught will render himself liable to the death penalty which will inevitably follow.'[82] Foreigners could go no further than the Court of Gentiles.

As the apostle to the uncircumcised, Paul knew the answer to overcoming such hostility, as his letter to the Ephesians shows. I quote *in extenso*:

> Therefore, remember that formerly you who are Gentiles by birth and called 'uncircumcised' by those who call themselves 'the circumcision' (that done in the body by the hands of men) – remember that at that time you were separate from Christ, excluded from citizenship in Israel and foreigners to the covenants of the promise, without hope and without God in the world. But now in Christ Jesus you who once were far away have been brought near *through the blood of Christ*.

---

[80] Noll 1993: 44; original emphasis. It is interesting to observe that Leon Morris's (2001b) *NBD* article 'Reconciliation' highlights the individual aspect alone, although two of the more expansive biblical references are cited (e.g. 'Eph. 2:11ff.; Col. 1:19ff').

[81] Gunton 2002: 72.

[82] Quoted in L. Morris 1983: 143.

> *For he himself is our peace* [*eirēnē*], who has made the two one
> and has destroyed the barrier, the dividing wall of hostility
> [*echthran*], by abolishing in his flesh the law with its command-
> ments and regulations. His purpose was to create in himself
> one new man out of the two, thus making peace, and in this one
> body *to reconcile* [*apokatallaxē*] *both of them to God through the
> cross, by which he put to death their hostility.* He came and
> preached peace to you who were far away and peace [*eirēnē*] to
> those who were near. For through him we both have access to
> the Father by one Spirit. (Eph. 2:11–18; my emphases)[83]

God's atoning project has more than the Jews in mind. The Father is
building through Christ and the Spirit a new temple as well as a new
humanity:

> Consequently, you are no longer foreigners and aliens, but
> fellow-citizens with God's people and members of God's
> household, built on the foundation of the apostles and proph-
> ets, with Christ Jesus himself as the chief cornerstone. In him
> the whole building is joined together and rises to become a
> holy temple in the Lord. And in him you too are being built
> together to become a dwelling in which God lives by his
> Spirit. (Eph. 2:19–22)

Jew and Gentile drawn to Christ are drawn to one another. As
Andrew Lincoln suggests, 'In accomplishing this, Christ has tran-
scended one of the fundamental divisions of the first-century world.'[84]
For Paul this was no mere theory but his practice, as his rebuke of
Peter's behaviour at Antioch shows (Gal. 2:11–21).

How then does the atonement actually break down the wall of hostility?[85] How does it bring peace on the horizontal level? The sacrifice

---

[83] Porter (2001b: 697) argues, 'The language of reconciliation in Colossians
1:20–22 and Ephesians 2:16 is slightly different from that in Paul's chief letters. The
verb translated "make peace" (*eirēnopoieō*) is used in its only instance in the Pauline
letters.' He is right about Col. 1.20–22 but mistaken about Eph. 2:16, where *katallassein* is used and not *eirēnopoiein*.

[84] Lincoln 2004, comment on Eph. 2:14–16.

[85] L. Morris (1983: 143) wisely comments concerning the temple superscription
directed at Gentiles (which I referenced previously), 'It would be too much to say that
Paul is writing about this wall. But the wall and its inscription allow us to see something of the depth of the division between Jew and Gentile and that is certainly before
us in Ephesians 2.' Porter (2001b) is less cautious: 'Paul employs a metaphor probably
drawn from the wall in the Jerusalem Temple, or the Temple itself, which prevented
Gentiles from proceeding into the inner courts.'

of Christ is integral to the process, as evidenced by the references to 'the blood of Christ' and 'the cross'. The apostle does not elaborate beyond arguing that through his death Christ abolished 'in his flesh the law with its commandments and regulations'. These rules constituted the heart of the barrier between Jew and Gentile. However, the rules of the law, especially purity and food rules, are now done away with.[86] J. D. G. Dunn also suggests that in view is 'ending an ancient blood feud, and echoes of the sacrifice which bonded the parties to the covenant in Gen. 15:7–21'.[87] This is speculative. What is not speculative is this: that the cross did in fact break down the dividing wall of hostility can be seen in Paul's case. He became the apostle to the non-Jewish world. Moreover, he exhibited demonstrable affection for his Gentile converts (1 Thess. 2:6–12). Again his practice is eloquent. He encouraged a collection for poor saints in Jerusalem from Gentile Christians, as he told the Romans: 'Now, however, I am on my way to Jerusalem in the service of the saints there. For Macedonia and Achaia were pleased to make a contribution for the poor among the saints in Jerusalem' (Rom. 15:25–26).

Christians who maintain walls of hostility between themselves and others at the interpersonal level need to revisit the cross, the Pauline practice and the words of Jesus himself 'Blessed are the peacemakers [*eirēnopoioi*]' (Matt. 5:9).[88]

Peace for the cosmos: reconciliation and pacification

Paul's letter to the Christians at Colosse makes an extraordinary contribution to our understanding of both the person and work of Christ against the backdrop of the false teaching troubling the church there. This false teaching offered a distorted Christology, which appears to have given Christ a lesser place in relation to God, creation and salvation. In contradistinction, Paul in Colossians 1:15–20 presents Christ as the mediator of creation and reconciliation. The apostle writes of Christ:

> He is the image of the invisible God, the firstborn over all creation. For by him all things were created: things in heaven

[86] Dunn 2000: 1170.
[87] Ibid.
[88] Vigorous debate about truth claims is not antithetical to interpersonal peacemaking. It can be a bona fide expression of love of neighbour and love of enemy.

and on earth, visible and invisible, whether thrones or powers or rulers or authorities; all things were created by him and for him. He is before all things, and in him all things hold together. And he is the head of the body, the church; he is the beginning and the firstborn from among the dead, so that in everything he might have the supremacy. *For God was pleased to have all his fulness dwell in him, and through him to reconcile to himself all things, whether things on earth or things in heaven, by making peace through his blood, shed on the cross.* (Col. 1:15–20; my emphasis)

This is high Christology indeed and Paul uses both a compound [*apokatallaxai*] of a familiar word for reconciliation [*apokatallaxai*], which we saw employed in Romans 5, 2 Corinthians 5 and Ephesians 2, and introduces a fresh one, 'peacemaking' [*eirēnopoiēsas*], in verse 20.

The scope of the reconciliation and peacemaking effected by Christ is breathtaking. 'All things [*ta*]' are touched by Christ's sacrifice ('through his blood shed on the cross'). The 'all things' include the earthly and the heavenly. As Robert Letham rightly notes with regard to Colossians 1:20, 'His death on the cross served not only to restore humanity to fellowship with God but also to renew the entire universe.'[89] The Colossians themselves, for example, are included:

Once *you were alienated from God and were enemies* in your minds because of your evil behaviour. But now *he has reconciled* [*apokatēllaxen*] *you by Christ's physical body through death to present you holy in his sight, without blemish and free from accusation* – if you continue in your faith, established and firm, not moved from the hope held out in the gospel. (Col. 1:21–23; my emphases)

Included also are the 'powers and authorities' in view in Colossians 2:15. Paul argues:

[89] Letham 1993: 147. Colossians 1:19–20 ('to reconcile to himself all things') is one of the texts used to argue for universalism (all will be saved) according to D. Fergusson (in Gunton 1997: 240). However, the universalist needs to face the weight of the biblical evidence, including the role of faith in Col. 1:23 and the reference to the coming wrath in 3:6. Furthermore, to look no further than the Paulines, Col. 1:19–20 needs to be read alongside Rom. 1 – 5 and 2 Thess. 1:5–10. Universalism fails to convince when the 'analogy of Scripture' (comparing Scripture with Scripture) is employed.

> When you were dead in your sins and in the uncircumcision of your sinful nature, God made you alive with Christ. He forgave us all our sins, having cancelled the written code, with its regulations, that was against us and that stood opposed to us; he took it away, nailing it to the cross. And having disarmed the powers [*tas archas kai tas exousias*] and authorities, he made a public spectacle of them, triumphing over them by the cross. (Col. 2:13–15)

The phrase 'Powers and authorities' refers to supernatural intelligences opposed to God's purposes.[90] People in the West may all too easily dismiss such references and in so doing exhibit what anthropologist Paul Hiebert termed 'the flaw of the excluded middle'. Hiebert confessed his own weakness at one stage of his life in this regard: 'The reasons for my uneasiness with the biblical and Indian worldviews should be clear: I had excluded the middle level of supernatural this-worldly beings and forces from my own worldview.'[91]

The good news is that Christ's cross not only saves us but additionally disarms those forces arraigned against us.[92] According to Jerome Murphy-O'Connor, Colossians 2:15 introduces a new image. God like a Roman emperor 'awards a Roman triumph to Christ (his victorious general), who, . . . stripped angelic beings of their power'.[93] And if Daniel G. Reid is correct, in the background is 'the Jewish archetype of the divine warrior vanquishing his foes' with its Old Testament roots.[94] The key to the disarmament is the forgiveness of sins on the basis of the cross (Col. 2:13). 'The powers and authorities' are thus deprived of their power now that 'the written code, with its regulations, that was against us and that stood opposed to

[90] Murphy-O'Connor 2000: 1194–1195. According to Twelftree (2001), most commentators understand Col. 2:8, 10, 15, 20 as referring in different ways to 'spiritual powers which are active within the physical and heavenly elements'. For an example of such a commentator see Lincoln 2002: 598.

[91] Hiebert 1994: 196. Carson and Moo (2005: 529) make a telling point: 'Some of us may miss part of the relevance of what he [Paul] is saying because we do not believe in those forces in the way the Colossians did.'

[92] O'Brien (2004) helpfully observes that although there is a cosmic dimension to reconciliation, the accent in Colossians falls on the Colossians themselves and their reconciliation (comment on Col. 1:21 and the significance of the emphatic position of the personal pronoun *hymas*, 'and you'). I have endeavoured to observe that weighting in this chapter by devoting the longest section to the 'peace dividend' for the individual.

[93] Murphy-O'Connor 2000: 1195. I take the view that God the Father and not Christ is the subject. For the alternative view see D. G. Reid 2001.

[94] Ibid.

us' is cancelled, taken away, nailed to the cross (Col. 2:14). These forces no longer have any grounds to accuse the Colossians and us who believe (cf. Col. 2:15).[95] In such accusation lay their power. Christ dying in our place robs them of their power (Rom. 8:31–34). Christus Victor needs the explanatory power of substitutionary atonement.[96]

In brief – no peace without disarmament.[97] The story of that disarmament though has yet to play out to its denouement. However, there is a day coming in Pauline perspective when Christ will put all his enemies under his feet, including 'all dominion, authority and power' (1 Cor. 15:24–25). Shalom is coming. The barriers to it are being removed.

Conclusion

The peace dividend works itself out in a variety of ways. Leon Morris usefully sums them up as follows:

> Peace means the defeat of evil. Peace means breaking down the barrier between man and God. Peace means the presence of God's rich and abundant blessing. Peace means positiveness; it is not the absence of anything – the barrier that separated us from God or anything else. Peace is presence, the presence of God. Christ 'is our peace.'[98]

Morris's statement covers the territory we have explored in this chapter: the cosmic (the devil), the individual (specifically God and the individual) and the corporate (analytically contained in 'anything else'). The devil and his minions are pacified. The believer is united with Christ, his or her sins are forgiven, is cleansed, justified,

---

[95] Some have suggested that in view are those spiritual intelligences that record human transgressions (cf. Ps. 56:8; Isa. 65:6; *1 Enoch* 81.2–4). See Murphy-O'Connor 2000: 1195. Also see A. T. Lincoln 2002: 625, who writes, 'The accusatory book has in effect been ruled out of court. It was canceled and set aside by being nailed to the cross.' For an alternative view see O'Brien 2004, comment on Col. 2:14, 'Our preference is to understand *cheirographon* as the signed acknowledgment of our indebtedness before God. Like an IOU it contained penalty clauses (see Job 5:3; Philem 19).'

[96] A point well argued by G. Williams (in Tidball, Hilborn and Thacker 2008: 187–188).

[97] Kaiser et al. (2001a), 'Here there is also a type of "reconciliation," in that these powers and authorities (spiritual beings) will no longer be in rebellion against God. Yet it is the "reconciliation" of a defeated enemy.'

[98] L. Morris 1983: 143–144.

redeemed, adopted and reconciled. The wall of hostility between Jew and Gentile is removed. One new man is created. Putting Morris's point another way, the Aaronic blessing (Num. 6:22–27) becomes the experience of all who are caught up in God's atoning project and who are the beneficiaries of Christ's vicarious sacrifice (the atonement). To be so caught up is to be blessed by God, to be kept by God, to have the divine face turned towards you, to have the divine face shine upon you, to experience God's grace and be given his peace (Heb. *šālōm*; Gr. *eirēnē*). To believe these things from the heart entails a distinctive way of life, and to that subject we now turn.

Chapter Eight

Life between the cross and the coming

In the previous chapter our focus was on the benefits of being caught up in God's atoning project, benefits such as the forgiveness of sins.[1] In this chapter we explore the responsibilities that come with being caught up in God's atoning project, responsibilities such as living for him who died for us. To be real, biblical religion needs expression in life. Both the Old and New Testaments make this point. Deuteronomy presents Moses on the plains of Moab addressing Israel in these terms: 'The secret things belong to the LORD our God, but the things revealed belong to us and to our children for ever, that we may follow all the words of this law' (Deut. 29:29). The purpose of revelation is not to feed *theoria* (the mere contemplation of divine things) but praxis (walking in God's ways). Jesus stood in this same tradition: 'If anyone loves me, he will obey my teaching' (John 14:23). Paul the great apostle of grace was also the great apostle of good works, as Ephesians 2:8–10 shows: 'For it is by grace you have been saved, through faith – and this not from yourselves, it is the gift of God – not by works, so that no-one can boast. For we are God's workmanship, created in Christ Jesus to do good works, which God prepared in advance for us to do.' James is of a piece with this Pauline emphasis: 'But someone will say, "You have faith; I have deeds." Show me your faith without deeds, and I will show you my faith by what I do' (Jas 2:18).[2]

How then are those who have appropriated the peace dividend at the personal level to live? Or, to use Kevin J. Vanhoozer's helpful

---

[1] In a letter to D. Jessup (5 Feb. 1954) C. S. Lewis wrote, 'How little they know of Christianity who think that the story *ends* with conversion' (in Ford 2008: 233; original emphasis).

[2] A way to throw fresh light on the apparent conflict between Paul and James, which Luther famously found so difficult, may benefit from a speech-act analysis. The key may be the illocutionary and perlocutionary differences involved in using the same Abrahamic locutionary material. To pursue this further, however, will take us too far from my brief.

idea, how are we to perform the theodramatic script?[3] This is the question that animates this chapter. But first we need to take our eschatological bearings before pursuing it.[4]

Eschatological location

As I type these words I am located in Libertyville, north-west of Chicago, in what is known to locals as Chicagoland. With regard to time it is 25 September 2008 and the autumn has begun. Leaves are turning red and golden, and some are falling. However, in biblical categories I am writing in the groaning creation as far as my location in space is concerned (Rom. 8:18–25). And with respect to time I am located as one 'on whom the end of the ages has come' (1 Cor. 10:11 ESV, NRSV), in 'the present evil age' (Gal. 1:4), or in 'these last days' (Heb. 1:2). As P. F. Jensen says, 'The new age announced in the New Testament has been inserted into time, the old age and the new run on together. It is the time of the two ages.'[5]

To change the biblical categories, I am on the road. In fact, the ultimate road trip! Pioneering missiologist Lesslie Newbigin suggests that there is a great divide between the major religions of the world. There are road religions and wheel religions. Wheel religions characteristically unify human experience by employing the wheel as a metaphor (e.g. Hinduism).[6] In contrast, using the road as a metaphor, there are other religions that as a rule unify human experience (e.g. Christianity). Indeed, Jesus famously described himself as the way (John 14:6, *hodos*). Early Christians were described as those 'who belonged to the Way' (Acts 9:2, *hodos*). What is typically in view with those religions that accent the wheel is a 'cycle of birth, growth, decay and death', which recurs endlessly.[7] Plants, animals, humans, and even institutions, are caught up in the cycle of endless recurrence. History is 'meaningless movement'.[8] With those religions that are teleological and favour the road metaphor, the 'perfect

---

[3] See Vanhoozer 2005: 30–33 for a summary of his theodramatic approach to Christian doctrine.

[4] The issues discussed in this chapter are pertinent to a variety of eschatological schemas, whether one holds to a rapture doctrine, as in classic dispensationalism (e.g. C. C. Ryrie), or one does not (e.g. historic premillennialist G. E. Ladd and amillennialist J. I. Packer).

[5] Jensen 1997: 26.

[6] Newbigin 1969: 65.

[7] Ibid. 66.

[8] Ibid.

goal is not timeless reality hidden now behind the multiplicity and change we experience; it is yet to be achieved; it lies at the end of the road'.[9] As I have written elsewhere, 'Christians are roadies not wheelies. God has a project and he will achieve it, and history is the arena for that achievement.'[10] Indeed, as the poet Robert Browning rightly affirmed, 'The best is yet to be.'[11]

In the meantime, how then should we live in 'these last days' between the cross and the coming again of Christ,[12] or, put another way, as we live in between the atonement and the reconciliation of all things?

Living by faith, not by sight

The Christ life begins and continues both in this life and the next as a life of faith. As D. B. Knox rightly notes, 'The whole of our Christian life is a life of faith.'[13] Appropriating the gospel is by faith. Jesus taught it: 'The kingdom of God is near. Repent and believe the good news!' (Mark 1:14).[14] John taught that eternal life comes through faith (trust) in Jesus Christ (John 3:16). That is why the Fourth Gospel was written (John 20:31).[15] Paul taught it: 'I have declared to both Jews and Greeks that they must turn to God in repentance and have faith in our Lord Jesus' (Acts 20:21). He tells the Corinthians that faith will continue in the age to come (1 Cor. 13:13). We never stop trusting God. This faith is God's gift (Eph. 2:8–9). This faith acts. It expresses itself through love (Gal. 5:6). The letter to the Hebrews is adamant that 'without faith it is impossible to please God' (Heb. 11:6). This faith believes not only in God's existence but also in God's benevolent character as a rewarder of 'those who earnestly seek him' (Heb. 11:6).

---

[9] Ibid.

[10] Cole 2007: 142.

[11] Ibid.

[12] Jensen 1997: 26. Technically speaking, this chapter's discussion involves in part the question of progressive sanctification rather than those of positional or final sanctification. See Cole 2005c: 720–722 and Grudem 1994: 746–762.

[13] Knox 1959: 15.

[14] In my view, following Calvin, repentance is an expression of faith. When a person repents, he or she is showing thereby that he or she is believing Jesus' command and the authority with which he states it. Calvin (2002e: 3.3.1) argues, 'Now it ought to be a fact beyond controversy that repentance not only constantly follows faith, but is also born of faith.'

[15] Comparing John 3:16, 'believing into him' (*pisteuōn eis auton*), and John 20:31, 'in order that you believe that Jesus is the Christ' (*hina pisteuēte hoti Iēsous estin ho Christos*), shows that the personal 'believing into' and the propositional 'believe that' ought not to be falsely opposed.

The New Testament, interestingly, does not contrast faith and reason. By 'reason' I mean the human ability to mount and refute arguments.[16] By 'reason' I am not referring to 'Reason' with a capital 'R', which sits in judgment on the things of God and emanates from the autonomous self, adrift from the service of God. The great contrasts in the New Testament are between faith and fear, as Jesus made plain (Matt. 8:26), and between faith and sight, as Paul taught (2 Cor. 5:7). The last contrast is an important one because the context is a two-ages one: life in the body here in contradistinction to life re-embodied in the hereafter (2 Cor. 4:16 – 5:10). So much we cannot see. For example, we cannot see physically just how God's atoning project is working itself out. We are told in Hebrews 2:5–8 that all things are subject to Jesus (á la Ps. 8:4–6). But, we are also told, 'In putting everything under him [Jesus], God left nothing that is not subject to him. Yet at present we do not see everything subject to him' (Heb. 2:8). How true the last statement is, as many who have suffered for the faith could testify! However, the letter to the Hebrews does not leave us there: 'But we see Jesus, who was made a little lower than the angels, now crowned with glory and honour because he suffered death, so that by the grace of God he might taste death for everyone' (Heb. 2:9).

In this life, living as we do between the cross and his coming again, Jesus is seen in the gospel. Believing is a way of seeing.

Faith appreciates the price

Paul's first letter to the Corinthians addresses a deeply troubling church: disunity, immorality, litigation, abuse of the Lord's Supper, corporate worship issues, spiritual gifts problems, and debate about the resurrection. One of the immorality issues Paul tackles is that of consorting with prostitutes (1 Cor. 6:12–20). He offers three arguments against the practice. The first is that, as members of Christ's body, such sexual unions are beyond the pale (1 Cor. 6:15–17). A second is that the believer is a temple of the Holy Spirit (1 Cor. 6:19). The inference to be drawn appears to be that the holiness of the temple is not to be so compromised. The last argument is the key one for our purposes. Paul writes, 'You are not your own; you were bought [ēgorasthēte] at a price [timēs]' (1 Cor. 6:19–20). Paul uses the aorist aspect for 'bought'. A definitive event is in view: the cross.

---

[16] Fideism is not the way forward. Think of Paul's cumulative argument in 1 Cor. 15:1–20 for the claim that Christ is risen.

A number of commentators both past and present note the implied reference to the cross. Calvin for instance writes, 'He proves this from the fact that the Lord has purchased us for himself, by paying the price of our redemption.'[17] He then cross-references 1 Corinthians 6:19–20 with Romans 14:9 and 1 Peter 1:18–19, with their clear references to the death of Christ. Craig Blomberg says likewise, 'Verse 20 alludes to Jesus' costly atonement.'[18] However, surprisingly, some contemporary scholars champion instead the idea of a person bought in the marketplace, as it were, who then as a result comes under new ownership, and they give no hint that there is any connection in this to the cross or atonement. For example, J. P. Sampley argues, 'Paul's concern is simply and directly to declare that the Corinthians have become subject to – that is, they belong to – a new Lord: Jesus Christ.'[19] This would be more convincing if Paul had merely written 'you were bought' and had made no reference to price.

The Pauline references to cost and to change of allegiance have a very practical application. The NRSV translation best preserves the logic of Paul's argument at this point: 'For [gar] you were bought with a price; therefore [dē] glorify [doxasate] God in your body' (1 Cor. 6:20). As Leon Morris says, 'This is the language of the market place. A price paid for the purchase of a slave. Paradoxically freed to belong to another . . . We are not to think of redemption as some remote, ethereal process. Redemption has effects in everyday experience and living.'[20] Given the larger context of 1 Corinthians 6:12–20 the motivation to glorify God in one's body as a believer is threefold. We do so as members of Christ's body, as temples of the Spirit and as those bought at great cost.[21] The last point Paul takes up, with a different application, in the next chapter. He writes in 1 Corinthians 7:23, 'You were bought [ēgorasthēte] at a price [timēs]; do not become slaves of men ['and women', anthrōpōn].' Morris is right to apply the text in these terms: 'The redeemed belong to God; they should not seek to have themselves enslaved to human opinions.'[22]

---

[17] Calvin 2002a, comment on 1 Cor. 6:19–20.

[18] Blomberg 1996, comment on 1 Cor. 6:19–20.

[19] Sampley 2002a: 864. Also see Barclay 2000: 1118.

[20] L. Morris 2001c.

[21] In contrast to the use of the temple-of-the-Spirit image in 1 Cor. 3:16–17 that is corporate, in 1 Cor. 6:19 the reference is better understood as to the individual believer. See the discussion in Mare 1997, comment on 1 Cor. 6:19.

[22] L. Morris 2001c. However, he follows the NRSV, which renders the text, 'do not become slaves of human masters'. Theologically true, but 'human masters' has been imported into the text.

To be caught up in God's atoning project with its centrepiece of the atoning death of Christ is to belong to another and to appreciate the cost.

Faith lives for him

Belonging to Christ means living for him – or at least it ought to. Paul reminds the Corinthians of this when he writes, 'For Christ's love compels us, because we are convinced that one died for all, and therefore all died. And he died for all, that those who live should no longer live for themselves but for him who died for them and was raised again' (2 Cor. 5:14–15). This rich passage thematizes the vicarious nature of Christ's sacrifice ('one died for all') and the divine motive behind it ('the love of Christ'), which is best understood as a subjective rather than objective genitive (v. 14).[23] In other words, Christ's love for his people, and not his people's love for him, is in view.[24] The passage also telegraphs the purpose of that sacrifice, which is to bring into existence a self-donating lifestyle that is the fitting response to Christ's love. Believers no longer live for themselves but for him (v. 15). Indeed, they have died to their old way of life ('all have died'). The difficult phrase 'all have died' constitutes no grounds for turning Paul into a universalist, however.[25] For earlier in the chapter Paul refers to the motive for his gospel ministry: 'Knowing therefore the fear [*phobon*] of the Lord we persuade men and women' (2 Cor. 5:11; my tr.). As Scott Hafemann argues, 'fear' here has the judgment of God in view given 2 Corinthians 5:10, 'the apostle seeks to persuade others to join him in fearing the Lord so that they too will escape his wrath'.[26]

---

[23] Paul's use of *hyper* (for, on behalf of) carries overtones of representation and substitution, according to Martin (2004, comment on 2 Cor. 5:14–15). For a contrary view see Sampley 2002b: 92, who argues that 2 Cor. 5:15 'should be taken, not in a substitutionary manner in the sense of Christ's taking everybody's place at his death, but in the sense of Christ's being for – that is, siding with – people'. This is far too anaemic in my view. Interestingly, it is the far more robust message of Christ's love seen in his taking our place on the cross (penal substitution) that those in lower economic circumstances find so liberating after a life trapped in 'low self-worth or even self-loathing and hatred', according to the pastoral experience of Gary Jenkins (1999: 17–19). The idea that someone loves me enough to take my punishment upon himself is extraordinarily powerful.

[24] This is the consensus position among commentators, according to Martin (2004, comment on 2 Cor. 5:14–15).

[25] Contra MacDonald 2000: 1140. She describes 2 Cor. 5:14–15 as 'one of the strongest statements of universal salvation in his epistles'.

[26] Hafemann 1996, '2 Corinthians: Paul's Motivation for Ministry (5:11–15)'.

Paul's own story fleshes out what it is to have died to the old way and been raised with Christ to a new way, that of the new creation (2 Cor. 5:17). No longer did he consider Christ 'from a worldly point of view' (2 Cor. 5:16). That is to say, as M. MacDonald suggests, 'Paul admits before his acceptance of Christ he judged Christ by worldly standards, perhaps according to the pathetic image of a crucified messianic imposter.'[27] Paul now lives for the risen Christ, as he informed the Philippians: 'For to me [*emou*, 'to me', in the emphatic position], to live is Christ and to die is gain' (Phil. 1:21). In fact, he is prepared to remain in this life for the benefit of the Philippians, even though his deeper desire is to be with Christ (Phil. 1:22–26). What then does 'to live is Christ' entail? H. A. Kent, Jr., sums it up this way: 'The very essence of Paul's present life was Christ and all that this entailed . . . Christ had become for him the motive of his actions, the goal of his life and ministry, the source of his strength.'[28] Living for him had put Paul in prison (Phil. 1:13–14). Living for Christ meant that Paul even rejoiced when the true gospel was preached for false reasons and to his personal detriment (Phil. 1:15–18). Living for Christ involved the courage to live in such a way that he was exalted (*megalynesthia*, 'to be magnified') in his body, whether by life or death in his service (Phil. 1:20). A question remains. Why then was 'to die' a gain in Paul's view? In brief – to depart the body was to be present with Christ in a far more intimate way than this life affords (Phil. 1:23).

Those caught up in God's atoning project live for Christ. He is worth it. This value judgment lies at the heart of Christian motivation as we live in between the cross and the coming again of Christ.

Faith walks worthy of the gospel

The Christian life is lived in ways that flow from the gospel. To use Pauline phrases, it is walking 'worthy of the calling you have received' and living 'a life worthy of the Lord' (Eph. 4:1 and Col. 1:10 respectively).[29] This gospel life is one that refracts the dying and rising of Christ as symbolized in a Christian's baptism.[30] Paul draws

---

[27] MacDonald 2000: 1140.

[28] Kent 1997, comment on Phil. 1:21.

[29] Some might prefer to speak of a 'cruciform life' that flows from the gospel. That is to say, a life shaped by the cross. However, the gospel is not only about the cross. It is also the good news of resurrection. 'Cruciform' is too restrictive.

[30] The early church appreciated the significance of Christian baptism as symbolizing the break between the old life and the new by holding many such baptisms at Easter, which, of course, celebrates Christ's own dying and rising. See Tucker 2000: 184.

out the implications of Christian baptism[31] in his letter to the Romans through a series of rhetorical questions:

> What shall we say, then? Shall we go on sinning so that grace may increase? By no means! We died to sin; how can we live in it any longer? Or don't you know that all of us who were baptized into Christ Jesus were baptized into his death? We were therefore buried with him through baptism into death in order that, just as Christ was raised from the dead through the glory of the Father, we too may live a new life. (Rom. 6:1–4)

This 'new life' involves breaking with sin (vv. 6–7), and living 'to God' (v. 10). Such a life requires believers to take responsibility. They are to 'count' themselves 'dead to sin but alive to God' (v. 11). In practice this means 'offering' oneself to God rather than one's body to sin. Paul's next point is that 'sin shall not be your master, because you are not under law, but under grace' (v. 14).

Clearly, for Paul such grace provides no opportunity for licence (antinomianism). He asks, 'What then? Shall we sin because we are not under law but under grace?' His answer is emphatic: 'By no means!' (v. 15). The believer is now a slave to God and not a slave to sin (vv. 14–23). The Christian is called to a holy life (v. 23). According to Luther's *Small Catechism*, baptism signifies that 'the old Adam in us, by daily repentance, be drowned and die, with all sins and evil lusts; and again a new man daily come forth and arise, who shall live before God in righteousness and purity for ever'.[32] To live between the coming and the cross of Christ is to live an other-person-centred life. Again the apostle Paul is our guide. The Philippians' church needed unity (cf. Phil. 2:1; 4:2). But unity will not come if these believers are looking only after their own interests. So Paul exhorts them in Philippians 2:4, 'Each of you should look not only to your own interests [*ta heautōn*, 'the things of themselves'], but also to the

---

[31] Whether there is an argument for infant baptism would take us beyond our brief. Suffice it to say that if the paradigm of baptism is the Ethiopian eunuch's experience in Acts 8:26–40, then it seems to me many baptisms conducted today are grounded on a different theology. That is to say, if the Ethiopian's baptism was an expression of a theology of repentance, then the baptism of junior teens in many baptistic churches is justified on the basis of a theology of witness before family and friends, while infant baptisms in other churches are defended on the basis of a theology of covenant, some understanding of prevenient grace or that the ritual is a form of prayer. These latter baptisms whether 'credo' or 'paedo' may be consistent with Scripture but are not necessarily demanded by Scripture.

[32] Luther in Kerr 1974: 164.

interests of others [*ta heterōn*, 'the things of others'].' But what does that look like in practice? What follows in Philippians is one of the richest Christological passages in all the New Testament. If I may use classic theological categories, Paul takes the reader through the journey of the Christ from the state of glory through the state of humiliation back to the state of glory. I quote *in extenso*:

> Your attitude should be the same as that of Christ Jesus:
>
> Who, being in very nature God,
> did not consider equality with God something to be grasped [his glory],
> but made himself nothing,
> taking the very nature of a servant,
> being made in human likeness.
> And being found in appearance as a man,
> he humbled himself
> and became obedient to death – even death on a cross! [His humiliation.]
> Therefore God exalted him to the highest place
> and gave him the name that is above every name,
> that at the name of Jesus every knee should bow,
> in heaven and on earth and under the earth,
> and every tongue confess that Jesus Christ is Lord,
> to the glory of God the Father [his return to glory].
>
> (Phil. 2:5–11)

In this extraordinary passage Paul presents *in nuce* the incarnation, the active and passive obedience of Christ, the atonement, resurrection ascension and exaltation. In returning to glory, Christ takes our humanity with him.[33]

Paul's point is a practical one, however. Informed by Christ's great stooping both in incarnation and atonement, the believer is to be like-minded (Phil. 2:5). Paul illustrates what he means. In Philippians 2:20–21 he refers to his co-worker Timothy, who

---

[33] An alternative proposal is that Paul has an Adam–Christ contrast in mind and that the incarnation per se is not in view in the passage. E.g. M. D. Hooker (2002: 504–505) takes this approach: 'The use of Adamic imagery elsewhere encourages us to suppose that it underlies Philippians 2–3, where we have similar ideas of Christ's becoming human, with the result that men and women become what he is.' For a fine discussion of the scholarly possibilities, and also his defence of the more traditional incarnational view, see R. Murray 2000: 1184–1186.

exhibits the Christlike mindset and practice Paul is commending. He writes of Timothy, 'I have no-one else like him, who takes a genuine interest in your welfare. For everyone looks out for his own interests, not those of Jesus Christ.' Paul contrasts Timothy as someone 'who will genuinely care for the things concerning them' [*ta peri hymōn*] with those who 'seek the things of themselves' [*ta heautōn*] (my tr.). Paul appears to be picking up the language of verse 4. Timothy is a true servant shaped by the Christ paradigm. How different to that modern mindset which reduces Christian ministry to a career choice!

One of the great twentieth-century theologians of the cross was Leon Morris, whose name has already featured at many points in this work. I recall a sermon of his during which he looked over the congregation and simply pointed to this person and that, saying, 'You have been died for! You have been died for! You have been died for!' It was electric. His point was about both the depths of Christ's love shown on the cross and what it says about human value. Importantly, the way he made his point also underlined the fact that others too were the beneficiaries of Christ's death. Paul needed to remind some at Rome of that fact against the backdrop of disputes over the religious observances such as sacred days and special diet. Such disputes strongly suggest that there was some kind of strife between Jewish-Christian and Gentile-Christian households.[34] He writes:

> Therefore let us stop passing judgment on one another. Instead, make up your mind not to put any stumbling block or obstacle in your brother's way. As one who is in the Lord Jesus, I am fully convinced that no food is unclean in itself. But if anyone regards something as unclean, then for him it is unclean. If your brother is distressed because of what you eat, you are no longer acting in love. Do not by your eating destroy your brother *for whom Christ died*. Do not allow what you consider good to be spoken of as evil. (Rom. 14:13–16; my emphasis)

Walking worthy of the gospel means respecting the weaker brother's or sister's conscience. To fail to do so is a failure in love (Rom. 14:15). Behaviourally, this means not doing anything that

[34] Moo 2001: 292.

constitutes a stumbling block for the other (Rom. 14:13). Why? One of Paul's imperatives captures the rationale: 'Do not by your eating destroy your brother for whom Christ died' (Rom. 14:15). Positively, Paul exhorts the Romans to 'make every effort to do what leads to peace and to mutual edification' (Rom. 14:19).

Faith suffers for the Name

Living in between the times may mean suffering for Christ in very real ways. It did for many in the early church period; and Paul knew such suffering, as the catalogue of the apostolic hardships, in 2 Corinthians 11:23–28 shows:

> I have worked much harder, been in prison more frequently, been flogged more severely, and been exposed to death again and again. Five times I received from the Jews the forty lashes minus one. Three times I was beaten with rods, once I was stoned, three times I was shipwrecked, I spent a night and a day in the open sea, I have been constantly on the move. I have been in danger from rivers, in danger from bandits, in danger from my own countrymen, in danger from Gentiles; in danger in the city, in danger in the country, in danger at sea; and in danger from false brothers. I have laboured and toiled and have often gone without sleep; I have known hunger and thirst and have often gone without food; I have been cold and naked. Besides everything else, I face daily the pressure of my concern for all the churches.

In this passage Paul is comparing his labours with those of the 'super-apostles' troubling the church at Corinth (2 Cor. 12:11). In Colossians language he was filling up in his flesh what was lacking 'in regard to Christ's afflictions, for the sake of his body, which is the church' (Col. 1:24). It is extremely unlikely that Paul meant by this difficult phrase that he was adding to the atonement in some way given the sweep of Colossians 1:15–20. Rather, Paul saw his own sufferings as 'part of the fulfillment of God's plan in bringing in the consummation through the worldwide proclamation of the gospel'.[35]

---

[35] I am following Lincoln (2002: 614) in this interpretation of a well-known exegetical crux. For a similar view see Kaiser et al. (2001b): 'Paul's suffering in the service of Christ and his gospel do not add anything to the perfection of Christ's atonement. They are, however, one of God's instruments to extend that atonement into the lives

His afflictions then were missionary, not redemptive. More generally, he expected that a godly life would attract opposition (2 Tim.
3:12).

This is not a uniquely Pauline perspective. 1 Peter holds out
similar expectations for those Christians scattered throughout Asia
Minor. The letter counsels:

> Dear friends, do not be surprised at the painful trial you are
> suffering, as though something strange were happening to
> you. But rejoice that you participate in the sufferings of
> Christ, so that you may be overjoyed when his glory is
> revealed. If you are insulted *because of the name of Christ*, you
> are blessed, for the Spirit of glory and of God rests on you. If
> you suffer, it should not be as a murderer or thief or any other
> kind of criminal, or even as a meddler. However, if you suffer
> *as a Christian*, do not be ashamed, but praise God that you
> bear *that name*. (1 Pet. 4:12–16; my emphases)

Suffering in general is not in view but that specific suffering which
arises when others take offence at the name. There is a world of difference in giving offence by unacceptable behaviour (e.g. the text
mentions murder, theft, meddling) and others taking offence because
of one's link to Christ. 1 Peter also offers this positive advice: 'So
then, those who suffer according to God's will should commit themselves to their faithful Creator and continue to do good' (1 Pet. 4:19).
'To do good' (*en agathopoiia*) may carry in this context the rich sense
of being good citizens who benefit the wider society by their
actions.[36]

---

of others. Only in that sense can it be said that Paul's sufferings fill up what is lacking
in regard to Christ's afflictions.' For a fine coverage of the options and another perspective see O'Brien 2004, comment on Col. 1:24, who writes, 'His [Paul's] contribut-
ing to the sum total of the messianic afflictions [the messianic woes], through his
service and suffering bound up with his calling as an apostle or minister to the
Gentiles, is on behalf of Christ's body.' In either view the finality and definitive nature
of Christ's atoning work is not under question.

[36] See the discussion in McKnight 2007: 139–140, who follows Bruce Winter's
work on this idea. There is no suggestion in 1 Peter that Christians ought to seek suffering. This stands in marked contrast to Ignatius of Antioch's plea (in his 'Epistle to
the Romans') early in the next century that the Roman Christians leave him to
embrace martyrdom: 'I must implore you to do me no untimely kindness; pray leave
me to be a meal for the beasts . . . Better still, incite the creatures to become a sepul-
chre for me; let them not leave the smallest scrap of my flesh' (quoted in Staniforth
1972: 104). This seems more like pathology than theology.

The term 'Christian' suggests someone whose allegiance is known to be given to Christ rather than to another, like Caesar. There is an implied political challenge to the empire in the term. That may have been one reason why to confess to be a Christian could be punished by death, as the governor Pliny's letter to the emperor Trajan shows (early second century). True Christians, he found, were prepared to suffer for that name. Moreover, they refused to curse Christ and worship Caesar instead.[37] Later in the early church period Tertullian of Carthage famously said, 'The oftener we are mown down by you, the more in number we grow; the blood of Christians is seed.'[38] Over many centuries the blood of the martyrs has indeed proved the seed of the church.[39] It still is. I recall an amazing conversation at the lunch table at a theological college. A Nigerian student and a Pakistani student in their last semester were discussing returning to their respective homelands. The Nigerian thought he would have to endure beatings and house burnings as he ministered in the northern part of the country. (Sadly, it is far more dangerous now.) The Pakistani student calmly said that he expected to be killed within the first five years of his return. Jesus said that those who follow him need to take up their cross (e.g. Mark 8:31–38). I merely spiritualize such dominical sayings in my comfortable affluent Western location. For these students, Jesus' discipleship sayings had an immediacy I have never known.

Faith resists the devil

In New Testament terms it would be a folly to think that opposition to the name emanates only from human hostility. 1 Peter 5:8–9 describes the devil as a roaring lion on the prowl, a devourer. He targets believers not only in Asia Minor but everywhere. He is behind the human hostility Peter's readers are experiencing, and is to be resisted. In stark contrast, Rudolf Bultmann infamously said last century, 'It is impossible to use electric light and the wireless and to avail ourselves of modern medical and surgical discoveries, and at

---

[37] Pliny to Trajan (in Bettenson 1967: 3).

[38] Tertullian, 'Apology', *NA* 50.

[39] Vanhoozer (2005: 426–434) describes the church as participating in the 'theater of martyrdom' when it faithfully lives out the imitation of Christ prophetically, even to the point of death. However, the notion of the church 'performing the doctrine of the atonement' (426), though suggestive, needs careful qualification. It is liable to misunderstanding. Although Vanhoozer regards Christ as 'the chief martyr', helpfully and clearly he affirms that 'Only Christ's death is redemptive' (see 429, 431).

the same time to believe in the New Testament world of spirits and miracles.'[40] In his view, biblical supernaturalism, including the belief in the demonic, needed demythologizing in order to find the kernel of existential truth relevant to modern life. However, the Bultmannian approach eviscerates the New Testament. Were Jesus' exorcisms (e.g. Mark 5:1–20) merely mind tricks? Was his binding the strong man (e.g. Mark 3:27) reducible to straightening out inner human psychological distortions? Shakespeare's Hamlet spoke more wisely:

> There are more things in heaven and earth, Horatio,
> Than are dreamt of in your philosophy.[41]

In a remarkable passage in his letter to the Ephesians, Paul exhorts his readers about spiritual warfare and reminds them that 'our struggle is not against flesh and blood, but against the rulers, against the authorities, against the powers of this dark world and against the spiritual forces of evil in the heavenly realms' (Eph. 6:12).[42] According to J. D. G. Dunn, the passage is 'one of the most vivid portrayals of the Christian life as a spiritual struggle, including the power of the hostile forces (vv. 10–12), the means of withstanding them (vv. 13–17), and the need for co-operative effort (vv. 18–20)'. He adds, 'The metaphor, be it noted, is of warfare, not of a school debate or of a business enterprise.'[43] The Christian is to stand against the evil one fully clothed in the armour of God, with regard to which D. G. Reid comments, 'Although the terminology is borrowed from the Roman world, it is in essence the armor of Yahweh the divine warrior (Eph 6:13; cf. Is 59:16–18; Wis 5:17–20), and the battle is engaged in "his mighty strength" (Eph 6:10).'[44]

The armour Paul speaks of consists of both defensive armour and

---

[40] Quoted in McGrath 2007b: 151. The reluctance to embrace the biblical world view is recognized by Perkins (2002: 463), who writes, 'Contemporary readers are less likely to see the demons as external beings than internal forces that infect the psyche.'

[41] Shakespeare, *Hamlet*, Act I, scene 5, lines 166–167.

[42] Keener (2001b) comments, 'Some pagan deities were called "world rulers," and terms for high ranks of good and evil angels were becoming popular in this period; "spiritual beings of wickedness" is idiomatic Greek for "evil spirits," a Jewish and New Testament term' ('Ephesians 6:10–20: Divine Armor').

[43] Dunn 2000: 1177.

[44] D. G. Reid 2001. A weakness in Vanhoozer (2005) is the lack of treatment of the role of Satan, demons and the demonic in the drama of salvation. There are, for example, no references to 'Satan', 'devil' and 'demons' in the index.

offensive weaponry. On the defensive side are the shield of faith, the breastplate of righteousness and the helmet of salvation (Eph. 6:14–17). The offensive weapon is the Word of God: the sword of the Spirit (Eph. 6:17). Pheme Perkins correctly comments, 'In this context, "word" . . . must refer to the Christian message, the gospel (as in Rom 10:8; 1 Pet 1:25).'[45] The believer is to take his or her stand (Eph. 6:11, 13). The passage appears to suggest that there is no need to look for the evil one. The evil one will come to the fight. Hence the need is to stay alert (Eph. 6:18). Although not listed as a weapon, prayer is crucial to the outcome of the conflict. In fact, Paul accents prayer (Eph. 6:18–20). He even includes his own needs as a subject of prayer. He calls upon the readers to pray for him. The prayer is to be specific and gospel focused: 'Pray also for me, that whenever I open my mouth, words may be given me so that I will fearlessly make known the mystery of the gospel, for which I am an ambassador in chains. Pray that I may declare it fearlessly, as I should' (Eph. 6:19–20; Col. 4:3–4). The impression given is that gospel ministry will especially attract spiritual opposition. This was also true of Jesus' messianic ministry. It was after the baptism by John and the descent of the Spirit that the tempter came to Jesus (Matt. 3:13 – 4:13).

Faith offers a living sacrifice

In Romans 12:1–2 the apostle Paul uses cultic language to articulate the believer's fitting response to the gospel in these powerful words:

> Therefore, I urge you, brothers, in view of God's mercy, to offer your bodies as living sacrifices, holy and pleasing to God – this is your spiritual act of worship. Do not conform any longer to the pattern of this world [lit. 'to this age', *tō aiōni toutō*], but be transformed by the renewing of your mind. Then you will be able to test and approve what God's will is – his good, pleasing and perfect will.

With regard to the idea of worship in view in this passage, as I have written elsewhere, 'That is to say, worship understood in that broad

[45] Perkins 2002: 462. Likewise, Keener 2001b ('Ephesians 6:10–20: Divine Armor'). Surprisingly, Dunn (2000: 1178) does not mention the gospel in his explanation of v. 17. He refers to Scripture and also to 'powerful speech' sourced in God that is suitable for particular occasions. However, Paul's prayer request suggests that the gospel is in mind (cf. vv. 17, 19–20).

201

New Testament sense of life lived in response to the Gospel (Rom 12:1–2) and not in the traditional but narrower sense of the corporate acknowledgment of the grandeur of God (as in Revelation 4–5).'[46]

What is involved in such worship? The key words and phrases are 'to offer', 'do not be conformed', 'be transformed' and 'to test and approve'. This language nestles within the eschatological framework of the two ages: the present evil age and the age to come. Believers are to be what they will be. That is to say, people characterized by Spirit-impelled resurrection life: as per Romans 8. Why so offer one's body? The mercies of God provide Paul's grounds for his appeal. These grounds he set out in Romans 1 – 11 and they climax with the doxological expression of the greatness of God:

> Oh, the depth of the riches of the wisdom and knowledge
> of God!
>> How unsearchable his judgments,
>> and his paths beyond tracing out!
> 'Who has known the mind of the Lord?
>> Or who has been his counsellor?'
> 'Who has ever given to God,
>> that God should repay him?'
> For from him and through him and to him are all things.
>> To him be the glory for ever! Amen. (Rom. 11:33–36)[47]

The Creator is reclaiming creation in general and rebellious men and women in particular, through Christ, his life, death and resurrection and the donation of his Spirit. He is not reclaiming only his ancient people, the Jews, but Gentiles as well, and the new identity marker of belonging is faith.

The temple system of the past has been replaced by living temples, namely believers indwelt by the Spirit, and the sacrifices to be offered are no longer bloody ones. Instead, believers are the sacrifices – and living ones at that. How does such worship show itself? On the one hand, this age no longer sets the agenda. Many translations render

---

[46] Cole 2007: 25. Gathered worship as a body of believers and lived out worship as individuals are not antithetical practices. Both are requisite.

[47] N. T. Wright (2002, 10: 703) argues that chs. 9–11 (which deal with Jew and Gentile in the plan of God) of Rom. 1 – 11 constitute especially important grounds for Paul's appeal in Rom. 12:1–2.

'this age' as 'this world' (e.g. ESV, NIV, NRSV).[48] However, this is to miss the Jewish two-ages eschatology that informs the text.[49] Paul's point is that the age to come and its values are determinative. According to N. T. Wright, 'Here is the interface, for Paul, between what scholars call "eschatology" and "ethics": because you are in fact a member of the age to come, if you are in Christ, new modes and standards of behavior are not only possible but commanded.'[50] Moreover, the believer has his or her responsibilities to pursue the will of God. To do so takes discernment. Such worship is not mindless; it is the worship of the whole person effected through a renewed mind. J. D. G. Dunn notes, 'There is no mind/body dualism in Paul; "renewal of mind" is bound up with "presenting of bodies" (v 1).'[51] Hence it is reflective or reasonable worship. In the rest of Romans 12 through to Romans 15 Paul spells out in relational terms what is involved, whether, for example, using one's gifts in the body of Christ or paying taxes or sensitivity to the weak conscience or in Paul's own case his ministry to the Gentiles as priestly labour.[52] As Douglas J. Moo argues, 'Paul encourages us to look at our entire Christian lives as acts of worship. It is not just what is done on Sunday in a church building that 'ascribes worth' to God, but what God and the world see in us every day and every moment of the week.'[53]

In the ancient world, temples were the expression of the grandeur of one's God, whether the temple in Jerusalem or the Parthenon in Athens. I developed a sense of this after visiting an exact replica of the Parthenon in Nashville, Tennessee. The goddess Athena stands helmeted at the far end of the building. She is 42 feet high and in her outstretched hand stands the 6-foot-high god Nikē (victory). Her other hand rests on a shield. Overwhelming in scale, impressive in colour. As J. D. G. Dunn says, 'The earliest Christian groups in the cities of the diaspora, however, must have stood out as strangely

---

[48] To their credit both the ESV and NRSV have 'age' in the margin as the Greek original.

[49] As Dunn (2004b) helpfully explains, 'Clearly implied is the contrast of Jewish eschatology between the present age and the age to come' (comment on Rom. 12:1–2).

[50] N. T. Wright 2002, 10: 705.

[51] Dunn 2004b, comment on Rom. 12:1–2. Likewise, N. T. Wright 2002, 10: 704.

[52] N. T. Wright (2002, 10: 706) rightly observes, 'Paul's transition from chapters 1 – 11 to 12 – 16 is a model of integrated theological and practical thinking and writing, and hence a notable standard for those who preach expository or doctrinal sermons.'

[53] Moo 2001, comment on Rom. 12:1–2.

distinctive by the fact that they practiced no sacrificial ritual, named no one as priest, and looked to no temple like that at Jerusalem.'[54] What did early Christians have to show? In brief, themselves. According to Paul, as individuals believers are temples (1 Cor. 6:19–20) and also as a group (1 Cor. 3:16–17). As for the sacrifices so typical of ancient temple worship, believers themselves are the sacrifices, as we have seen above in Romans 12:1–2. 1 Peter 2:4–5 tells a similar story: 'As you come to him, the living Stone – rejected by men but chosen by God and precious to him – you also, like living stones, are being built into a spiritual house to be a holy priesthood, offering spiritual sacrifices acceptable to God through Jesus Christ.'

Charles Spurgeon, that great preacher of the nineteenth century, saw clearly the personal implications of Paul's words in Romans 12:1–2 for any who came after: 'It is our duty and our privilege to exhaust our lives for Jesus. We are not to be living specimens of men in fine preservation, but living *sacrifices*, whose lot is to be consumed.'[55] Likewise, the missionary C. T. Studd said, 'If Jesus Christ be God, and died for me, then no sacrifice can be too great for me to make for him.'[56] Oddly, the language of living sacrifice has largely disappeared from Christian thought and speech, even in evangelical circles.

An eschatological community: mercy-showing and shalom-making

The world to come has a beachhead in this one. The church is that beachhead. Believers are kingdom people, to use Jesus' kingdom idiom. They constitute an eschatological community living according to the values of the world to come.[57] Or, to change the descriptor and use Pauline language, believers live under the lordship of Christ, not under that of any Caesar. Kevin J. Vanhoozer raises an urgent question though in a broken world: '*What has the church to say and do that no other institution can say and do?*'[58] In this section we shall consider the *doing* answer to the question, and in the next the *saying* answer.

---

[54] Dunn 2004b, comment on Rom. 12:1–2.

[55] Spurgeon, quoted in Packer and Dever 2007: 110; original emphasis.

[56] Studd, quoted in Packer and Dever 2007: 110.

[57] I owe the phrase 'eschatological community' to Boring (2002: 175).

[58] Vanhoozer 2005: 402; original emphasis. His own answer (443) is that '*Only* the church can rehearse the kingdom of God; *this, the kingdom of God, is what the church has to say and do that no other institution can say or do*' (original emphasis). He unpacks in his ch. 12 what this means.

In the celebrated Sermon on the Mount of Matthew 5 – 7, Jesus uses two startling metaphors to describe his disciples in relation to the watching world. First, he informs his listeners that they are 'the salt of the earth' (Matt. 5:13). The language is emphatic (*hymeis*, 'you' pl.). It is beyond my brief to explore the many suggestions offered as to why Jesus used the metaphor of salt.[59] According to Donald A. Hagner, 'it may be best simply to take the metaphor broadly and inclusively as meaning something that is vitally important to the world in a religious sense, as salt was vitally necessary for everyday life'.[60] Suffice it to say then that given the variety of salt's use in the ancient world Jesus is making the general point that in some way the world needs his followers.[61] Secondly, he describes his followers as 'the light of the world' (Matt. 5:14). Like 'a city set on a hill' that cannot be hidden. The task of the light is to shine and not be like a lamp hidden under a measuring bowl (Matt. 5:15). In its form of life they are to be 'a display people' – to use Durham's phrase – just like ancient Israel was meant to be.[62] As Dietrich Bonhoeffer says, 'Flight into the invisible is a denial of the call. A community of Jesus which seeks to hide itself has ceased to follow him.'[63] A feature then of this form of life is the disciples' engagement with the world. Disciples are not counselled by Jesus to be like Essenes or like a Simeon Stylites withdrawn from the world. Simeon Stylites, for example, constructed a stone column upon which he lived for thirty-seven years until his death in 458.[64] Nor are disciples simply to be culturally captive to the folkways and mores of the day. Disciples are to be salt and light. Both metaphors assume contact. Salt in contact with the earth and light in contact with the darkness.

But just how is the salt to do its work and the light to shine before others? What are the good works of which Jesus speaks? A thorough answer would require visiting all the beatitudes of Matthew 5:3–12 at length. Usefully, M. Eugene Boring sums these beatitudes up in the following way:

[59] There is an excellent coverage of the many suggestions in Wilkins 1996, comment on Matt. 5:3–16.

[60] Hagner 2004a, comment on Matt. 5:13.

[61] Jesus speaks of salt losing its saltiness, which has occasioned much varied comment. For the possibilities see Wilkins 1996, comment on Matt. 5:3–16.

[62] J. I. Durham, quoted in Bartholomew and Goheen 2005: 66.

[63] Bonhoeffer, quoted in Carson 1997, comment on Matt. 5:13–16.

[64] For Simeon Stylites see Davies 1981: 245, 274. Unfortunately, if Simeon wanted solitude he was to be disappointed. He became a religious tourist attraction instead!

The nine pronouncements are thus not statements about general human virtues – most appear exactly the opposite to common wisdom. Rather, they pronounce blessing on authentic disciples in the Christian community. All the beatitudes apply to one group of people, the real Christians of Matthew's community. They do not describe nine different kinds of good people who get to go to heaven, but are nine declarations about the blessedness, contrary to all appearances, of the eschatological community living in anticipation of God's reign. Like all else in Matthew, they are oriented to life together in the community of discipleship, not to individualistic ethics.[65]

The beatitudes are not pronouncements concerning human psychological well-being, as though Jesus is talking about inner states of contentedness. Rather, the accent falls on what God does. Again Boring is helpful:

The beatitudes declare an objective reality as the result of a divine act, not subjective feelings, and thus should be translated with the objective 'blessed' instead of the subjective 'happy.' The opposite of 'blessed' is not 'unhappy,' but 'cursed' (cf. Matt. 25:31–46; Luke 6:24–26).[66]

Importantly, the plural nature of the beatitudes ('blessed are', *makarioi*, with 'are' understood) shows that Jesus is forming a people in his restoration of Israel and not simply individuals here and there.

Although there are nine pronouncements, for our purposes two stand out for comment. First, Jesus said, 'Blessed are the merciful' (cf. Matt. 5:7; 25:31–46). When believers live this kingdom value, the impact can be remarkable. In 362 Julian the Apostate lamented to Arsacius, high priest of Galatia, 'For it is disgraceful that, when no Jew ever has to beg, and the impious Galileans [Christians] support not only their own poor but ours as well, all men see that our people lack aid from us.'[67] He exhorted his fellow pagans, 'Then let us not, by allowing others to outdo us in good works, disgrace by such remissness, or rather, utterly abandon, the reverence due to the

---

[65] Boring 2002: 178.
[66] Ibid. 177.
[67] Quoted in Stevenson 1976: 67.

gods.'[68] Secondly, Jesus pronounced, 'Blessed are the peacemakers [*eirēnopoioi*]' (Matt. 5:9). This is what it means to be sons of God in that to be shalom-bringers is to act like God in character. D. A. Carson offers this helpful comment:

> Our peacemaking will include the promulgation of that gospel. It must also extend to seeking all kinds of reconciliation. Instead of delighting in division, bitterness, strife, or some petty 'divide-and-conquer' mentality, disciples of Jesus delight to make peace wherever possible.[69]

Such peacemaking is not appeasement Carson rightly notes. In this same Gospel of Matthew, Jesus speaks of the peace he is not bringing to the earth, and of the sword he is bringing, and the division that follows (Matt. 10:34–39). His messianic ministry would be rejected by many in Israel.[70] His followers face similar rejection (Matt. 5:10–12). Importantly, peacemaking is not at the expense of the pursuit of justice. As Stanley Hauerwas says of biblical peacemaking, 'it is an active way to resist injustice by confronting the wrongdoer with the offer of reconciliation. Such reconciliation is not cheap, however, since no reconciliation is possible unless the wrong is confronted and acknowledged.'[71] Neighbour love demands no less.[72]

The current Prime Minister of Australia, my home country, is Kevin Rudd. He is a professed Christian who is deeply influenced by the thought of Dietrich Bonhoeffer. Early in 2008, as the newly elected leader of the country, he did something that had been talked about by politicians for years. He told the parliament:

> There comes a time in the history of nations when their peoples must become fully reconciled to their past if they

---

[68] Ibid. In fact, Julian sought to create a pagan alternative to Christian welfare, organized through his priests, but failed. Time was not on his side. He was emperor only from 361 to 363, when he died from a spear thrust received in battle against the Persians. See Davies 1981: 159–161.

[69] Carson 1997, comment on Matt. 5:13–16.

[70] See the discussion in ibid., comment on Matt.10:34–36.

[71] Hauerwas 2005: 325–326. 'The task of peacemaking cannot ignore real wrongs, past or present' (323).

[72] McKnight (2007: 125) provocatively develops the justice theme in his treatment of atonement: 'Justice is structural at some level: it refers to the establishment of conditions that promote loving God and loving others or living in the Spirit.' However, I find his notion (134) that 'Missional work is *atoning*' and that 'Atonement is the work God calls the church to do in its praxis of healing' quite problematical because of the possibilities of considerable misunderstanding (original emphasis).

are to go forward with confidence to embrace their future. Our nation, Australia, has reached such a time. That is why the parliament is today assembled: to deal with this unfinished business of the nation, to remove a great stain from the nation's soul and, in a true spirit of reconciliation, to open a new chapter in the history of this great land, Australia.[73]

In the course of his address he repeatedly apologized to the indigenous peoples of Australia for the great wrongs done to them by white settlement. The history is a sorry one and includes the forcible removal, from the 1930s to the 1970s, of indigenous children from their mothers. These children have come to be known as the 'stolen generation'. The film *Rabbit Proof Fence* depicts one such story. Rudd acknowledged at length the character of the wrongs done, asked for forgiveness and committed the nation to positive steps of reconciliation. His speech to the parliament resonated with biblical language and ideas. For example, he said, 'For us [Australians] symbolism is important but, unless the great symbolism is accompanied by an even greater substance, it is little more than a clanging gong.'[74] The echoes of 1 Corinthians 13:1 are unmistakable. Is this not what it is to be salt and light, and a shalom-maker, in as much as it lies within one's orbit of influence?

Telling and defending the story of the project

We now turn once more to Kevin J. Vanhoozer's question '*What has the church to say and do that no other institution can say and do?*'[75] In brief, to quote the old hymn, the church has 'a story to tell to the nations', a public truth.[76] Some are especially gifted by the risen Christ and equipped by his Spirit to tell that story (Eph. 4:11–13). These are the *evangelists*. However, every believer has a story to tell of how he or she has been caught up in God's reclamation project. Every believer is a *witness*. Moreover, any believer who identifies with the project might find himself or herself asked to defend that identification and the story itself. This is *apology*. Let us look at each of these categories in turn.

---

[73] Rudd 2008.
[74] Ibid.
[75] Vanhoozer 2005: 402; original emphasis.
[76] For a stimulating article on the gospel as public truth see Drew 2006.

The evangelist

Evangelism is the Christian practice of communicating the evangel. D. W. B. Robinson sums up the evangel in these terms: 'THE EVANGEL is the divine word addressed to all men [and women] everywhere to bring them to repentance and thus to salvation by faith. It is a proclamation of God's kingdom, a revelation of his sovereignty and also of his purpose to judge the world.'[77] He points out that to translate *euangelion* as 'good news' needs to be rethought. Whether it is good news or not depends upon its content and how it is received.[78] Good news to those who embrace it, but not all do. For them it is bad news indeed. According to Paul, for some it has 'the fragrance of life', but for others 'the smell of death' (2 Cor. 2:14–16). In fact, *euangelion* with its Old Testament background of Isaiah 40 is an 'authoritative, "properly delivered" proclamation'.[79] In New Testament evangelism the accent falls on the verbal, as the book of Acts shows. As more and more believe, the language of Acts is striking in describing the progress of the gospel, whether Jewish or Gentile audiences are in view. The 'word of God spread' (Acts 6:7); 'the word of God continued to increase and spread' (Acts 12:24); 'the word of the Lord spread' (Acts 13:49); 'the word of the Lord spread widely and grew in power' (Acts 19:20).[80] This word formed congregations. As Wolfhart Pannenberg observes, 'The church is a creature of the Word.'[81] But what is the content of this word?

The book of Acts displays the content of the gospel as apostle and evangelist spread the message from Jerusalem (Acts 1) to Rome itself

---

[77] Robinson 1971: 2; original capitals.

[78] E.g. the NRSV and NIV translate *euangelion* in Mark 1:14 as 'good news', but in Rev. 14:6 as 'gospel'. N. T. Wright (2004: 168) seems to prefer 'good news', understood as a deliberate contrast to the kind of message that announced the Roman emperor's accession or birthday. Jesus, not the emperor, is Lord (*kyrios*). However, Rev. 14:6 shows the need for nuance.

[79] Robinson 1971: 2–3. For a more traditional approach that defines evangelism as sharing 'the good news' see Tidball 2001. For a more expansive view of evangelism see Abraham 1989 and 1994. Abraham argues (unconvincingly in my view) for evangelism understood as initiation into the kingdom (1994: 117). Abraham's idea of evangelism bears a strong resemblance to the recent Roman Catholic one of evangelization. According to Broderick (1987: 201), 'evangelization' after Vatican II has come to mean 'the whole mission of the church and the activities of the apostolate through which she announces, implants and brings to maturity the Kingdom of God'.

[80] This point is well made by Stott (1969: 6).

[81] Pannenberg 1994: 462–463. He warns against reducing the gospel to the forgiveness of sins and not including the proclamation of the reign of God.

(Acts 28).[82] Those without the benefit of the Jewish Scriptures needed to hear of the Creator, his providential goodness, the folly of idolatry, and his demand upon their existence. In Acts 17:22–29 the apostle Paul gives the Gentile sophisticates on Mars Hill a lesson in Old Testament 101, but without making explicit his source of knowledge.[83] By way of contrast, Philip in Acts 8:30–35 did not need to give the Ethiopian eunuch such a lesson since the eunuch was a god-fearer and a reader of Jewish Scripture. Instead, Philip preached Jesus to him from Isaiah 53. Returning to Acts 17 we find that Paul likewise preached Jesus to the Epicureans and stoics gathered there, but elicited a very mixed response (Acts 17:32–34). However, unlike Philip, he does not mention Jesus by name but accents his resurrection as the guarantee of a coming judgment to which the fitting response is repentance and faith (cf. Acts 17:30–34; 20:21). The message calls for conversion: a turning away from sin, which is *repentance* (Acts 3:26), and a turning to God, which is *faith* (Acts 15:19; 26:20). Offering a hope is also a key feature of the message, as Paul's encounter with the Roman governor Felix shows (Acts 24:14–15). In the next century the future cast of the evangel was underlined by the way the pagans of Lyons and Vienne attempted to defeat it. Having murdered the Christians, they displayed their bodies for six days. Next they burned the bodies and threw the ashes into the river Rhone. They explained the rationale for their actions as 'that they [the Christians] may not even have hope of a resurrection, in faith of which they introduce into our midst a certain strange and new-fangled cult, and despise dread torments, and are ready to go to their death, and that too with joy'.[84]

The note of coming judgment sits uneasily with people, but it would be false to the New Testament to pretend that it is not there or that it is a minor motif. For example, when Paul sums up the evangel in writing to the Thessalonians, he crisply declares, 'you turned to God from idols to serve the living and true God, and to wait for his Son from heaven, whom he raised from the dead – Jesus,

---

[82] In my view, evangelism and social action (or social aid or social service) are not to be confused. Social action should be an expected fruit of the gospel. Discipling teaches followers of Jesus to obey all that Jesus commanded, which includes the great commandments (Matt. 22:34–40). Evangelism, according to Tidball (2001), should result in 'obedience to Christ, incorporation into his church and responsible service in the world'. Well said! Also see the excursus at the end of this chapter.

[83] Drew (2006: 56) rightly characterizes Paul's address in Athens as 'a paradigm case' of what it is to communicate the gospel as 'public truth'.

[84] Stevenson 1970: 40.

who rescues us from the coming wrath (1 Thess. 1:9–10; my emphasis). What a contrast with much that passes for evangelism in the Western world today. Indeed, one contemporary theologian summed up some well-known televangelism ministries in these terms: God is nice; you are nice; I am nice. The God of this evangelism is too nice to judge anyone.

The witness

The idea has grown up, in evangelical circles especially, that every Christian is an evangelist or at least should be. There are books and training programmes predicated on that assumption. Like a number of ideas and practices found in today's churches it is hard to find explicit biblical justification for them. For example, praying a sinner's prayer to accept Christ as Saviour and Lord is difficult to find in the New Testament. The publican's prayer is the nearest to it: 'God have mercy on me the [*tō*] sinner' (Luke 18:13; my tr.). However, a theological rationale may be found if such a practice is seen as a way of calling on 'the name of the Lord' (Rom. 10:12–17). Likewise, there is a good reason for desiring that every believer be trained in evangelism (it helps, at the very least, to ground participants in the gospel), but to think that every Christian is an evangelist in the Ephesians 4:11–13 sense of a gift of the risen Christ to the church is to make such a text opaque in the extreme. D. W. B. Robinson concurs: 'We must not say that every Christian is given the gift of evangelism, even though all may have fellowship or partnership with those to whom this ministry has been given.'[85] However, a good case can be made from the New Testament that every Christian is a witness. Every believer has a story to tell – like the man born blind in John 9, accused before the Pharisees. His story was a simple one: 'One thing I do know. I was blind but now I see!' (John 9:25). Some of these stories may be spectacular, like the Damascus road experience of Paul (Acts 9:1–18); others less so, as in Timothy's case, who appears to have been nurtured in the faith from infancy (2 Tim. 1:5; 3:14–15).

Witness may entail great suffering and even death, as it did for Stephen in Acts 7, and as it did for Polycarp, Bishop of Smyrna in AD 155. The proconsul commanded him to swear by the genius of Caesar and to denounce the atheists (i.e. Christians, since they had

---

[85] Robinson 1971: 3. G. Reid (1996: 45) in his article 'The Decay of Evangelists?' provocatively argues, 'Chief among the casualties is the evangelist in a church-culture where evangelism is seen as the responsibility of the whole body.'

no visible god). According to one ancient account, Polycarp went to his death in the stadium with these stirring words: 'Eighty and six years have I served him [Christ], and he hath done me no wrong; how then can I blaspheme my king who saved me?'[86] Unsurprisingly, a close association soon developed between the ideas of witness, suffering and martyrdom. According to D. J. Graham:

> In the *Martyrdom of Polycarp* . . . the meaning of 'witness' is specifically tied to martyrdom. It is here, more than in any other text we have considered, that the concept of testifying to the faith becomes a specific reference to dying for the faith, a connection that would be made in many other writers thereafter.[87]

Martyrdom is not simply an episode in the history of Christian testimony now long past. Sadly, martyrdom is a contemporary phenomenon.[88]

God will have his witnesses, who tell of his ways and deeds. In the Old Testament, Israel was to be that witness to the nations (Isa. 43:10, 12; 44:8), and in the New Testament it is the followers of Israel's hoped for Messiah. Israel was to testify before the world that there is only one God, and without rival (Deut. 6:4); the church as restored Israel is to testify that Jesus is Lord (2 Cor. 4:5). As R. G. Maccini says, 'The church's mission consists of worldwide witness to God's decisive act in Jesus; this witness is thus foundational for New Testament thought.'[89]

The apologist

The gospel raises questions.[90] How is Jesus Lord? Why believe that he was raised from the dead? How credible is the idea of a coming

---

[86] Bettenson and Maunder 1999: 11.

[87] Graham 2001.

[88] The numbers of recent martyrs is hard to calculate with any accuracy, as Byassee (2008: 20–23) points out. However, as he also contends, the reality of contemporary and recent martyrdoms is undeniable.

[89] See Maccini 2001 for a helpful discussion of the continuities and discontinuities between testimony in the Old Testament and the New. Also see Vanhoozer 2005: 354–359, 396–397, 429, 434–435, for a creative treatment of witness. He writes, 'Our vocation thus becomes our identity: we achieve genuine selfhood precisely as witnesses to Jesus Christ, to the gospel truth about God and humankind alike' (397).

[90] In my view, communicating the gospel through evangelism and witness are first-order activities. Apology as a practice is a second-order activity. For more on this see Cole 2006: 325.

judgment? Is not your hope wishful thinking? Apostles in particular and followers of Jesus in general had to face questioning. For example, think of Paul before King Agrippa: 'King Agrippa, I consider myself fortunate to stand before you today as I make my defence [*apologeomai*] against all the accusations of the Jews, and especially so because you are well acquainted with all the Jewish customs and controversies' (Acts 26:2–3). Paul then proceeds to tell the story of his zeal for the law, the Damascus road experience (in my view both a conversion and call) and his commission from the risen Christ to evangelize the Gentiles (Acts 26:4–23).

Apology was not only for apostles such as Paul, though. The task of answering questions is for all Christians, as 1 Peter 3:13–16 shows:

> Who is going to harm you if you are eager to do good? But even if you should suffer for what is right, you are blessed. 'Do not fear what they fear; do not be frightened.' But in your hearts set apart Christ as Lord. Always be prepared to give an answer [*apologia*, 'defence', as in ESV and NRSV is preferable to the NIV] to everyone who asks you to give the reason for the hope that you have. But do this with gentleness and respect, keeping a clear conscience, so that those who speak maliciously against your good behaviour in Christ may be ashamed of their slander.

The text presupposes persecution of some kind because of the gospel, which is summed up in terms of hope.[91] In the face of hostility the believer is to have the right relation to Christ as Lord, and the right manner in addressing questioners ('gentleness and respect'). Again there is a world of difference between giving offence and others taking offence. Apology is to be backed up by right conduct ('a clear conscience' and doing good). Lesslie Newbigin was right to describe the church as 'the hermeneutic of the gospel'.[92] At least it ought to be.[93] It is as believers individually and corporately live in

---

[91] According to D. L. Bartlett (2002: 291), 'For 1 Peter, the whole content of the Christian faith can be summed up as "hope" – a motive and motif that runs through the whole epistle (see explicitly 1:3, 13, 21[3:5]; implicitly 1:8–9; 2:12; 4:13; 5:4, 6, 10).'

[92] Quoted in Hunsberger 1994: 142. However, the individual and corporate behaviour of professing Christians can cloud the gospel.

[93] As Drew (2006: 55) points out, 'the history of Christianity's social dominion has been a mixed bag'. He cites the advent of hospitals and the Thirty Years War, the emancipation of slaves and anti-Semitism as evidence in a much longer list.

Christlike ways that the grand ideas of the gospel (e.g. forgiveness, mercy, reconciliation, peace, love, grace and hope) take on flesh before the watching world.[94] One of those words, 'forgiveness', came alive for many as the world watched how an Amish community in Pennsylvania responded to the massacre of five of their children in a schoolhouse in 2006. They forgave the killer and offered support to his family. A CBS reporter wrote, 'In just about any other community, a deadly school shooting would have brought demands from civic leaders for tighter gun laws and better security, and the victims' loved ones would have lashed out at the gunman's family or threatened to sue.'[95] Not so this Christian one, and the world took notice.

The scandal

The roles of evangelist, witness and apologist are involved in what is a scandalous story. There is a name (Jesus Christ) and a narrative (the gospel) that the church takes to the world. The world's problem with that name and narrative was stated centuries ago by a pagan senator of Rome. Symmachus (c. 340–402) was a Roman orator and official. As a pagan aristocrat he argued against the increasing Christian dominance of Roman life. A celebrated cause was the removal of the pagan Altar of Victory in 382 by the emperor Gratian. Symmachus argued for its restoration. He lamented, 'every man has his own customs, his own rites . . . We cannot by one and the same path arrive at so great a secret [the truth of religion].'[96] The scandal of the Christian claim concerning the sufficiency, supremacy and finality of Christ remains to this day, especially in the pluralist West.[97]

---

[94] Hunsberger (1994: 141–142) says of 1 Pet. 3:15, 'The assumption is that the presence of such a hope is an observable thing, demonstrable to public view by the community that embodies the gospel.'

[95] 'Amish Forgive, Pray and Mourn', accessed 23 Oct. 2008.

[96] Quoted in Stevenson 1976: 122.

[97] As Trites (2006) rightly suggests, 'The person and place of Jesus in the present pluralistic theological climate is still very much a contentious issue. The claims of Christ as the Son of God are currently widely disputed. In such an environment a brief must be presented, arguments advanced and defending witnesses brought forward, if the Christian case is to be given a proper hearing. To fail to present the evidence for the Christian position would be tantamount to conceding defeat to its opponents. That is to say, the controversy theme, so evident in the NT, appears to be highly pertinent to the missionary task of the church today.'

The role of the Spirit

Life in between the cross and the coming again of Christ does not start with grace and then continue as an exercise in DIY (do it yourself). The book of Acts relates the story of how the exalted Christ poured out the Spirit at Pentecost and now directs the reconciling project through the Spirit. In Johannine terms, the Spirit continues Christ's mission as the Paraclete. The Spirit, for example, continues Christ's case against the world through the disciples (John 14 – 16). A. A. Trites sums up the evidence as follows:

> Similarly in the Fourth Gospel and Acts when the apostles are witnessing for Christ in the face of antagonism and hostility, they do not witness in their own strength but rather in the convincing power of the Spirit. They are reassured that the Spirit is active in challenging the world with the truth of what they say. John underscores the inner witness of the Spirit . . . while Luke in Acts focuses on the outward manifestation of the Spirit's work in signs and wonders which confirm the apostolic testimony.[98]

Trites's summary is helpful but more needs to be said concerning the Spirit and mission.

A particular feature of the testimony of Luke-Acts is the language of the filling of the Spirit. Repeatedly in Luke-Acts we read of those filled with the Spirit. This expression is often followed by or follows the conjunction 'and'.[99] Well before Pentecost and at the beginning of Luke we find that John the Baptist will be filled with the Spirit *and* will turn many to the Lord (Luke 1:15–16). Elizabeth was filled with the Holy Spirit *and* exclaimed a blessing upon Mary (Luke 1:41–42). Again, Zechariah was filled with the Holy Spirit *and* prophesied (Luke 1:67). Similarly, in Acts we read of those gathered together on the day of Pentecost that they were filled with the Spirit *and* spoke in other tongues (Acts 2:4). Some time later in the Acts' account the believers, facing hostility, were filled with the Holy Spirit *and* continued to speak the word of God (the gospel) with boldness (Acts 4:31). Paul, in confronting Elymas the magician at Paphos, was filled with the Holy

---

[98] Ibid.
[99] See Knox in Payne 2000: 217–272. I am very much indebted to Cole (2007: 218) for this paragraph and especially my theological teacher D. B. Knox for observing the conjunction.

Spirit *and* pronounced a rebuke (Acts 13:9–10). These instances of filling are linked with speech acts of various kinds: prophesying, blessing, speaking in tongues, speaking the word of God, rebuking.

Basil of Caesarea (c. 330–379) has much to say to us with regard to reflecting theologically on the Spirit's role in realizing the divine project. He understood the persons of the Trinity to have particular roles in the economy of salvation.[100] In his view the Father is the 'original cause of all things made', the Son is the 'creative cause', while the Spirit is the 'perfecting cause'. Colin Gunton accurately captures Basil's thought: 'The Spirit as the perfecting cause of the creation is one who enables things to become what they are created to be; to fulfill their created purpose of giving glory to God in their perfecting.'[101] In assigning the Spirit such a role Basil was deploying the doctrine of appropriation that we considered in chapter 4. Father, Son and Holy Spirit are each involved in the divine project, as Augustine taught.[102] However, there is merit in regarding the Spirit as the great applier of salvation given Jesus' teaching on the Paraclete in John 14 – 16, the account of Pentecost and the testimony of the New Testament letters. In other words, there is a certain appropriateness in accenting the Spirit's role in bringing the divine plan to its appointed end. In this view, the Holy Spirit for example uses our evangelism, witness, apology, shalom-making and mercy-showing (the list is not exhaustive but is indicative) to bring to fruition the divine plan.

How the Spirit works in evangelism is illustrated by the story of Lydia in Acts 16. By the river at Philippi she hears Paul preach. In classic theological terms, through her outward ears she experiences the external call of God through the gospel proclaimed. But as well, she experiences the inward call of God. The text says, 'The Lord opened her heart to respond to Paul's message' (Acts 16:14). The response was real, as can be seen in the hospitality she soon shows to Paul. The 'Lord' in view in the text is presumably Jesus, for we know from the overall argument of Acts that what happens in Acts is the work of the risen Christ through the Spirit (cf. Luke 1:1–4; Acts 1:1–2; 2:32–33; 26:15–18). Acts has sometimes been described as the Acts of the Holy Spirit.[103] But it would be more accurate to describe

---

[100] Basil of Caesarea (in Bettenson 1977: 72).

[101] Quoted in Cole 2007: 73.

[102] In classic expression, *opera Trinitatis ad extra sunt indivisa* ('the Trinity's works on the outside are undivided'; my tr.). See Muller 1986: 212.

[103] E.g. Stott 1969: 4.

this New Testament book as the Acts of the exalted Christ through the Spirit.[104] Nowhere does Scripture explain how divine sovereignty and human agency connect. The biblical writers are not interested in such metaphysical matters. Theologically reflected upon though, it can be said that the story of Lydia shows how divine providence acts concursively. Paul's agency is the instrument the Spirit uses to engage Lydia. The causal story is mysterious in the sense of incomprehensible, since not enough is revealed to allow anything but speculation at this point as to the precise nature of the causal joint in this phenomenon of double agency. As Bernard of Clairvaux suggests, 'Remove freewill and there will be nothing to save; remove grace, and there will be nothing to save with.'[105]

Conclusion

Christians live by faith, not by sight. Moreover, appreciating the cost, the believer recognizes that he or she has been bought with a price. Now life is lived for him, controlled by Christ's love. This new life is one that walks worthy of the gospel. In so doing, this life is to reflect in one's own life the way of Christ in death and resurrection: dead to sin but alive to God. It is an other-person-centred life that expresses itself in self-donation on behalf of others rather than the selfish pursuit of one's own interests. This is a life prepared to suffer for Christ's sake and to take its part in spiritual warfare. It is a sacrificial life lived in response to the mercies of God expressed in the gospel. Importantly, it is not a life lived solo. It is lived as part of a great company of salt and light that pursues mercy-showing and shalom-making as agents of peace, and that tells the story both in evangelism and in witness of God's great reconciling project and Jesus who stands at the heart of it. He is the Christ, who came in humility and will come again, but this time in glory. This also is the company of those prepared to give a defence of the hope within them. This is how life ought to be lived in between the comings of Christ, during these last days. Yet this is no brief for any version of Pelagianism. Put another way, the Christian life is not reducible to

---

[104] Vanhoozer (2005: 32) describes the Spirit as the 'director' of the theodrama (the divine project, in my terms); however, if I am right, the exalted Christ, using his analogy, is the director, while the Spirit is more like the dramaturge (the one who advises the director).

[105] Hammond 1956: 97. Like Hammond I see Bernard of Clairvaux's statement through the lens of 'a modified form of Calvinism'. In this view, free will is understood in voluntarist rather than libertarian terms.

deism in world view and stoicism in ethics. As far as Scripture is concerned, we do not live in an abandoned creation pitifully worshipping an absentee landlord. Nor do we simply do the commandments with a stiff upper lip as though God's Spirit is on vacation. The fact is that the risen Christ is seated at the right hand of the Father in the place of executive power and has poured out the Spirit.

Excursus: the three commissions lifestyle

How the Christian is to live in between the cross and the coming again of Christ is a vast subject, a book project in itself. I have only touched on some key aspects. However, in this excursus I offer a more expansive formal framework for understanding the calling to be God's person in his creation.

If the testimony of the entire canon of Scripture is taken into purview, the Christian task in the world involves three commissions.[106] The creation commission of Genesis 1:28 (in some circles called the cultural mandate) has never been rescinded: 'Be fruitful and increase in number; fill the earth and subdue it. Rule over the fish of the sea and the birds of the air and over every living creature that moves on the ground.' The exercise of dominion – however frustrated by sin – is still our creaturely task. Yet this is no brief for the rape of the earth. The picture of what that commission looks like in Genesis 2 is of Adam exercising both care and control in the garden (v. 15). Creation care as a project has exegetical warrant.[107] The Great Commission of Matthew 28:18–20 is the discipling one: 'All authority in heaven and on earth has been given to me. Therefore go and make disciples of all nations, baptizing them in the name of the Father and of the Son and of the Holy Spirit, and teaching them to obey everything I have commanded you.' God is saving a people for his praise. The labours of Peter and Paul in Acts exhibit this commission, with Peter spreading the news of Christ from Jerusalem

[106] Liu, Preece and Li (2005: 23–24) adopt a similar schema to mine. However, they speak of the 'Creation Commission', the 'Evangelistic Commission' and the 'Relational Commission'. Moreover, they assign a Person of the Trinity to each: the Father with creation, the Son with evangelism and the Spirit with the relational. This, in my view, risks overtheologizing. For a two-commissions approach (creation and evangelism) see Macauley (n. d.).

[107] For a stimulating treatment of the creation task see Wolters 1985. This slim work has great insight into a Christian approach to world-view thinking in terms of the interplay of creation, fall and redemption.

(Acts 2) to Caesarea (Acts 10), and Paul to Rome itself (Acts 28). Both the creation commission and the discipling commission are to be informed by the moral commission of Matthew 22:37–39: '"Love the Lord your God with all your heart and with all your soul and with all your mind." This is the first and greatest commandment. And the second is like it: "Love your neighbour as yourself." All the Law and the Prophets hang on these two commandments.' That is to say, the creation commission and the discipling commission are to be shaped by love of God and love of neighbour. For some believers, because of their life context, the creation commission is to the fore (e.g. they may work in agriculture, medicine or education). Even so, the discipling commission is not out of mind (e.g. praying for opportunities at work to witness in appropriate ways). For others, because of their calling, the discipling commission is to the fore (e.g. a student worker on campus or a pastor). Even so, the creation commission is not absent (e.g. responsibly exercising the privileges of citizenship at election time or establishing a home). In both life contexts the moral commission is the common denominator.[108] Without love, creation care and discipling others become vacuous. We gain nothing (1 Cor. 13:1–3).

---

[108] I attempt to apply these categories to education in Cole 2001: 21–31.

Chapter Nine

The grand purpose: glory

In this chapter we briefly consider the point of God's project of atonement. What is its purpose? To answer this question we shall briefly review the biblical teleology that gives Scripture its narrative unity. As P. F. Jensen says, 'The Bible presents God as a purposive Creator and Redeemer, one with an End in view.'[1] Next we shall consider the truth in Irenaeus' and Athanasius' claim that Christ became what we are that we might become what he is. In the second century Irenaeus wrote in his critique of gnosticism, 'In his [God's] unbounded love He was made what we are, that He might make us what He is.'[2] In the fourth century Athanasius in his great work on the incarnation said, 'He became man that we might be made God.'[3] Lastly, our attention turns to the goal of the project, summed up as glory, and the question of whether the divine pursuit of glory is simply celestial egotism.

Scripture's narrative unity

Scripture meets Aristotle's definition of a plot. Formally speaking, it has a beginning, a middle and an end. Materially considered, it tells a story that moves from creation to fall through redemption to consummation. The triune God is the chief actor in the story and its architect. The conflict between good and evil organizes the plot. Human beings are constantly challenged to decide to align themselves with him (his character, will and ways). As the *Dictionary of Biblical Imagery* suggests:

> Almost every story, poem and proverb in the Bible fits into this ongoing plot conflict between good and evil. Every human act or attitude shows people engaged in some

---

[1] Jensen 1997: 19.
[2] Irenaeus, *Against Heresies* 5, preface, quoted in K. Ware 1996: 56.
[3] Athanasius, *On the Incarnation* 54, quoted in K. Ware 1996: 57.

movement, whether slight or momentous, toward or away from God in this story of the soul's choice.[4]

Salvation history is also decision history and, for some, disaster history.[5] Again the *Dictionary of Biblical Imagery* is helpful with regard to salvation history:

> This history focuses on God's great plan to save people from their sin and its eternal consequences. Human history in the Bible unfolds within the providential framework of God's acts of redemption and judgment, as God deals with evil in the universe.[6]

The disorder that evil brings is met with grace, which not only restores order but, in regard to human beings, does an amazing thing for those who entrust themselves to the God of such grace.

Little 'Christs'

C. S. Lewis understood the amazing thing that God is up to. In his well-known book *Mere Christianity* he expresses it as follows:

> [T]he Church exists for nothing else but to draw men [and women] into Christ, to make them little Christs. If they are not doing that, all the cathedrals, clergy, mission, sermons, even the Bible itself, are simply a waste of time. God became man for no other purpose. It is even doubtful, you know, whether the whole universe was created for any other purpose. It says in the Bible that the whole universe was made for Christ and that everything is to be gathered together in him.[7]

Lewis is right about the biblical testimony, although he gives no actual chapter and verse. (This is unsurprising since *Mere Christianity* is made up of what were originally BBC radio talks.) Paul informs the Colossians concerning Christ that 'all things were created by him

---

[4] Ryken, Wilhoit and Longman 2001a. I am much indebted in this section to their discussion.

[5] For the idea of decision history see Daniel 1990: 8; and for disaster history see Hasel 1991: 175.

[6] Ryken, Wilhoit and Longman 2001a.

[7] C. S. Lewis 1958: 166. Lewis, of course, was writing for a popular audience.

and for him. He is before all things, and in him all things hold together' (Col. 1:16–17). And to the Ephesians, Paul writes:

And he made known to us the mystery of his will according to his good pleasure, which he purposed in Christ, to be put into effect when the times will have reached their fulfilment – to bring all things in heaven and on earth together under one head, even Christ. (Eph. 1:9–10)

Lewis also has biblical support when he writes of 'little Christs', although nuancing is necessary.[8] According to Paul in his letter to the Romans, God has a purpose:

For those God foreknew he also predestined to be conformed to the likeness of his Son, that he might be the firstborn among many brothers. And those he predestined, he also called; those he called, he also justified; those he justified, he also glorified. (Rom. 8:29–30)

Glorification is Christification. Paul tells the Corinthians that the Spirit is the agent of this transformation: 'And we, who with unveiled faces all reflect the Lord's glory, are being transformed into his likeness with ever-increasing glory, which comes from the Lord, who is the Spirit' (2 Cor. 3:18).[9] Underlying such New Testament language may be the ancient epistemological principle of connaturality: like knows like. Believers will not be able to experience the vision of God (*visio Dei*) unless ontologically changed to be Godlike (cf. Matt. 5:8; Phil. 3:19–21; 1 John 3:1–3).

In Eastern Orthodoxy the way to speak of the believer's transformation into a little Christ is to speak of 'theosis', 'deification' or 'divinization'. God is making little gods. The key text for Eastern

[8] A more sophisticated theological articulation of the idea would insist on preserving the ontological distinction between Christ's natural sonship and the believer's adoptive one, as in Gal. 4:4–7, and would make it clear that the term 'Christ' has Jesus in view and not the title and role of messiah of Israel per se. As much as I admire Lewis he is not to be read uncritically. E.g. is the incarnation as central to the gospel as the atonement? Has Lewis characterized accurately the relation of faith to works in Christian soteriology? How well grounded are his theological proposals in the exegesis of Scripture as opposed to anchored in the tradition of the church? It has been said that the patron philosopher of Eastern Orthodoxy is Plato, for Roman Catholicism, Aristotle, and for Protestants, Augustine. These days, for many evangelicals, it is Lewis.

[9] See the discussion in Gaffin 2001.

Orthodoxy is 2 Peter 1:4, which speaks of participating in the divine nature. Importantly, the Orthodox do not blur the Creator–creature distinction in their theology. Believers participate in the energies of God, not his essence. As The Orthodox Study Bible says, '*What deificiation is not*. When the Church calls us to pursue godliness, to be more like God, this does not mean human beings then become divine.'[10] Even so, I am not convinced that texts such as 2 Peter 1:4 can bear the exegetical weight the Orthodox place on them.[11] For example, the idea that 2 Peter 1:4 can be explained as the way a sword in a fire is interpenetrated by the fire so as to glow is theological speculation at best.[12] However, the general idea that the destiny of believers is to be conformed to the image of the Son has sound biblical warrant, as we saw above in Paul's letters to the Romans and Ephesians. P. F. Jensen soundly sums up the biblical presentation: '*In* Christ we are; *with* Christ we shall be; *like* Christ completes our hope.'[13] Perhaps then it would be wiser to speak of 'becoming like God' or 'becoming like Christ' than 'becoming gods or a god'.

Significantly, the end-time picture is not that of the traditional *visio Dei* (vision of God) as in Eastern Orthodoxy and Catholicism but of these 'little Christs' serving and reigning in a new heaven and earth (Rev. 22:4–5).[14] As Christopher C. Rowland comments with regard to Revelation 22:5, 'So, as in the millennium, God's servants share God's reign (cf. 3:21); they are a kingdom as well as priests who serve (1:5; cf. 7:15).'[15] The vision of God is only half the eschatological story.

Glory the goal

Why create? Why salvation history? Why the cross? Why a new heavens and a new earth? What is the divine goal? According to

[10] 'Deification', TOSB, 561; original emphasis.

[11] See Cole 2007: 230–232 for a discussion and critique of the Eastern Orthodox view and bibliography on the subject both Eastern Orthodox and evangelical. Some evangelicals are very attracted to deification as a way of understanding soteriology (e.g. Boersma 2004).

[12] TOSB, 560–561. Although the analogy is an ancient one, it is hardly exegesis to apply it to 2 Pet. 1:4, nor to see partaking of the Eucharist as the means as some Eastern Orthodox do.

[13] Jensen 1997: 35; original emphases.

[14] For Eastern Orthodoxy see K. Ware 1981: 141, 170–172, 176–177; and for Catholicism see CCC, para. 610. Likewise, Boersma (2004: 261), who ends his work with this quote from Irenaeus: 'For the glory of God is a living man; and the life of man consists in beholding God.' This may account for Rev. 22:4, but what of v. 5?

[15] Rowland 2002: 721.

W. J. Dumbrell, 'the entire Bible is moving to, growing according to a common purpose and towards a common goal (thus we can say that the whole Bible is "eschatological")'.[16] The formal answer, in a word, is 'glory'.[17] Love is the motivation; glory is the goal.[18] But what does that term 'glory' mean? And is such a goal unworthy even of God? For example, according to D. A. Carson, 'God is passionately (if I dare use this word) concerned for his own glory. His glory is something God does not yield to another (Isa. 42:8; 48:11).'[19] J. I. Packer maintains, 'Certainly, God wants to be praised for his praiseworthiness and exalted for his greatness and goodness; he wants to be appreciated for what he is.'[20]

First then let us attend to the meaning of the term 'glory'. It is an important biblical concept. According to the *Dictionary of Biblical Imagery*, 'With references in English Bibles ranging from 275 (NIV) to 350 (RSV), glory is one of the master images that helps to tell the story of the Bible.' [21] 'Glory' (Hebr. *kābôd*; Gr. *doxa*) is the transcendent majesty that shines out of God's very being.[22] This is the God, to use Pauline language, 'who lives in unapproachable light' (1 Tim. 6:16).[23] 'Glory' refers not so much to an attribute of God, unlike 'omnipotence', but is the term that when theologically considered encapsualtes the eminence of all God's attributes viewed together in the light of the *tota Scriptura* (the whole biblical testimony).[24]

'Glory is a way of speaking of God's presence with his people in the historical order,' according to Charles H. H. Scobie.[25] This glory was revealed in the exodus deliverance (Exod. 16:7), the Sinai theophany (Deut. 5:24), the tabernacle (Exod. 40:34) and the temple (1 Kgs 8:11). The loss of the presence of Yahweh was the loss of his glory. Israel lost the ark to the Philistines in a disatrous campaign.

---

[16] Dumbrell 2001a: introduction, no page.

[17] The material answers offered by biblical theologians differ. Goldsworthy (1981) argues for 'kingdom'. Dumbrell (2001a) in *The End of the Beginning* contends for 'new creation'. C. J. H. Wright (2006) suggests 'God's mission'. The scriptural testimony is rich enough to accommodate these and other views.

[18] As Packer (1993: 59) rightly notes, 'God's goal is his glory.'

[19] Carson in McCormack 2008: 51.

[20] Packer 1993: 59.

[21] Ryken, Wilhoit and Longman 2001b.

[22] According to Scobie (2003: 368), when used of humans 'glory' refers to their 'fame, reputation, honor, prestige'.

[23] For a good discussion see Burge 2001.

[24] Milne (1982: 64) rightly says, 'His glory carries us to the heart of all that is essential to his being as God, his divine majesty.'

[25] Scobie 2003: 368.

Eli the priest collapsed and died at the news of its loss (1 Sam. 4:12–22). His grandson was subsequently named 'Ichabod' or 'no glory'. Eli's daughter-in-law lamented, 'The glory has departed from Israel, for the ark of God has been captured' (1 Sam. 4:22). Likewise, Judah lost the glory from the temple because of her sin, an event that presaged the exile to Babylon (Ezek. 11:22–23). Part of Judah's hope was for the glory to return to the midst of God's people, as Ezekiel prophesied (Ezek. 43:1–5). Supremely, it is revealed in the face of Jesus Christ (2 Cor. 4:6), who is 'the radiance of God's glory' (Heb. 1:3). He is the definitive expression of divine glory.[26] Until such time the believer is metamorphosed into the very likeness of God (the priniciple of connaturality is relevant here); the revelation of divine glory is a humbling experience that produces 'fear and trembling'. It did so to Isaiah in the temple in Jerusalem (Isa. 6:1–5) and to the disciples of Jesus on the mount of transfiguration (cf. Mark 9:2–8; 2 Pet. 1:16–18). And there is so much more revelation of glory to come. Indeed, the eschatological revelation of the divine glory is the finale of both humanity's and nature's history. There is a day coming when, according to the prophet Habukkuk,

> the earth will be filled with the knowledge of the glory of the
> LORD,
> as the waters cover the sea.
>
> (Hab. 2:14)

In fact, the glory of God provides the light in the world to come (cf. Rev. 21:11; 22:23). Light, fire and cloud are symbols of the divine glory. These are not competing symbols. As Charles H. H. Scobie argues, 'The visual imagery is not self-contradictory, for a cloud can be suffused with light.'[27] The *Dictionary of Biblical Imagery* sums up that future in these helpful terms: 'The eschatological revelation of glory enacts a series of unparalleled transformations – a transformation of human relationships, society at large, the human heart and even the whole world.'[28]

Second, as for the goal of glory and the question of *digno Dei* and whether such a goal is unworthy of God, D. A. Carson relates a story that poses the issue starkly. He was asked this question in a university mission setting:

---

[26] See the excellent discussion in ibid. 384–386.
[27] Ibid. 368.
[28] Ryken, Wilhoit and Longman 2001b.

In human relationships, we learn to distrust and despise anyone who always wants to be number one, who is offended if he or she is not number one. So why should we not take umbrage at a God who wants to be number one, who is offended if he or she is not number one?[29]

One can see the point that the student was raising. The pursuit of glory for oneself is usually regarded as narcissistic. This is behaviour that is seldom approved. Such a pursuit expresses a hubris (pride) that, according to the ancient historian Herodotus, can only lead to a nemesis (a disastrous fall), as in the case of Croesus 'in all likelihood for thinking that he was the most fortunate man [*olbiōtatos*] in the world'.[30] Many film plots have such a theme. However, human analogy does not help here, as Carson points out.[31] Thus one answer given is that although such a goal is unworthy of the creature, it is not so for the Creator. The Creator is *sui generis* (unique) by definition. The Reformation cry *soli Deo gloria* (Glory to God alone) makes sense with such an answer. Given the transcendent greatness of God he is deserving of praise in ways we shall never be.

However true the above may be, there is another answer that I find worth considering, which turns the flank of the objection. This answer has to do with the triune reality that is God. In the Johannine testimony we find that the Father glorifies the Son and the Son glorifies the Father and that this is not merely true of the Trinity operating economically (*ad extra*) in creation, revelation and redemption. It is also true of the Trinity relating essentially (*ad intra*). In his famous high priestly prayer of John 17 Jesus prays to the Father, 'I have brought you glory on earth' (v. 4), and, 'Father, glorify me in your presence with the glory I had with you before the world began' (v. 5). In an earlier chapter Jesus teaches that the Spirit is the one who will glorify the Son (John 16:14). The life of the triune God appears to be from these biblical hints one of mutual glorification.[32] If I am correct, other-person-centredness has always been true of the inner life of God. Love and glory are not in antithesis. If so, the

---

[29] Carson in McCormack 2008: 52.
[30] Quoted in Bakker, De Jong and Wees 2002: 174.
[31] Carson in McCormack 2008: 52.
[32] B. A. Ware (2005: *passim*) posits an asymmetry in the mutual glorifying within the triune Godhead. The Father has the highest honour, glory and authority, the Son less so and the Spirit less that either. I find this extremely problematical unless its speculative nature is duly acknowledged and the dogmatic weight Ware gives to it is moderated dramatically.

triune God is no narcissus, no lonely monad in need of praise. Rather, when we as creatures are commanded to glorify God (e.g. Rev. 14:6–7) we are called to a practice that is true to the very nature of God. Moreover, if C. S. Lewis is correct, then 'Fully to enjoy is to glorify. In commanding us to glorify Him, God is inviting us to enjoy Him.'[33] And if I am right, when we are so commanded to glorify God (e.g. 1 Cor. 10:31), we enjoy him, albeit in a creaturely mode, in an analogous way to how the uncreated persons of the triune Godhead enjoy each other.

Conclusion

According to Cross, Lamm and Turk, three things epitomize the late Middle Ages: in architecture, Chartres cathedral; in philosophy, Aquinas's *Summa Theologica*; and in literature, Dante's *Divine Comedy*.[34] With regard to the last, Dante ends his trilogy on the note of 'The love that moves the sun and the other stars.'[35] Dante has captured the divine motivation in this last line of his magnificent poem, but not the divine goal. The divine goal is to make 'little Christs' to his glory. The motive of divine love and divine pursuit of glory gives the Scriptural narrative its unity. If the God of the Bible is understood in non-trinitarian terms, then such a goal seems prima facie unworthy even of God. God is the celestial egotist. However, if God is really triune, that divine dance of mutual love and glorying, then glory is other-person-centred, even within the Godhead.

[33] C. S. Lewis 1969: 82. This is Lewis's conclusion to 'A Word about Praising'. His whole argument (77–83) repays study. Interestingly, Lewis anticipated John Piper's influential thesis concerning Christian hedonism. See Piper 1986: 14.

[34] Cross, Lamm and Turk 1973: 310.

[35] Dante 1977: 347, Canto 33, line 145.

Chapter Ten

Conclusion

Implicit in the title of this work is a question. How then does atonement bring shalom? Atonement brings shalom by defeating the enemies of peace, overcoming the barriers both to reconciliation and to the restoration of creation. This is God the peacemaker's mission. The biblical presentation of God's atoning project in general and the atonement in particular is multifaceted. Consequently, any delineation of the atonement centrepiece needs to do justice not only to penal substitution but also to the Christus Victor motif, in the light of the *protoevangelium*. However, as Garry Williams maintains, 'Deny penal substitution and *Christus Victor* is hamstrung' – because it leaves unexplained why Jesus died in our place as he did.[1] Moreover, one needs to appreciate that there is no spiritual maturity without reflecting deeply on both the priestly and sacrificial work of Christ as adumbrated in the letter to the Hebrews.

Even more basic is the need to understand both the character of God and who we are, as revealed by Scripture. The God of the Bible is the righteous God of holy love. The trouble is, however, that we have become paradoxically the glory and garbage of the universe. Our great need is peace with God, and not just with God but also with one another. The 'peace dividend' that atonement brings ranges from the forgiveness of sins for the individual to adoption into the family of God. The 'peace dividend' is appropriated by faith in the strong sense of trust and not merely the weak one of assent. And such peace also brings responsibilities to those who live in between the times, and has not only personal but also interpersonal entailments. These entailments include truth-telling (e.g. witness) and truth-doing (e.g. showing mercy). Faith works through love (Gal. 5:6).

There is no shalom, however, without sacrifice. Peace is made through the blood of the cross. The atoning life, death and vindication of the faithful Son bring shalom by addressing the problem of

---

[1] G. Williams in Tidball, Hilborn and Thacker 2008: 187.

sin, death the devil and wrath definitively. Sacrifice, satisfaction, substitution and victory are key terms for understanding God's atoning project in general and the cross in particular. Eschatologically speaking, the realization of the triune God's reconciling project will see *God's people in God's place under God's rule living God's way enjoying shalom in God's holy and loving presence to God's glory.*[2] The life to come will be replete with doxology, as the *Westminster Shorter Catechism* famously instructs: 'The chief end of man [and woman] is to glorify God and to enjoy him for ever' or, as John Piper nuances it, 'by enjoying him forever'.[3] Both the broad idea of atonement and the narrower one of the atonement are essential for understanding the scriptural story. And both ideas also have deep existential implications. The broad notion should humble us at the thought of a righteous God of holy loving purpose who, in love, has never abandoned his wayward creatures but in a plan of rescue has begun to reclaim the created order and will in the end restore creation to himself and to his glory. Love is the motive, glory the goal. The narrow one brings us to Christ and his cross. He is the linchpin of the plan. We are brought to a real Christ, to a real cross, to a real cost. We are indeed brought to a person whose 'Love so amazing, so divine / Demands [rightly] my soul, my life, my all,' as Isaac Watts taught the church of Jesus Christ to sing, living sacrifices no less.

W. J. Dumbrell finely sums up God's atoning project in these terms as he reflects on the theological significance of Revelation 22:6–11:

> The history of salvation has ended, and the journey has been long. We have moved from creation and Adam to Israel and redemption, to Jesus as suffering Israel, to the creation of a new people of God through the cross and resurrection of Jesus . . . The biblical search for order is now at an end. Though the divine intention for humankind and the world had been signaled by Genesis 1–2, God patiently bore with sinful humankind until imposing order at the end of the canon. The movement from creation to the new creation was

[2] See Goldsworthy 1981: 47. I have expanded Goldsworthy's summation of the biblical story, which he takes to be a kingdom-of-God story. His formulation runs, 'God's people in God's place under God's rule.'

[3] Piper 1986: 14. A caveat – I would prefer to be called a Christian doxologist than a Christian hedonist. I am not sure what Christian hedonism could look like in the context of a violent persecution for the faith.

made possible only by the fact that God was in Christ, in the historical factor of the cross outside the city of Jerusalem in the midpoint of salvation history, reconciling the world to himself.[4]

Is the project worth it? Yes! If it glorifies the triune God and results in a creature as close to being God as a creature can logically possibly become, a creature who is not merely innocently good but morally good, a creature who is not merely God's servant but God's child. Creation is on tiptoe, awaiting that very revelation (Rom. 8:19).

---

[4] Dumbrell 2001b: 346. Biblical theology works with the whole canon and does so with a sensitivity to its storyline. In the light of it, an old evangelical adage needs expansion. Ruin through Adam, redemption through Christ and regeneration through the Spirit (the three R's of redemption) needs expansion to become ruin through Adam, redemption through Christ, regeneration through the Spirit and restoration of creation through the triune God.

Appendix

Questioning the cross: debates, considerations and suggestions

In this appendix a number of controversial aspects of the atonement will be addressed, questions that have been raised in the course of this study. For example, in an earlier chapter I argued for penal substitution as an exegetically grounded doctrine. Such a commitment to substitutionary atonement invites many questions, however. For example, how central should this view be in any articulation of a fully orbed doctrine of the atonement? Other issues we shall consider in this appendix include the morality of substitutionary atonement, the fittingness of moral influence and exemplarist theories as atonement theories per se, healing in the atonement, the Holy Saturday controversy and non-violent atonement theories. In asking such questions we move more obviously into the area of systematic theology. Since this is an appendix, the exploration of these matters will be suggestive rather than exhaustive. Likewise, the list of issues themselves is indicative rather than complete.

Debate about the centrality of penal substitution

When it comes to examining an atonement tradition, there are a number of possible outcomes. Penal substitution provides a case in point. The tradition may be *repudiated* (e.g. J. Denny Weaver; see below). The tradition may be *interpreted afresh* (e.g. J. I. Packer's use of the idea of model, canvassed in an earlier chapter). The tradition may be *reaffirmed* (e.g. Jeffery, Ovey and Sach; see below). The tradition may be *rebalanced* in the light of other traditions (e.g. Hans Boersma; see below). This last possibility is our concern at this point of the discussion. How important is the doctrine of penal substitution in relation to other putative doctrines of the atonement?

The history of the doctrine is an interesting one. J. I. Packer argues that it was only in the nineteenth century that the language of penal substitution eclipsed that of satisfaction in the theologies of 'all conservative Protestants'.[1] And if Stephen Holmes is right, it was not until the second half of the nineteenth century that there were evangelicals, for example, who argued that penal substitution was not only central, but also 'the one and only correct way of talking about the atonement'.[2] Significantly, these evangelicals were in a minority at the time. Substitutionary atonement has always been integral to the evangelical position, Holmes contends, but the penal articulation of it has never been made the sine qua non of the evangelical position in all the major pan-evangelical doctrinal statements, with the exception of the Universities and Colleges Christian Fellowship (UCCF).[3] His survey covers 1736 to 2004.

Of course, the historical account is one thing. The theological account is another. The theological account is about what ought to be central, if anything, given the testimony of special revelation. More precisely put, 'How does the penal substitution view relate to Christus Victor, to moral influence, to exemplarist doctrines, to governmental and to non-violent perspectives?' Advocates of penal substitution use a variety of metaphors to convey their sense of the importance of the doctrine. Some speak of penal substitution as the heart of the atonement.[4] In this view, 'heart' functions as another way of saying 'centre', or this doctrine supplies the blood supply as it were to the whole body of divinity (to use a Puritan expression). Others speak of penal substitution as 'absolutely central' to the atonement.[5] Here the metaphor may suggest either that all other atonement views revolve around this one much like a satellite around the earth, or that all other 'theories' must be related to penal substitution and not the reverse. Still others write of penal substitution as the 'essence' of the atonement. The idea here seems to be that without penal substitution the atonement is not the atonement.[6] However, it may be that the language of 'heart', 'core' or 'centre' is simply a way of stating the singular theological importance of the

---

[1] Packer in Packer and Dever 2007: 91–92, esp. n. 41.

[2] S. R. Holmes in Tidball, Hilborn and Thacker 2008: 267–292. His examples are Charles Hodge, R. L. Dabney, George Smeaton and T. J. Crawford. He even says (276) that this exclusive emphasis on the penal substitution 'seems to be a new theme within evangelical writings'. Elsewhere Holmes writes, 'penal substitution was the *dominant* way of talking about the cross among Protestant Christians between 1600 and 1800' (2007: 110; my emphasis).

[3] S. R. Holmes in Tidball, Hilborn and Thacker 2008: 283.

[4] Bloesch 1997: 158.

[5] Jeffery, Ovey and Sach 2007: 211.

[6] Letham 1993: 175, and Packer in Packer and Dever 2007: 25.

doctrine. That is to say that one cannot deeply understand the significance of Christ's sacrifice apart from it. Importantly for its advocates, the language of 'heart', 'core', 'centre' or 'essence' – used with reference to penal substitution – does not eliminate other atonement perspectives. But it does tend to relegate other interpretations to a lesser place.[7]

There are critics of the language of 'core', 'heart' or 'centrality', however, when used of penal substitution. For example, Joel B. Green prefers the metaphor of kaleidoscope. In fact, he describes his approach as the 'Kaleidoscopic View'.[8] He argues that Scripture presents multiple views of the atonement, none of which is to be privileged.[9] However, penal substitution is to be rejected. He believes that Romans 3:25 and 2 Corinthians 5:21 present substitution, but economic exchange rather than penal satisfaction is on display.[10] He will have none of retributive justice. To understand God's wrath in such terms is 'a mistaken concept'.[11] Penal substitution is the view of only 'one strand in evangelicalism'. He has Calvinists in mind. He quotes Harold Greenlee with approval, who maintains that 'Reformed theology (Calvinism) says that Christ paid the penalty for sins . . . Arminianism says that Christ's death provided an alternative to the penalty.'[12] But if Arminian theologian Roger E. Olson is correct, then both Green and Greenlee are promoting a myth about Arminianism because many Arminians embrace penal substitution – including Arminius and Wesley no less.[13] Importantly, kaleidoscope is a highly problematical metaphor. In common parlance the term 'kaleidoscope' refers to a continually shifting pattern of colours as seen through an instrument of some kind. There is no stable image. All is in motion. Our insights on the atonement, however, are found in Scripture and Scripture by definition is canonically *fixed*.

Two other approaches worth considering, albeit briefly, are those of Kevin J. Vanhoozer and Hans Boersma. Vanhoozer does not

---

[7] Letham 1993: 175; Packer in Packer and Dever 2007: 25.

[8] This is the title of his contribution to Beilby and Eddy (2006: 157–185).

[9] J. B. Green in Beilby and Eddy 2006: 167.

[10] Ibid. 176–177.

[11] Green and Baker 2000: 147. For a fair-minded critique of Green and Baker see Holmes 2007: 122–125.

[12] Quoted in J. B. Green in Beilby and Eddy 2006: 110, n. 1.

[13] Olson (2006: 231) writes, 'Even the harshest Calvinist critics of Arminianism admit that John Wesley believed in the penal substitution theory of the atonement and not the governmental theory.'

make penal substitution alone central, nor does he seek to relegate it to a lesser place. Instead, he argues, '*The death of Jesus appears as it really is only in canonical-linguistic context, where it is the climax to a covenantal drama in which penal substitution and relational restoration are equally important and equally ultimate.*'[14] I find myself asking where Christus Victor features in this account and how coherent the notion of two ultimates is. Boersma, on the other hand, argues that 'There is a sense, therefore, in which the Christus Victor theme is the ultimate metaphor. Moral influence and penal representation are subordinate to Christus Victor, inasmuch as they are the means to an end.'[15] However, according to the New Testament witness, the love of God is seen in substitution (Rom. 5:8; 1 John 4:9–10). The New Testament does not link in a clear way Christus Victor with the love of God. This is no small point with regard to the importance of penal representation.

A fresh way forward may be to consider the exhortation that the writer of the letter to the Hebrews lays on the consciences of its readers in Hebrews 6:1: 'Therefore let us leave the elementary teachings about Christ and go on to maturity [*teleiotēta*] . . .' The list of elementary teachings in Hebrews 6:1–2 include 'the foundation of repentance from acts that lead to death, and of faith in God, instruction about baptisms, the laying on of hands, the resurrection of the dead, and eternal judgment'. The writer in Hebrews 6 – 10 proceeds to expound *at more depth* the work of Jesus as the Melchizedekian high priest and the sacrifice to end all sacrifices: offerer and offering. In so doing the writer is keeping his earlier promise: 'We have much to say about this' (Heb. 5:11). Immediately prior to that statement the writer had introduced the priestly theme with its Melchizedekian twist (Heb. 4:14 – 5:10).[16] According to the writer, the subject matter of Hebrews 6 – 10 does not contain 'elementary teachings' but 'solid food' (cf. Heb. 6:1 and 5:14). The solid food has to do with dealing with the problem of sins. As Leon Morris argues:

> He put sins away so that God remembers them no more (8:12; 10:17). He bore sin (9:28), he offered a sacrifice (*thysia*) for sins (10:12), he made an offering (*prosphora*) for sin (10:18), and brought about remission of sin (10:18). He annulled sin

[14] Vanhoozer 2005: 387; original emphasis.
[15] Boersma 2004: 182.
[16] Attridge (2000: 1244) is right to see Heb. 5:11 – 10:18 as dealing with 'The Priestly Work of Christ' (hence my emphasis).

by his sacrifice (9:26). He brought about redemption from transgressions (9:15). In other passages the author speaks of a variety of things the former covenant could not do with respect to sin, the implication in each case being that Christ has now done it (e.g., 10:2, 4, 6, 11). It is clear from all this that the author sees Jesus as having accomplished a many-sided salvation. *Whatever had to be done about sin he has done.*[17]

Moreover, Jesus has done all that needed to be done about judgment on behalf of sinners who believe. I quote *in extenso*:

It was necessary, then, for the copies of the heavenly things to be purified with these sacrifices, but the heavenly things themselves with better sacrifices than these. For Christ did not enter a man-made sanctuary [under the old covenant] that was only a copy of the true one [under the new covenant] he entered heaven itself, now to appear for us in God's presence. Nor did he enter heaven to offer himself again and again, the way the high priest enters the Most Holy Place every year with blood that is not his own [under the old covenant]. Then Christ would have had to suffer many times since the creation of the world. But now he has appeared once for all [under the new covenant] at the end of the ages to do away with sin by the sacrifice of himself. Just as man is destined to die once, and after that to face judgment, so Christ was sacrificed once *to take away* [*anenenkein*, 'to carry away'] *the sins of many* people; and he will appear a second time, not to bear sin [lit. 'without sin', *chōris hamartias*], but to bring salvation to those who are waiting for him. (Heb. 9:23–28; my emphasis)

The key phrase is 'to take away the sins of many' with its echoes of the fourth servant song of Isaiah (Isa. 53:12). W. L. Lane persuasively argues that, in drawing upon the fourth servant song, the writer sees that the 'vicariously redemptive quality of Jesus' death was of paramount importance to the argument. It permitted Jesus to enter the heavenly sanctuary and to appear in the presence of God as high priestly mediator.'[18] Clearly, in his first coming Christ did bear

---

[17] L. Morris 1997, comment on Heb. 1:3; my emphasis.
[18] W. L. Lane 2004a, comment on Heb. 9:28.

our sins as our substitute. In view of Hebrews 9:28 and the Isaianic reference, B. C. Joslin is right to suggest there is 'strong evidence that for Hebrews the death of Christ is not only a *substitutionary* sacrifice, but a *penal substitutionary* sacrifice'.[19] Hence, according to the logic of Hebrews, there is no need for him to so deal with sin a second time.

In the light of Hebrews 6 – 10 there may be a better question than 'Is penal substitution central?' The fresh question is, 'Can there be Christian maturity without grasping penal substitution?' To fail to incorporate the argument of Hebrews concerning the nature of Christ's priesthood and substitutionary sacrifice into one's theology risks locking oneself into an arrested theological development. Existentially speaking, the biblical testimony to the penal substitutionary death of Christ may not have been our entry point into coming to understand the significance of the cross – for example, it may have been the exemplarist theme or Christus Victor – but it needs to be the ending point.[20] As James Denney argues:

> It always comes to this in the long run. Men [and women] may come into contact with Christ at different places. They may approach Him from all quarters of the compass, under

[19] Ably argued by Joslin (2007: 90; original emphases), who offers (90–95) other arguments in support of penal substitution in Hebrews, including the instances of the wrath motif and how the writer understands that Christ's death was for our sins. Contra Swinburne (1989: 152, n. 6), who regards Hebrews as important testimony to the atonement model of sacrifice, but in a footnote argues that penal substitution is not explicit in the New Testament but developed later by Luther and Calvin from hints in Paul. Swinburne neglects Augustine: 'Christ, though guiltless, took our punishment, that He might cancel our guilt, and do away with our punishment' ('Reply to Faustus the Manichean', *NA* 14.4). Penal substitution can be found taught by the Fathers.

[20] Interestingly, the call to maturity in Heb. 6:1 and subsequent argumentation concerning Christ's priestly work and his sacrifice for sins does not refer to the devil, even though there is an earlier Christus Victor reference to the devil in Heb. 2:14–15. Boyd (in Beilby and Eddy 2006: 24) argues that Christus Victor provides 'a unifying framework' for Christ's work. Even if there is merit in this thesis, I would argue penal substitution still lies at the heart or, to change the metaphor, constitutes the centre of that work. Boyd himself is somewhat agnostic as to how the cross and the resurrection defeat Satan and evil. He is reluctant to press the details. He argues (ibid. 37, n. 23) that humility is needed here because 'our understanding is severely limited'. Point taken. However, I believe that Scripture has light to throw on the question, as my treatment of expiation and propitiation in chapter 6 endeavoured to show. Henri Blocher (1999: 31) puts it well: 'the *Christus Victor* scheme depends on the forensic one as soon as one realizes that the Devil's weapon is accusation, that the satisfaction of justice deprives him of his hold (Rv 12.10f)'. For if the problematic for us of divine judgment and concomitant wrath is not addressed through propitiation and expiation, then the devil's sway over humanity remains unbroken.

various impulses, yielding to a charm and constraint in Him as manifold as the beatitudes or as gracious as the words and deeds of the gospel. But if they are indeed earnest as He is, they will come sooner or later to the strait gate. And the ultimate form the strait gate assumes – for it is a gate that goes on straitening till the demand for death is made as the price of life – is that to which Jesus leads His disciples in His last lessons.[21]

The argument of Hebrews still applies and the right question to ask is, 'Shall we go on to maturity?'[22]

Debate about the morality of penal substitution

The Unitarian classic the Racovian Catechism of 1605 poses the difficult question 'For what is that justice, and what too is that mercy, which punishes the innocent, and absolves the guilty?'[23] This question persists, especially in more liberal theological circles. For example, Keith Ward asserts, 'The moral problem is that it is quite unjust for an innocent person, however well intentioned, to pay the debt of a guilty person.'[24] This is a serious question and it is important to ask how it might be addressed. One could simply exegete a raft of relevant biblical passages that present both God as just and Jesus as sinless, yet Jesus is described as bearing the sins of the guilty. Some might argue, since Scripture teaches it that is enough for the godly. But what Scripture does not do is anticipate moral criticism like that of the later Socinians.

Addressing the question requires in my view both a theological and a philosophical treatment. The attempted answer needs to be consistent with the canonical testimony, although, by definition, going beyond what is written. The theological treatment might draw attention to the biblical witness that the cross is a trinitarian event. For example, Keith Ward contends, 'And it is a very unjust God

---

[21] Denney 1973: 164.

[22] P. T. O'Brien ('Hebrews 5:11–6:12', unpublished MS) defines *teleiotēta* (maturity, perfection) as follows: 'In a final sense, however, perfection is the acquisition of all that God has promised as he brings his work to completion.'

[23] As found in the English translation from the Polish of 1818 in McGrath (2007b: 367). Other objections to penal substitution are addressed at length in Jeffery, Ovey and Sach (2007: 205–324), so I do not engage in them here.

[24] Ward 2004: 112. For similar criticisms see philosopher McCullagh (1988: 392–400) and theologian Thomas Smail (in Goldingay 1995: 85).

who can say, "You owe me a debt which must be paid, but I do not mind if someone else pays it."'[25] That God was in Christ reconciling the world to himself is part of the answer to Ward's criticism. A theological response would also ask what the implications of our union with Christ are. Put another way, how realistic – in some ontological sense – is Christ's union with us?[26]

The philosophical approach would ask other questions about the nature of human solidarity and the relation of the one to the many. For example, recall the Kevin Rudd story from chapter 8. As the Prime Minister of Australia, Rudd apologized to the aboriginal peoples on behalf of the nation. How could he do that when so many in the nation have had nothing to do with the misery of indigenous people that began in 1788 with British colonization? In his apology the one acted for the many.[27] And so far as I know he has never personally harmed any aboriginal person. One may ask whether the Socinian objection is rooted in a nominalist-like individualism that fails to reckon with corporate realities and responsibilities.[28] Again, does the Socinian objection arise, at least in part, from the emergence of Western individualism that makes biblical culture seem so alien in its understanding of the one and the many?[29]

---

[25] Ward 2004: 112. Ward adds, 'Further, there is something very odd in the idea that God pays a debt to God.' What Ward calls 'odd', others might call 'grace'.

[26] Jeffery, Ovey and Sach (2007: 242–246) very helpfully make much of our union with Christ and its relevance to the objection: 'The doctrine of penal substitution thus does not propose a transfer of guilt between unrelated persons. It asserts that guilt is transferred to Christ from those who are united to him' (243). Union with Christ was treated in its own right in chapter 7 of this work.

[27] Of course, this illustration has limitations if used to illustrate more than the phenomenon of the one acting on behalf of the many. E.g. Rudd acted as an elected representative of the Australian people. Australia became a nation state in 1901. Until 1901 Australia was a British colony, so Rudd arguably substituted for, rather than represented, the former colonial power in making his apology.

[28] On the relation of Socinianism to nominalism see Muslow and Rolls 2005: vii. But also see the more nuanced assessment by Mason (2000: 731). Pannenberg (1982: 87–88) argues that substitution or representation is a universal phenomenon of human social life without which 'the Christian doctrine of the vicarious efficacy of Jesus' death would remain a futile assertion'. He maintains that the chief weakness of the Socinian critique is the failure to reckon with this universal phenomenon.

[29] See the discussion of this point in Boyd and Eddy 2002: 119–120. Cultural shifts can render a view less plausible than it once was. I see the shift from the traditional retributive philosophy of eighteenth-century criminal justice to a more Benthamite reformative approach in the nineteenth century as one such shift that made penal substitution less plausible. See Cole 1991, which on this matter contrasts among others William Paley (d. 1805) and Jeremy Bentham (d. 1832). Making a somewhat similar point about cultural plausibility, but drawing on Foucault, S. R. Holmes in Tidball, Hilborn and Thacker 2008: 273–274.

Moreover, one might ask, 'Does it make any difference that Scripture does not describe Jesus merely as innocent?' He is also described as righteous. Both ideas are present in the passion account in Luke (cf. Luke 23:41, 47). What may a righteous person do as opposed to what an innocent person may do on behalf of others? Biblically speaking, a righteous person does what is appropriate in a relationship. Is bearing the sins of others appropriate for the incarnate God-man, who is both *homoousion* with God and with us? Someone who was merely human may not have been qualified to atone, whether innocent or righteous.[30] Hans Urs von Balthasar – probably the greatest Roman Catholic theologian of the twentieth-century – expresses the point well:

> For this *pro nobis* to be effective, Jesus Christ has to be, unconditionally, truly human, for only in that way could he take on himself and suffer from within the vicarious experience of the world's sin. But he must also be more than a human being, for within the world no being can completely assume the place of another free fellow nature: this would offend against the dignity of the self-responsible person.[31]

In other words, we need to ask, 'Who did what?' A final comment: it may well be that because the substitution that took place on the cross was *sui generis*, looking for analogies from modern criminal justice takes us only so far and could easily mislead. So great caution is needed. There is mystery here.

With debts to Alvin Plantinga, let me suggest then with regard to penal substitution that all that may be offered is a defence rather than a theodicy.[32] A theodicy gives *the* reason God allows or does X. A defence offers a more moderate proposal. A strong defence would give reasons for trusting in God's moral integrity (e.g. the love of God expressed through the cross) and also offer a theory of how that integrity is not compromised by penal substitution. A weak defence

[30] T. V. Morris (in Noll and Wells 1988: 125) writes, 'An individual is *fully human* just in case that individual has all essential human properties composing basic human nature. An individual is *merely human* if he has all those properties *plus* some additional limitation properties as well, such as being less than omnipotent, less than omniscient, and so on' (original emphases). In this view, Christ is fully human but not merely human.

[31] Von Balthasar in Kehl and Löser 1982: 150. Von Balthasar, to Finlan's dismay (Finlan 2007: 76–77), strongly defends both Anselm and an expiatory atonement.

[32] Plantinga 1980: 10–11, 26–29.

would likewise give reasons for trusting in God's moral integrity (e.g. the love of God expressed through the cross), but unlike the strong defence offer no account of how penal substitution comports with that integrity. I would argue that because of the limitations in scope of special revelation (not all has been revealed: Deut. 29:29), only some kind of strong defence is possible.[33] As that great 'theologian' Clint Eastwood says, 'A man [or woman] needs to know his limitations.' We shall return to matters of theodicy and defence when we consider the debate about violence in the atonement.

Are moral influence and exemplarist theories atonement theories?

Space is given in many discussions of the history of the doctrine of the atonement to what are sometimes described as subjective theories of the atonement.[34] That is to say, unlike the so-called objective theories (such as Christus Victor, satisfaction, penal substitution or governmental theories), the death of Christ is directed at impacting us in the first instance rather than God (as in penal substitution) or evil (as in Christus Victor).[35]

The medieval theologian Abelard (1079–1142) made the moral influence theory famous in his rejection of Anselm's satisfaction one. In the light of the cross he argues, 'our hearts should be set on fire by such a gift of divine grace, and true love should not hold us back from suffering anything for his sake'.[36] In other words, the cross should move us to love. There is ostensible biblical grounding for

[33] For a contrary view to mine see Tierno 2006: 167, who is unconvinced that defence is better than theodicy.

[34] For helpful though brief overviews of the history of discussion of the atonement see Demarest 1997: 149–166; G. Allison 2007: 4–190; and Letham 1993: 159–175. Beilby and Eddy (2006: 11–12) distinguish Christus Victor from objective and subjective 'paradigms'. However, since Christus Victor focuses on Satan and evil, I find it hard not to see it as an example of an objective interpretation of the cross.

[35] K. Ware (1996: 50) offers Christ as Teacher as his first model of the atonement. In this he claims to be following Justin Martyr. How such a view qualifies as an atonement model is not at all clear. In fairness to Ware he has four other models that he works with.

[36] Quoted in McGrath 2007b: 359, who helpfully points out that Abelard highlights this aspect of the cross within a broader context that includes a full sacrificial understanding of the cross. Not all readers are as helpful and nuanced as McGrath's. One can gain the impression from some that Abelard held only to the moral influence view or that Augustine maintained only the Christus Victor approach. In fact, Abelard (quoted by Mozley 1915: 132, n. 4) in a sermon preached 'the notion of vicarious penalty' (penal substitution) and in his *Retractions* claimed 'Christ delivers us from the yoke of the devil' (Christus Victor).

this idea in 1 John. The letter reads, 'We love because he first loved us' (1 John 4:19). As Robert Murray McCheyne preached, 'Love begets love.'[37] More recently, the moral influence view has found a champion in Paul Fiddes. Fiddes argues that the cross constitutes 'an event which has a unique degree of power to evoke and create a human response to the forgiving love of God'.[38] There is arguably an exemplarist theory as well as moral influence in Abelard. Christ died as an example to humanity of what 'supreme love' looks like in action. Abelard cites John 15:13, 'Greater love has no-one than this . . .'[39] In the early twentieth century Abelard found a champion in the British theologian Hastings Rashdall, who regarded Christ as his moral ideal and that life was to be lived under its influence.[40] He wrote of Abelard, 'At last we have found a theory of the atonement which thoroughly appeals to reason and to conscience.'[41]

The Socinians of the sixteenth century are especially associated with the exemplarist theory of the atonement. Faustus Socinus (1539–1604) argued in his work *De Jesu Christo Servatore* 'that Jesus Christ is our Saviour, because he proclaimed to us the way eternal life, confirmed it and clearly showed it forth, both by example of his life and by rising from the dead, and because he will give eternal life to us who have faith in Him'.[42] Socinians were persecuted and found in the example of Christ how to face such suffering. In expounding Socinus' theology, Marion Hillar adds, 'By dying on the cross Jesus proved that no sacrifice should prevent people from fulfilling God's commands.'[43] After all he was raised from the dead and so will those who follow him and 'in this sense only Christ can be called Savior'. As with the moral influence theory there is some biblical warrant for seeing in the death of Christ an example for the Christian to follow. Slaves are counselled in 1 Peter 2:20–21, 'But if you suffer for doing good and you endure it, this is commendable before God. To this you were called, because Christ suffered for you, leaving you an example.'

Exemplarist and moral influence theories draw attention to important aspects of Christ's death and its significance for Christian

---

[37] McCheyne 1961: 9.
[38] Fiddes 1989: 29.
[39] McGrath 2007b: 359.
[40] Rashdall 1919: 463–464.
[41] Ibid. 360.
[42] Quoted by Mozley 1915: 150.
[43] Hillar, accessed 7 Mar. 2007.

conduct. They both have some exegetical support. However, to describe either as a theory of the atonement is something of a misnomer. Robert Letham argues with regard to the atonement, 'any exemplary elements do not strictly belong to the atonement as such, but are consequences of it'.[44] Finely said! In fact, his argument applies equally to moral influence theory. However, I suspect that the idea of the atonement as both exemplary and moral influence is now so well enshrined in discussion after discussion that there is little point in not considering both in this work. What would be a great folly would be to collapse the significance of the death of God's faithful Son into just one or both of these views.[45]

Healing in the atonement?

Some argue that one of the benefits to be appropriated from the atonement is healing for the body, if we have the faith to believe it.[46] This claim is based on texts such as Isaiah 53:5 ('by his wounds we are healed') and the quotation of Isaiah in Matthew 8:17. However, using the analogy of Scripture and comparing Scripture with Scripture, this claim fails to do justice to Pauline texts such as 2 Corinthians 12:7–8 ('a thorn in my flesh') and 2 Timothy 4:20 ('I left Trophimus sick in Miletus'). These texts give no hint that the great apostle lacked faith. Clearly, physical healing in this life lies in God's sovereign good pleasure. Healing may be prayed for, as Paul did in 2 Corinthians 12:8 ('Three times I pleaded with the Lord to take it away from me'), but not presumed upon. Charismatic theologian J. Rodman Williams rightly concludes, 'We ought not therefore confuse the salvation made possible through Christ's atonement with the healing also made available through divine resources.'[47] Anyone who has a robust Christian theism believes that God can

---

[44] Letham 1993: 152.

[45] The inadequacy of an exemplarist theology with its Socinian and Enlightenment debts is powerfully articulated by Gunton (in Webster and Schner 2000: 121–124).

[46] Bruce R. Reichenbach (in Beilby and Eddy 2006: 117–142, esp. 139) goes much further and argues for a 'Healing View' of the atonement to rank with other atonement models. He draws heavily on the suffering servant of Isaiah in his argumentation. Healing in his view restores a person to God by dealing with both sin *and sickness* (my emphasis). He argues that physical healing is available in the atonement. However, Joel B. Green (in Beilby and Eddy 2006: 155) offers an incisive critique: 'In short, it is far easier to argue that salvation itself must be understood as healing or that healing is really a consequence of salvation than to argue that healing is the means by which salvation through Christ's (life and) death is made available.'

[47] J. R. Williams 1996: 364–365, n. 36.

indeed heal, including cessationists, who maintain that some of the Spirit-inspired gifts of the New Testament era have been withdrawn. What has not been withdrawn, whether one is a cessationist or a continuationist, is the promise found in James 5:13–18.[48] Moreover, there is a day coming when death will be no more. The tension between 'the now and the not yet' will be relieved by the resurrection of the body, and by establishment of the new heavens and new earth. The final answer to the healing question will be the glorified body of which Paul writes (Phil. 3:20–21).

The Holy Saturday debate

At the end of 2006 an interesting debate broke out in the pages of the journal *First Things* between A. L. Pitstick and E. T. Oakes on the theological soundness of Hans Urs von Balthasar's view that on so-called Holy Saturday Jesus descended to hell and experienced there in his abandonment by the Father all that the damned sinner endures. But, more than that, Christ experienced the judicious wrath of God as he became the sinner's substitute.[49] Both Pitstick and Oakes are Roman Catholic theologians.[50] At issue was the proper Catholic interpretation of the phrase in the creed 'he descended into hell'. Pitstick argued that Balthasar had departed from both the tradition and the present official teaching of the Catholic Church as found in the *Catechism of the Catholic Church*. The *Catechism* states that the descent into hell 'is the last phase of Jesus' messianic mission', and as Saviour Christ proclaimed there 'the Good News to the spirits imprisoned there'.[51] This is the so-called harrowing of hell.[52] Balthasar had in effect veered in a Protestant direction. The

---

[48] On the cessationist versus continuationist debate see Cole 2007: 248–258.

[49] Pitstick and Oakes 2006: 25–32; 2007a: 16–19; 2007b: 5–20. Pitstick (2006: 28) argues that Balthasar held to penal substitution. For Balthasar's view see Kehl and Löser 1982: 150–153; Oakes 2005: 237–247.

[50] For a study of Holy Saturday theology from a different perspective see A. E. Lewis 2001. Lewis understands Holy Saturday in a thoroughly trinitarian way.

[51] CCC, paras. 164–165. The identity of the spirits in prison in view in 1 Pet. 3:19 is an exegetical crux. For a thorough discussion of the scholarly possibilities see D. L. Bartlett 2002: 291–295; Michaels 2004, comment on 1 Pet. 3:19. The three main possibilities are these: the pre-incarnate Christ preached through Noah to the flood generation, the incarnate Christ preached to the unbelievers of Noah's day in hell or he preached to fallen angels.

[52] Belief in the harrowing of hell is very early. Hippolytus (AD 170–236) says, 'The jailers of Hades trembled when they saw Him. And the gates of brass and the bolts of iron were broken. For look! The Only-Begotten, God the Word, had entered Hades with a soul – a soul among souls' (quoted in Bercot 2002: 207).

official Roman Catholic doctrine, Pitstick maintains, is that Christ descended to that part of hell which is the limbo of the fathers, where he 'then liberated the just from the limbo of the fathers, conferring on them the glory of heaven'.[53] Oakes rejected Pitstick's criticisms of Balthasar, although he granted that Balthasar was a 'disturbing theologian'. Elsewhere he argues that Balthasar's theology of Holy Saturday is 'absolutely crucial to Balthasar's thought and perhaps constitutes his single greatest innovation to the tradition'.[54]

The details of this debate need not detain us. In fact, more recent translations of the Apostles' and Nicene Creeds state, 'he descended to the dead', instead of 'descended to hell'.[55] What the controversy does do is raise the question of how Holy Saturday features in a theology of the atonement. Calvin is provocative:

> The point is that the Creed sets forth what Christ suffered in the sight of men, and then appositely speaks of that invisible and incomprehensible judgment which he underwent in the sight of God in order that we might know not only that Christ's body was given as the price of our redemption, but that he paid a greater and more excellent price in suffering in his soul the terrible torments of a condemned and forsaken man.[56]

In other words, to human sight Christ's death on the cross was just another first-century expression of Roman brutality. However, the phrase in the creed signals that something extraordinary took place.[57] Christ bore the wrath due us. As Pannenberg suggests, Jesus experienced 'the fate brought about by sin'.[58] Christ did not descend to hell per se. The Reformed tradition has tended to follow Calvin on this point and sees the creedal phrase as referring to 'the final stage of Christ's state of humiliation'.[59]

Some recent theology takes a different direction when dealing

[53] Pitstick and Oakes 2006: 26.

[54] Oakes 2005: 237.

[55] *A Prayer Book for Australia* 1999: 489.

[56] Calvin 2002e: 2.16.10.

[57] 'Descended into hell' was not part of the earliest versions of the creeds. See the excellent discussion of this whole topic in Grudem 1994: 583–594.

[58] Pannenberg 1982: 90. 'To be fully conscious of the nearness of God and yet to be excluded from him is what ancient dogmas saw as the tortures of hell' (91). Pannenberg follows Luther's interpretation closely that the descent into hell was Christ's experience of God's forsakenness.

[59] Muller 1986: 89.

with the biblical passages (Acts 2:27; Rom. 10:6–7; Eph. 4:8–9; 1 Pet. 3:18–20; 4:6) that are the putative basis for the traditional view of an actual descent of Christ to the place of the dead. The key text is the very difficult 1 Peter 3:18–20: 'He was put to death in the body but made alive by the Spirit, through whom also he went and preached to the spirits in prison who disobeyed long ago when God waited patiently in the days of Noah while the ark was being built.' Robert Letham writes with specific regard to 1 Peter 3:18–22, 'a growing appreciation seems to be developing on syntactic, structural, semantic and theological grounds that what Peter is teaching is that Christ pronounced judgment on the spirits in prison in his resurrection'.[60] There is merit in this proposal. Such scholarship has affinities with the classic Lutheran position of the subject; namely, the so-called descent was actually the first stage of Christ's exaltation. 1 Peter 3:19 thus refers to Christ's announcement to the satanic realm of his victory over the demonic.

In my view, the Reformed tradition has the better of the argument with regard to how best to interpret the creedal phrase. Even better, speaking as one involved in the worship of a liturgical church, would be to return to the earlier versions of the creed that do not include the question-raising phrase at all.[61] Indeed, what is striking about the biblical account of the passion and resurrection of Christ is the silence concerning Holy Saturday. Some silences are worth observing to this day.

Non-violent atonement theories

Let us begin with definitional matters. Hans Boersma offers a 'definition' of violence that is broad enough to encompass what follows in this discussion. He argues that any 'use of force or coercion that involves some kind of hurt or injury – whether the coercion is physical or nonphysical – is a form of violence'.[62] Strictly speaking, this is

---

[60] Letham 1993: 150.

[61] As mentioned in n. 57 above, the phrase does not appear in the earliest creeds. E.g. it is missing from the following creeds: the Old Roman Creed, Creed of Caesarea, Creed of Nicaea and Nicene Creed. However, it does appear late in a Gallican Creed of the sixth century (see Bettenson 1967: 23–26). I find Grudem (1994: 593–594) convincing on this matter, esp. his treatment of Luke 23:43, 46 and John 19:30 in relation to the issue. Grudem (1994: 587) thinks that the phrase was added to the Apostles' Creed around 650. However, Pelikan (1971: 151) suggests as early as 370.

[62] Boersma 2004: 47. This statement is found in a section listed in the index as 'violence: definition of' (280). This 'definition' is gaining wider acceptance. See e.g. Sanders 2006: xii.

not so much a definition of violence; rather, it is illustrating one form that it may take. If there are other forms of violence, then a strict definition will endeavour to show the totality of necessary conditions sufficient for the use of the term 'violence' in any context. However, his 'definition' will suffice for our purposes and with it in mind we consider the critics.[63]

Critics of violence in the atonement

A vociferous critic of traditional atonement theory is Joanne Carlson Brown. She understands the 'classic orthodox' position to be as follows: 'Jesus died on the cross to save us from sin . . . the death of Jesus is required by God to make God's plan of salvation effective.'[64] This theology, she argues, 'glorifies suffering', and presents 'a blood-thirsty God'. In fact, Christianity needs to 'throw out the atonement'.[65] Her concern is with the abuse of women by men who embrace the theology she rejects. She wants to liberate them from 'this abusive patriarchy'. Women are abused, in her view, when told to embrace suffering just like Jesus did. She sums up the traditional view, which she construes as 'Divine Child Abuse'.[66] Some feminist theologians, however, are not persuaded by the Carlson argument. Margo G. Houts points out that Brown construes the cross in non-trinitarian terms, which leads to distortion. She maintains, 'we can expect abusive imagery to run rampant when the controls which Trinitarian doctrine places on atonement imagery are removed'.[67] Reta Haltemann Finger rightly points out that the Christ who died on the cross 'was an adult, not a child without power or choice'.[68]

Another critic of the traditional view of the atonement that accents sin, sacrifice and divine wrath is Steve Finlan. According to Finlan, 'Atonement is a millstone around the neck of Christianity,

---

[63] Interestingly, the question of violence and the atonement is not a new one. Aquinas deals with this objection in *Summa Theologica*, *NA* 3.46.3.2, 'Further, natural actions are more suitably performed than deeds of violence, because violence is "a severance or lapse from what is according to nature" as is said in De Coelo ii. But Christ's Passion brought about His death by violence. Therefore it would have been more appropriate had Christ died a natural death rather than suffer for man's deliverance.'

[64] Brown 1992: 25.

[65] Ibid. 28.

[66] Ibid. 24.

[67] Houts 1992: 30.

[68] Finger 1992: 38. According to Finger, the phrase 'divine child abuse' was minted first by feminist theologian Alice Miller and made popular by Rita Nakishima Brock.

preventing further advance in psychological health and family ethics.'[69] Violent atonement theology needs to be replaced with 'the truth of parental love'.[70] He regards texts such as 4 Maccabees 6.29 and 17.21–22, which he links to Romans 3:25 and 1 Timothy 2:6, with their emphases on 'heroism and self-sacrifice', vicarious benefits for others, and retributive justice as predicated on 'the anger and violence of God'.[71] He argues, 'The notion that God requires a human sacrifice is fatal to all tender values.'[72] Substitutionary atonement in particular is unacceptable to him. It is based 'on an abusive mentality, the result of having suffered brutality as a child'.[73] (How he knows this is not explained.) Luther and Calvin assume that God is 'an angry parent who is ready to destroy all his children since all are unworthy'.[74] His alternative is to 'abandon the idea of God as judge and sacrifice demander' and replace it with 'God as parent and as director of human growth'.[75] His treatment of Scripture is highly selective. I looked in vain in his book for any real sustained consideration of the biblical testimony to the love of God expressed in the cross, or a robust trinitarian understanding of the cross.[76]

Interpreters of violence in the atonement

J. Denny Weaver is a critic of traditional atonement theories, including Christus Victor, and sees satisfaction and moral influence as intrinsically violent and therefore to be rejected.[77] Penal substitution is particularly offensive. He concludes that these atonement theories 'portray an image of God as either divine avenger or punisher and/ or as child abuser, a Father who arranges the death of one child for the benefit of the others'.[78] The details of his argument would take us beyond the scope of this section. Suffice it to say that large portions of the biblical testimony have to be jettisoned to accommodate his

---

[69] Finlan 2007: 117.
[70] Ibid.
[71] Ibid. 16.
[72] Ibid. 50.
[73] Ibid. 61.
[74] Ibid.
[75] Ibid. 127.
[76] Danaher (2004) is also highly selective, but in contrast to Finlan treats only texts that speak of or are consistent with divine love.
[77] Weaver in Sanders 2006: 1–29. This recent volume contains a handy bibliography (161–164) on what is a publishing growth industry. Other volumes that survey the non-violent atonement scene through multiple contributors are Trelstad (2006) and Jersak and Hardin (2007).
[78] Weaver in Sanders 2006: 7.

critical claims, as well as the concepts of retributive justice, double-agency or concursus (more below), seemingly the doctrine of the essential Trinity and Chalcedonian Christology.[79] He calls his own positive interpretation of the cross 'Narrative Christus Victor' to distinguish it from the early church ransom version. In this view Christ faithfully confronts those forces that oppose the reign of God and suffers in the process. But 'his death was not willed or needed by God'.[80] Christ's example consequently is not one of the passive embrace of suffering, as in penal substitution. Penal substitution fosters the acceptance of abuse. Rather, in his faithful death at the hands of evil, Jesus exemplifies a liberating activism that is vindicated by the resurrection. He maintains that his theory is a non-violent one.[81] This seems to mean that in no way does God induce or direct violence in the violent event that the cross undoubtedly was. His position raises a question. Since the cross was a violent event, has divine providence not effectively allowed violence? In the light of his thesis, I am left wondering whether God could have allowed a different way of accomplishing his restorative purpose that did not involve the death of Jesus at all.

Hans Boersma advocates an interpretation of the cross that he describes as 'a modified reformed view'.[82] Unlike Weaver he believes in concursus. This is the idea that God and ourselves may be involved in the same event but with different intentionalities and in different ways. He cites Acts 2:23 in evidence.[83] He believes that the hospitable God (recall that divine hospitality is a key organizing idea for him) does use violence to accomplish his loving purposes in

[79] Finely argued by Boersma (in Sanders 2006: 33–36). Weaver may question my assertion that he rejects the essential Trinity. However, I am puzzled by statements such as 'According to standard interpretation, each Person in some way reveals the fullness of God, and there is nothing in the Godhead or in any of the Persons of the Trinity that is not in the others' (16). 'Standard interpretation?' This is sloppy at best. What of paternity, filiality and procession? At worst, there is no way to distinguish the Persons from one another.

[80] Weaver in Sanders 2006: 26.

[81] Others are not so sure that Weaver's theory actually is a non-violent atonement theory. E.g. A. W. Bartlett in Jersak and Hardin (2007: 412) contends that Weaver's theory 'still utilizes the currency and language of violence, even if the means of triumph are nonviolent'.

[82] Boersma in Sanders 2006: 47–69. His modifications include e.g. emphasizing unrestricted divine love rather than love only for the elect, emphasizing restorative rather than retributive justice, and the use of N. T. Wright's exile-of-Israel theology. He believes that high Calvinism (e.g. Theodore Beza and William Perkins) with its double-predestination doctrine posits a God of violent love whose limited hospitality draws violence into the heart of God (cf. 56, 73). These are large claims.

[83] Boersma in Sanders 2006: 51.

a fallen world.[84] In fact, he contends strongly that 'There is simply no hospitality in our world without violence.'[85] He accepts then a notion of divine violence paradoxically in the service of divine hospitality. Importantly though, he argues that 'the Christian faith does not, however, commit to a God who has violence inscribed in the heart of his being'.[86] Even so, in the end a creation without boundaries and their enforcement would be chaos. He acknowledges that traditional atonement theories may poorly articulate the role of violence in the divine economy, especially high Calvinism's limited atonement theory, which on his view locates 'divine violence in the very heart of God'.[87] However, faithfulness to the testimony of Scripture means acknowledging that God does punish sin. Drawing on Irenaeus' theory of recapitulation and N. T. Wright's view that Christ recapitulates Israel's exile and restoration in his death and resurrection, he impressively offers a theory that prioritizes the divine love, has a place for God's historical dealings with Israel, retains a notion of punishment and accents restorative justice. The divine project intends to bring about 'the restoration of shalom'.[88]

Unlike both Weaver (2001) and Boersma (2004), T. Scott Daniels has not written a book-length treatment of the violence question. What he does though is provide an example of an interpretation of the cross that draws upon the increasingly influential scapegoat theory of renowned French literary critic René Girard.[89] Daniels argues that our worship shows our real theology.[90] Evangelical worship, in particular as expressed in baptism, Eucharist and praise songs, is informed by a substitutionary view of the atonement. A debt has been paid by Christ on the cross. He bore our punishment. Such worship places God at a distance from us and makes problematical Jesus' own idea that disciples are to take up their cross and follow him. How can they when all has been done at the cross?

[84] Boersma (2004: 37, n. 46) argues with regard to the Old Testament, but it applies *mutatis mutandis* more broadly: 'God's entry in restricted and inhospitable surroundings required the use of violence.'

[85] Ibid. 18.

[86] Ibid. 54.

[87] Ibid. 18.

[88] Boersma in Sanders 2006: 66.

[89] Daniels in Sanders 2006: 125–148. Another example is Peters 2005. For Girard's theory see Girard in J. G. Williams 1996. Also see Girard 1996. For a recent contribution on violence and religion from Girard see Girard 2004. He describes his view as 'the mimetic theory of religion' (19).

[90] This is the famous and venerable *lex orandi lex credendi* (the rule of praying is the rule of believing) principle.

Drawing on a variety of Girard appropriators (Robin Collins and Raymond Schwager in particular) and Girard himself, Daniels sees two important ideas in Girard's theory for atonement theology.[91] First, he follows Girard in the idea that violence comes from rivals in a community, state or nation imitating (mimesis) one another in the pursuit of the same goal. Such a pursuit would ordinarily lead to violence towards one's rival. It is a contagion. However, secondly, a scapegoat is found to be the object of that violence so that communal peace is maintained. The scapegoat is the victim of redirected violence, and as a result communal catharsis takes place. Such peace is so tension reducing that scapegoating becomes ritualized as a communal habit. According to Girard, mimetic rivalry is a social phenomenon found in all cultures. However, in the story of Jesus, God becomes the victim of the scapegoating mechanism. Thus God unmasks its false basis. The object of scapegoating violence is innocent, not guilty, and thus breaks the cycle of scapegoating violence in all those who embrace the story. The cross then is not an expression of the wrath of God or the judgment of God. The cross is not about penal substitution.

For Daniels, Girard provides help in interpreting the sacraments of baptism and Eucharist. With regard to baptism he argues:

> In Girardian terms in baptism we have participated in the death of the scapegoat through mutual identification with Christ-as-victim, and in that practice have not only exposed but put to death the previous mimetic patterns of our sinful existence whose ultimate wages are death.[92]

With regard to the Eucharist he contends, 'Again to use Girardian terms, when the church gathers around the table of the Lord we are made keenly aware that our life together is not possible apart from the peacemaking scapegoating of the one whose body was broken and whose blood was shed.'[93] He concludes, 'It is our hope that our practices of worship and evangelism follow the pattern of the sacraments and call believers to participate daily in the peacemaking, Spirit-empowered reconciling work of God in the world.'[94]

Daniels's treatment of the atonement leaves me wondering how to

---

[91] Daniels in Sanders 2006: 129–134.
[92] Ibid. 139.
[93] Ibid. 140.
[94] Ibid. 145.

make sense of biblical testimony to divine wrath and judgment and to the cross as an expiatory and propitiatory sacrifice. He sees his view as a species of Christus Victor. God defeats evil as its victim, not as its perpetrator. He also sees an element of moral influence theory in it, but as a minor note.[95] However, Hans Boersma rightly questions whether Christus Victor is a correct descriptor and whether Girard and Daniels are actually offering a moral influence theory.[96] I question too – as have others – whether Girard has got the cultural anthropology right.[97] Daniels also wants to make sense of the violence described in the Old Testament. Girard gives him an answer. Over time the violence in Israel became the necessary background for the divine exposure at the cross of the lie it was built upon. He follows Schwager in maintaining that the Old Testament contains 'the residue of false ideas about God carried over from the general human past'.[98] I am left asking, 'What kind of Word of God then is the Old Testament?'

Some critics of the critics

Penal substitution in particular is the subject of criticism, but it has its defenders: there are critics of the critics.

Jeffery, Ovey and Sach address the cosmic child abuse and myth of redemptive violence criticisms. With regard to the first they point out what a caricature the rhetoric of child abuse constitutes. The Jesus who endured the cross was no child. He went willingly to the cross to glorify himself and his Father and to save his people. They appeal to numerous biblical references to support this claim. The cross was part of the divine plan of salvation. To reject this idea is to reject the word of God.[99] Moreover, the rhetoric of 'cosmic child abuse' is 'misleading, disturbing – even blasphemous – and should be abandoned'.[100] With regard to the second line of objection, our authors argue that the myth of redemptive violence criticism rests on

---

[95] Ibid. 136.

[96] Boersma in Sanders 2006: 154–156.

[97] Daniels is aware of the criticism and seems to be sympathetic to it, as his quote from Walter Wink shows. Daniels in Sanders 2006: 147, n. 30.

[98] R. Schwager, quoted with approval by Daniels in Sanders 2006: 134. Girard (2004: 14) himself sees some positive anticipations of Jesus' reversal of the mimetic myth with its 'all-against-the-one structure' in the suffering servant of Isa. 52 – 53 and in other places in the Old Testament.

[99] Jeffery, Ovey and Sach 2007: 228–233. In this section the critical contentions of Chalke and Mann are in view.

[100] Jeffery, Ovey and Sach 2007: 230.

the work of Girard. The myth of redemptive violence is the view that violence can overcome violence. Girard, they contend, dismisses much of the biblical evidence to the contrary as legendary in order to maintain his thesis.[101] This dismissal of so much Scripture is a cost that Jeffrey, Ovey and Sach are unwilling to bear.

Derek Tidball makes four points in his pastoral response to criticisms of violence in the atonement.[102] He argues that penal substitution does not glorify violence; rather, it overcomes it. First, he acknowledges that the cross was a bloody and violent event. Secondly, the violence in the atonement was 'a necessary evil, which God took upon himself'.[103] It does not provide a model for how we are to treat others. He embraces Boersma's point that not all divine actions are imitable (e.g. creation and the pouring out of the Spirit). Thirdly, 'child abuse' he argues is a term that 'is misleading and inappropriate' given trinitarian doctrine.[104] Lastly, he contends that the alleged connection between penal substitution and 'harsh penal policy is often asserted but not often demonstrated'.[105] He notes that harsh practices are to be found in the Catholic tradition that link 'passively enduring suffering and the violence borne by Jesus'.[106] However, penal substitution is not part of this picture.

A personal response: some considerations towards a strong defence

Christians believe in a good God, but there is violence in the world. How can this be? The question remains, whatever atonement view one holds. If God had not created, then obviously there would be no creaturely violence. Why then, at the very least, has God permitted creaturely violence? Christian critics of atonement theories they regard as violent ones still face this question, as do the critics of the critics. Theodicy as we have seen suggests *the* answer. A strong defence offers a possible answer. Because of epistemic limitations ('the secret things belong to the LORD', Deut. 29:29), I believe only a defence is possible. What considerations might go into such a defence with specific regard to violence in the atonement?

First, the cross was a trinitarian event. Father, Son and Holy Spirit

---

[101] Ibid. 235–239.
[102] Tidball in Tidball, Hilborn and Thacker 2008: 348–350.
[103] Ibid. 349.
[104] Ibid.
[105] Ibid.
[106] Ibid. 350.

were subjects (2 Cor. 5:18 – 19; Gal. 2:20; Heb. 9:14). The Son cannot be reduced to a mere object: 'No-one takes it [his life] from me, but I lay it down of my own accord' (John 10:18). 'Unitarian' understandings of the cross invite the kinds of caricaturing of substitutionary atonement that I find in much of the literature. To return briefly to a point made earlier in this appendix in the discussion of the morality of substitution, some popular evangelical presentations of the atonement may invite such caricaturing. Perhaps trying to illustrate, for example, penal substitution is like trying to illustrate the idea of Trinity. The analogies and illustrations fail at crucial points because the Trinity and its involvement in the atonement is *sui generis*.

Secondly, divine action in the world is mysterious. God works in ways that preserve the agency and therefore accountability of his creatures, whether angelic or human. Thus in the Old Testament story of Joseph we find that in the evil of his sale into slavery God was at work as well as his bothers. In the account Joseph, looking back on the incident, concludes, 'You [his bothers] intended to harm me, but God intended it for good to accomplish what is now being done, the saving of many lives' (Gen. 50:20). More to the point, in Peter's Pentecost address he affirms double-agency with regard to the cross: 'This man was handed over to you by God's set purpose and foreknowledge; and you, with the help of wicked men, put him to death by nailing him to the cross' (Acts 2:23). Interestingly, at the end of the address the crowds do not conclude, 'Well if God was sovereignly involved, that lets us off the hook!' Rather, 'cut to the heart' they respond, 'Brothers, what shall we do?' (Acts 2:37). How divine sovereignty and human agency asymmetrically comport I can only guess.

Thirdly, at the cross I would argue God in Christ absorbs the violence to end the violence to bring about eventual shalom.[107] Andrew Lincoln, in his commentary on Colossians 1:11–20, is insightful here:

> The hymnic material in Colossians tells a story of Christ's role in the cosmos from creation to consummation. In our postmodern context, we frequently encounter an aversion to overarching stories or grand metanarratives. Such narratives are seen as making absolute claims that are inevitably oppressive and violent. We need to acknowledge that various formulations of the Christian story have had such lamentable

---

[107] Migliore (2004: 190) says, 'In Jesus God takes the sin, the hatred, and the violence of the world into God's own being and extinguishes them there.'

consequences. But the key question is whether the overarching christological narrative implied by the hymn in Colossians necessarily perpetuates violence toward others.[108]

He is obviously aware of the postmodern criticism that grand narratives are inherently hegemonically violent in their imperialism. He adds with regard to Colossians 1:11–20 in particular:

> This [Col. 1:11–20] is a reminder that in Colossians, too, the cosmic Reign of Christ, meant to effect not uniformity but a harmonious unity, is described as being accomplished through violent means – 'through the blood of his cross.' *But this violence is not perpetrated by Christ but rather the violence is perpetrated on him.* This cosmic narrative has at its heart not a pantocrator's tyranny or benevolent dictatorship but the brutal death of a victim. There can be no universal statements without at the same time focusing on someone bleeding and suffocating on a cross. Paradoxically, this victim is the cosmic ruler; his rule is achieved through the experience of suffering, *and his peacemaking is accomplished through the absorption of violence.*[109]

Human violence does not defeat the peacemaking intent of God and his Christ.

Fourthly, the triune God knows suffering, and not only in the human nature of Christ. According to biblical testimony, God knows grief over human violence (Gen. 6:5–6) and human moral dereliction (Eph. 4:30). The implications of this testimony are captured in one of B. B. Warfield's sermons, who preached with regard to Philippians 2:5–11:

> Men [and women] tell us that God is, by very necessity of His nature, incapable of passion, incapable of being moved by inducements from without; that he dwells in holy calm [the apathy axiom] and unchangeable blessedness, untouched by human suffering or sorrows . . . Let us bless our God that it is not true. God can feel; God does love. But is not this gross anthropomorphism [more precisely, anthropopathism]? We

---

[108] Lincoln 2002: 609.

[109] Ibid.; my emphases. Holmes (2007: 107) argues that 'God has so ordered the world that the inevitable consequence of sin is violence, suffering and death; and rather than let us suffer these things, God takes them on himself.' Holmes's statement would be biblically stronger if judgment were also listed as a consequence of sin.

are careless of names; it is the truth of God. And we decline to yield up the God of the Bible and the God of our hearts to any philosophical abstraction.[110]

Living as we do in this post-holocaust, post-the-arrival-of-Aids, post-9/11 world, Warfield's message is particularly relevant. The God of biblical portrayal is no remote frozen absolute without emotion.[111]

Lastly, there is still violence in the world. Sadly, at times Christians have been among the perpetrators in the name of the Prince of Peace. For example, at the beginning of the fourth century Christianity was proscribed by pagan imperial power; by the end of that same century paganism was proscribed by Christian imperial power.[112] Again Andrew Lincoln provides a helpful comment:

This christological narrative [Col. 1:11–20] actually subverts violence. It is always open to misuse, but those who profess allegiance to it can have no excuse for employing it in a narrow partisan fashion that encourages the marginalization or exclusion of those who do not share the particular christo-logical formulations of their own tradition.[113]

In canonical perspective, however, there is a day coming when shalom will be established. Lincoln once more:

The reference to his death is now set in the context of Christ's role in creation and his cosmic rule means that it was not just one more act in a cycle of unending violence. Rather, there are grounds, through the vindication of his resurrection, for the hope that alienation and suffering throughout the creation will cease.[114]

The problem of evil and the violence that exemplifies it ultimately require an eschatological resolution. As Wolfart Pannenberg affirms, 'Violence is not the last word.'[115] The Lord of glory is coming again!

---

[110] Warfield 1970: 570.
[111] For a defence of divine passibility, albeit carefully qualified, see Cole 2000.
[112] Cf. Stevenson 1970: 287, 289; 1976: 161.
[113] Lincoln 2002: 609.
[114] Ibid.
[115] Pannenberg 2001.

Bibliography

A Prayer Book for Australia: Shorter Edition, Sydney: Broughton, 1999.

Abraham, W. J. (1989), *The Logic of Evangelism*, Grand Rapids: Eerdmans.

—— (1994), 'A Theology of Evangelism: The Heart of the Matter', *Int* 48.2: 117–130.

'Alexamenos *Graffito*', <http://penelope.uchicago.edu/~grout/encyclopedia_romana/gladiators/graffito.html>, accessed 17 Dec. 2007.

Allen, W. (1976), *Without Feathers*, <http://www.quotationspage.com/quotes/Woody_Allen/31>, accessed 18 July 2008.

Allison, Jr., D. C. (2000), 'Matthew', OBC.

Allison, G. (2007), 'A History of the Doctrine of the Atonement', *SBJT* 11: 4–19.

'Amish Forgive, Pray and Mourn', <http://www.cbsnews.com/stories/2006/10/04/national/printable2059816.shtml>, accessed 23 Oct. 2008.

Aquinas (1963), '*Summa Theologica*', in P. J. Glenn (ed.), *A Tour of the Summa*, St. Louis: Herder.

Attridge, H. W. (2000), 'Hebrews', OBC.

Augustine (1958), *City of God*, abr. and tr. G. G. Walsh, D. B. Zema, G. Monahan and D. J. Honan, Garden City, N. Y.: Image.

—— (1977), *Confessions*, tr. R. S. Pine-Coffin, Harmondsworth: Penguin.

—— (1992), *Four Anti-Pelagian Writings*, tr. J. A. Mourant and W. J. Collinge, Washington, D. C.: Catholic University Press.

—— (2005), *The Trinity*, tr. E. Hill, Hyde Park, N. Y.: New City.

—— (2007), 'Tractates on the Gospel of John (John 17:21–23)', *NA*.

Aulén, G. (1931), *Christus Victor*, tr. A. G. Hebert, London: SPCK.

Aune, D. E. (2004), *Revelation*, WBC.

Averbeck, R. E. (1996), '*KPR*', *NIDOTTE* 2: 692–693.

Bakker, E. J., I. J. F. De Jong and H. V. Wees (eds.) (2002), *Brill's Companion to Herodotus*, Leiden: Brill.

Barclay, J. (2000), '1 Corinthians', OBC.

Bartholomew, C. G., and M. W. Goheen (2005), *The Drama of Scripture: Finding Our Place in the Biblical Story*, Grand Rapids: Baker Academic.

Bartlett, A. W. (2001), *Cross Purposes: The Violent Grammar of Christian Atonement*, Harrisburg: Trinity Press International.

Bartlett, D. L. (2002), *1 Peter*, NIBC 12.

Beasley-Murray, G. R. (2001), *Revelation*, NBCRev (EIRC).

Beilby, J., and P. R. Eddy (eds.) (2006), *Four Views: The Nature of the Atonement*, Downers Grove: IVP.

Bell III, A. G., 'Byzantine Catholic Culture – Mel Gibson and the Eastern Church', <http://www.byzantines.net/byzcathculture/melgibson.html>, accessed 29 Aug. 2008.

Bercot, D. W. (ed.), (2002), *A Dictionary of Early Christian Beliefs*, Massachusetts: Hendrickson.

Berkhof, H. (1979), *Christian Faith: An Introduction to the Study of Faith*, tr. S. Woudstra, Grand Rapids: Eerdmans.

Berkhof, L. (1969), *Systematic Theology*, London: Banner of Truth Trust.

'Bertrand Arthur William Russell', <http://www.gigausa.com/quotes/authors/bertrand_arthur_russell_a001.htm>, accessed 6 Sept. 2007.

Bettenson, H. (ed.) (1967), *Documents of the Christian Church*, London: Oxford University Press.

—— (ed. and tr.) (1978), *The Early Christian Fathers*, Oxford: Oxford University Press.

Bettenson, H., and C. Maunder (1999), *Documents of the Christian Church*, 3rd ed., London: Oxford University Press.

Black, C. C. (2002), *The First, Second, and Third Letters of John: Introduction, Commentary, and Reflections*, NIBC 12.

'Blind Justice, Lady Justice, Scales of Justice, or Themis Statues', <http://www.statue.com/lady-justice-staues.html>, accessed 17 July 2008.

Blocher, H. A. G. (1997), *Original Sin: Illuminating the Riddle*, Leicester: Apollos.

—— (1999), 'The Sacrifice of Jesus Christ: The Current Theological Situation', *EJT* 8: 23–36.

—— (2001), 'Sin', *NDBT* (EIRC).

—— (2008), 'God and the Cross', in B. L. McCormack (ed.),

Engaging the Doctrine of God: Contemporary Protestant Perspectives, Edinburgh: Rutherford House; Grand Rapids: Baker Academic, 125–141.

Bloesch, D. G. (1995), *God the Almighty: Power, Wisdom, Holiness, Love*, Downers Grove: IVP.

—— (1997), *Jesus Christ: Saviour and Lord*, Carlisle: Paternoster.

Blomberg, C. L. (1996), *1 Corinthians*, NIVACNT.

—— (2007), 'Matthew', CNTUOT.

Blum, E. A. (1997), *1 Peter*, EBC.

Boersma, H. (2004), *Violence, Hospitality and the Cross: Reappropriating the Atonement Tradition*, Grand Rapids: Baker.

Boff, L., and C. Boff (1989), *Introducing Liberation Theology*, tr. P. Burns, Tunbridge Wells: Burns & Oates.

Boring, M. E. (2002), *The Gospel of Matthew: Introduction, Commentary, and Reflections*, NIBC 8.

Boyd, G. A., and P. R. Eddy (2002), *Across the Spectrum: Understanding Issues in Evangelical Theology*, Grand Rapids: Baker Academic.

Bridges, J., and B. Bevington (2007), *The Great Exchange: My Sin for His Righteousness*, Wheaton: Crossway.

Broderick, R. C. (ed.) (1987), *The Catholic Encyclopedia*, Nashville: Thomas Nelson.

Bromiley, G. (1955), 'Doctrine of the Atonement: A Survey of Barth's *Kirchliche Dogmatik* IV', *SJT* 8: 175–187.

Brown, J. C. (1992), 'Divine Child Abuse', *Daughters of Sarah* 18: 24–28.

Buechner, F. (1992), 'The Good Book as a Good Book', in *The Clown in the Belfry: Writings on Faith and Fiction*, New York: HarperSanFrancisco, 31–44.

Bultmann, C. (2000), 'Deuteronomy', OBC.

Burge, G. M. (1996), *The Letters of John*, NIVACNT.

—— (2001), 'Glory', *DJG* (EIRC).

Burke, T. J. (2006), *Adoption into God's Family: Exploring a Pauline Metaphor*, Nottingham: Apollos.

Burrow, R., Jr. (1998), 'The Love, Justice, and Wrath of God', *Enc* 59.3: 379–407.

Burtner, R. W., and R. E. Chiles (eds.) (1954), *A Compend of Wesley's Theology*, Nashville: Abingdon.

Butterworth, M. (2001), *Hosea*, NBCRev (EIRC).

Byassee, J. (2008), 'How Martyrs Are Made: Stories of the Faithful', *ChrCent* 125: 15, 20–23.

Calvin, J., (2002a), *1 Corinthians, CCJC.*

—— (2002b), *1 John, CJCC.*

—— (2002c), *Hebrews, CJCC.*

—— (2002d), *Hosea, CJCC.*

—— (2002e), *Institutes of the Christian Religion*, ed. J. T. McNeill, tr. F. L. Battles, Philadelphia: *CJCC.*

Cameron, A., and B. Rosner (eds.) (2007), *Still Deadly Ancient Cures for the Seven Deadly Sins*, Sydney: Aquila.

Campbell, J. M. (1996), *The Nature of the Atonement*, Edinburgh: Handsel; Grand Rapids: Eerdmans.

Carson, D. A. (1997), *Matthew*, EBC.

—— (2000), *The Difficult Doctrine of the Love of God*, Wheaton: Crossway.

—— (2008), 'The Wrath of God', in B. L. McCormack (ed.), *Engaging the Doctrine of God: Contemporary Protestant Perspectives*, Edinburgh: Rutherford House; Grand Rapids: Baker Academic, 37–63.

Carson, D. A., and D. J. Moo (2005), *An Introduction to the New Testament*, 2nd ed., Grand Rapids: Zondervan.

Carson, D. A., P. T. O'Brien and M. A. Seifrid (eds.) (2004), *Justification and Variegated Nomism*, vol. 2, Tübingen: Mohr Siebeck; Grand Rapids: Baker.

Chalke, S., and A. Mann (2003), *The Lost Message of Jesus*, Grand Rapids: Zondervan.

Ciampa, R. E. (2001), 'Adoption', *NDBT* (EIRC).

Coggins, R. (2000), 'Isaiah', OBC.

Cole, G. A. (1991), 'Theological Utilitarianism and the Eclipse of the Theistic Sanction', *TynB* 42.2: 226–244.

—— (2000), 'The Living God: Anthropomorphic or Anthropopathic?', *RTR* 59: 16–27.

—— (2001), 'Theological Education – a Personalist Perspective', *Journal of Christian Education* 44.3: 21–31.

—— (2005a), 'God, Doctrine of', *DFTIB*, 259–263.

—— (2005b), 'Lord's Supper', *DFTIB*, 464–465.

—— (2005c), 'Sanctification', *DFTIB*, 720–722.

—— (2006), 'Holy Spirit in Apologetics', *NDCA*, 324–327.

—— (2007), *He Who Gives Life: The Doctrine of the Holy Spirit*, Wheaton: Crossway.

—— (2008), 'Exodus 34 and the Doctrine of God: The Importance of Biblical Theology to Evangelical Systematic Theology', *SBJT* 12.5: 4–23.

Craddock, F. B. (2002), *The Letter to the Hebrews, Introduction, Commentary, and Reflections*, NIBC 12.

Cross, N. M., R. C. Lamm and R. H. Turk (1973), *The Search for Personal Freedom: A Text for a Unified Course in the Humanities*, vol. 1, 4th ed., Dubuque: W. C. Brown.

Cullmann, O. (1956), *The Early Church*, London: SCM.

Culpepper, R. A. (2002), *The Gospel of Luke: Introduction, Commentary, and Reflections*, NIBC 9.

Danaher, J. (2004), 'A Contemporary Perspective on Atonement', *ITQ* 69: 281–294.

Daniel, D. R. (1990), *Hosea and Salvation History: The Early Tradition of Israel in the Prophecy of Hosea*, Berlin: de Gruyter.

Dante, A. (1977), *The Comedy of Dante Alighieri the Florentine, Cantica III, Paradise (Il Paradiso)*, tr. D. L. Sayers and B. Reynolds, Harmondsworth: Penguin.

Davies, J. G. (1981), *The Early Church: A History of Its First Five Centuries*, Grand Rapids: Baker.

Dawkins, R. (2006), *The God Delusion*, Boston: Houghton Mifflin.

Day, J. (2000), 'Hosea', OBC.

Demarest, B. (1997), *The Cross and Salvation: The Doctrine of Salvation*, Wheaton: Crossway.

Dempster, S. G. (2007), 'The Servant of the Lord', in Hafemann and House 2007: 128–178.

Denney, J. (1973), *The Death of Christ*, London: Tyndale.

Dillenberger, J. (ed.) (1961), *Martin Luther: Selections from his Writings*, Garden City, N. Y.: Anchor.

Drew, G. (2006), 'The Gospel as Public Truth in a Pluralistic World: A Reflection on Lesslie Newbigin's Thought', *Evangel* 24.2: 53–61.

Duguid, I. M. (2001), 'Exile', *NDBT* (EIRC).

Dumbrell, W. J. (1988), *The Faith of Israel: Its Expression in the Books of the Old Testament*, Grand Rapids: Baker.

—— (2001a), *The End of the Beginning: Revelation 21–22 and the Old Testament*, Eugene: Wipf & Stock.

—— (2001b), *The Search for Order: Biblical Eschatology in Focus*, Eugene: Wipf & Stock.

—— (2005), *Romans: A New Covenant Commentary*, Eugene: Wipf & Stock.

Dunn, J. D. G. (1977), *Baptism in the* Spirit, London: SCM.

—— (2000), 'Ephesians', OBC.

—— (2004a), *Romans 1–8*, WBC.

—— (2004b), *Romans 9–16*, WBC.

Durham, J. I. (2004), *Exodus*, WBC.

Dyk, L. V. (1993), 'Vision and Imagination in Atonement Doctrine', *ThTo* 50: 1, <http://theologytoday.ptsem.edu/apr1993/v50-1-article1.htm>, accessed 24 Sept. 2003.

Eco, U. (1999), 'Signs of the Times', in C. David, F. Lenoir and J. P. de Tonnac (eds.), tr. I. Maclean and R. Pearson, *Conversations about the End Times*, Harmondsworth: Penguin, 215–216.

Eliot, T. S. (1935), *Murder in the Cathedral*, New York: Harcourt Brace.

Ellul, J. (1985), *The Humiliation of the Word*, Grand Rapids: Eerdmans.

Erickson, M. J. (1993), *Christian Theology*, Grand Rapids: Baker.

Fairweather, E. R. (ed. and tr.) (1956), *A Scholastic Miscellany: Anselm to Ockham*, Philadelphia: Westminster.

Fernando, A. (1996), *Acts*, NIVACNT.

Fiddes, P. S. (1989), *Past Event and Present Salvation: The Christian Idea of Atonement*, London: Darton Longman & Todd.

—— (2007), *Options on Atonement in Christian Thought*, Collegeville: Liturgical.

Finger, R. H. (1992), 'Liberation or Abuse?', *Daughters of Sarah* 18: 37–38.

Finlan, S. (2007), *Options on Atonement in Christian Thought*, Collegeville, Minnesota: Liturgical Press.

Flewelling, R. T. (1946), *The Things That Matter Most: An Approach to the Problems of Human Values*, New York: Ronald.

Ford, P. F. (ed.) (2008), *Yours, Jack: Spiritual Direction from C. S. Lewis*, New York: HarperCollins.

Forsyth, P. T. (1909), *The Cruciality of the Cross*, London: Hodder & Stoughton.

—— (1957), *God the Holy Father*, London: Independent; repr. of Hodder & Stoughton, 1897 ed.

—— (1981), 'Positive Preaching and the Modern Mind', repr. in D. G. Miller, B. Barr and R. S. Paul, *P. T. Forsyth the Man, the Preachers' Theologian, Prophet for the Twentieth Century: A Contemporary Assessment*, Pittsburgh: Pickwick.

France, R. T. (1970), *The Living God: A Personal Look at what the Bible Says about God*, London: Inter-Varsity Fellowship.

Fretheim, T. E. (2002a), *Genesis*, NIBC 1.

—— (2002b), 'Theological Reflections on the Wrath of God in the Old Testament', *HBT* 24: 25–26.

—— (2004), 'God and Violence in the Old Testament', *WW* 24: 1.

Furedi, F. (2002), 'Making a Virtue of Vice', *Spectator*, 12 Jan., <http://findarticles.com/p/articles/mi_qa3724/is_200201/ai_n9048096/print>, accessed 14 June 2008.

Gaffin, Jr., R. B. (2001), 'Glory, Glorification', *DPHL* (EIRC).

Gathercole, S. (2007), 'What Did Paul Really Mean?', *Christianity Today*, Aug., 22–28.

Geddert, T. J. (2001), 'Peace', in *DJG* (EIRC).

Gentry, P. J. (2007), 'The Atonement in Isaiah's Fourth Servant Song (Isaiah 52:13–53:12)', *SBJT* 11: 20–47.

Girard, R. (1996), 'Are the Gospels Mythical?', *First Things* 62: 27–31.

—— (2004), 'Violence and Religion: Cause or Effect', *Hedgehog Review: Critical Reflections on Contemporary Culture* 6: 1, 8–20.

Goldingay, J. (ed.) (1995), *Atonement Today: A Symposium at St. John's College, Nottingham*, London: SPCK.

Goldsworthy, G. (1981), *Gospel and Kingdom: A Christian Interpretation of the Old Testament*, Exeter: Paternoster.

González, J. L. (1987), *A History of Christian Thought: From the Beginnings to the Council of Chalcedon*, vol. 1, rev. ed., Nashville: Abingdon.

—— (1989), *Christian Thought Revisited: Three Types of Theology*, Nashville: Abingdon.

Grabbe, L. L. (2000), 'Leviticus', OBC.

'Grace', <http://acronyms.thefreedictionary.com/God's+Riches+At+Christ's+Expense>, accessed 26 Aug. 2008.

Graham, D. J. (2001), 'Witness', *DLNTD* (EIRC).

Green, E. M. B. (1974), *2 Peter and Jude*, London: Inter-Varsity Press.

Green, J. B., and M. D. Baker (2000), *Recovering the Scandal of the Cross: Atonement in New Testament and Contemporary Contexts*, Downers Grove: IVP.

Grider, J. K. (1983), 'Governmental Theory of the Atonement', *BDT*.

—— (1994), *A Wesleyan-Holiness Theology*, Kansas City: Beacon Hill.

Griffith-Thomas, W. H. (1963), *The Principle of Theology: An Introduction to the Thirty-Nine Articles*, London: Church Book Room.

Grogan, G. W. (1997), *Isaiah*, EBC.

Groom, S. (2008), 'Why Did Christ Die? An Exegesis of Isaiah 52:13–53:12', in Tidball, Hilborn and Thacker 2008: 96–114.

Grudem, W. (1994), *Systematic Theology: An Introduction to Biblical Doctrine*, Leicester: IVP; Grand Rapids: Zondervan.

Guinan, M. D., 'Adam, Eve and Original Sin', <http://www.americancatholic.org/Newsletter/CU/ac0507.asp>, accessed 10 June 2008.

Gunton, C. E. (2002), *The Christian Faith: An Introduction to Christian Doctrine*, Oxford: Blackwell.

—— (ed.) (1997), *The Cambridge Companion to Christian Doctrine*, Cambridge: Cambridge University Press.

Guthrie, G. H. (1996), 'A Positive Example: Jesus' Faithfulness as a Son (3:1–6)', *Hebrews*, NIVACNT.

—— (2001), 'John', NBCRev (EIRC).

Hafemann, S. J. (1996), *2 Corinthians*, NIVACNT.

—— (ed.) (2002), *Biblical Theology: Retrospect and Prospect*, Leicester: Apollos.

Hafemann, S. J., and P. R. House (eds.) (2007), *Central Themes in Biblical Theology: Mapping Unity in Diversity*, Leicester: Apollos; Grand Rapids: Baker Academic.

Hagner, D. A. (2004a), *Matthew 1–13*, WBC.

—— (2004b), *Matthew 14–28*, WBC.

Hamilton, J. (2006), 'The Skull Crushing Seed of the Woman: Inner-Biblical Interpretation of Genesis 3:15', *SBJT* 11: 30–55.

Hammond, T. C. (1956), *In Understanding Be Men: A Handbook on Christian Doctrine for Non-Theological Students*, 4th ed., London: Inter-Varsity Fellowship.

Harrison, C. (2000), 'Truth in a Heresy? 1. Pelagianism', *ExpTim* 112: 78–82.

Harvey, V. A. (1997), *A Handbook of Theological Terms*, New York: Simon & Schuster.

Hasel, G. (1991), *Old Testament Theology: Basic Issues in the Current Debate*, 4th ed., Grand Rapids: Eerdmans.

Hauerwas, S. (2005), *The Hauerwas Reader*, ed. J. Berkman and M. Cartwright, Durham, N. C.: Duke University Press.

Hawthorne, G. F. (2001), 'Faith', *DPHL* (EIRC).

Hays, R. B. (2002), *The Letter to the Galatians: Introduction, Commentary, and Reflections*, NIBC 11.

Heschel, A. J. (1951), *Man Is Not Alone: A Philosophy of Religion*, New York: Jewish Publication Society.

Hiebert, P. G. (1994), *Anthropological Reflections on Missiological Issues*, Grand Rapids, Baker.

—— (2000), 'Spiritual Warfare and Worldview', *ERT* 24.3: 240–256.

Hill, C. C. (2000), 'Romans', OBC.

Hill, C. E., and F. A. James III (eds.) (2004), *The Glory of the Atonement: Biblical, Theological and Practical Perspectives*, Downers Grove: IVP.

Hillar, M., 'Laelius and Faustus Socinus, Founders of Socinianism, their Lives and Theology', <http://www.servetus.org/newsletter/newsletter3/links/faustus-socinus.htm>, accessed 7 Mar. 2007 (taken *from The Journal from the Radical Reformation: A Testimony to Biblical Utilitarianism* 10.2 and 10.3).

Hitchens, C. (2007), *God Is Not Great*, New York: Hachette.

Holmes, S. R. (2007), *The Wondrous Cross: Atonement and Penal Substitution in the Bible and History*, London: Paternoster.

Hooker, M. D. (2002), *The Letter to the Philippians: Introduction, Commentary, and Reflections*, NIBC 11.

Hooker, R., 'The European Enlightenment Jean Jacques Rousseau', <http://www.wsu.edu/-dee/enlightenment/rousseau.htm>, accessed 13 June 2008.

Hopko, T., 'Mel Gibson's Messiah', <http://svots.edu/index2. php?option=com_content&task=view&id129&pop=1&pag e=0>, accessed 28 Aug. 2008.

Houts, M. G. (1992), 'Atonement and Abuse: An Alternative View', *Daughters of Sarah* 18: 29–32.

Hubbard, Jr., R. L. (2001), 'Redemption', *NDBT* (EIRC).

Hunsberger, G. R. (1994), 'Is There Biblical Warrant for Evangelism?', *Int* 48.2: 131–144.

Hunter, A. M. (1974), *P. T. Forsyth: Per Crucem ad Lucem*, London: SCM.

Jacobs, A. (2008), *Original Sin: A Cultural History*, New York: HarperCollins.

Jeffery, S., M. Ovey and A. Sach (2007), *Pierced for our Transgressions: Rediscovering the Glory of Penal Substitution*, Nottingham: IVP.

Jenkins, G. (1999), *In my Place: The Spirituality of Substitution*, Cambridge: Grove.

Jensen, P. (1997), *At the Heart of the Universe: The Eternal Plan of Salvation*, Wheaton: Crossway.

Jersak, B., and M. Hardin (eds.) (2007), *Stricken by God? Nonviolent Identification and the Victory of Christ*, Grand Rapids: Eerdmans.

Joad, C. E. M. (1952), *The Recovery of Belief: A Restatement of Christian Philosophy*, London: Faber & Faber.

Joslin, B. C. (2007), 'Christ Bore the Sins of Many: Substitution and the Atonement in Hebrews', *SBJT* 11: 74–103.

Jowers, D. W. (2001), 'The Theology of the Cross as Theology of the Trinity: A Critique of Jürgen Moltmann's Staurocentric Trinitarianism', *TynB* 52.2: 245–266.

Kaiser, W. C., et al. (2001a), '1:19 Universalism?', *HSOB* (EIRC).

—— (2001b), 'Colossians 1:24: Lacking in Christ's Afflictions?', *HSOB* (EIRC).

Kärkkäinen, V.-M. (2006), 'Salvation as Justification and *Theosis*: The Contribution of the New Finnish Luther Interpretation to our Ecumenical Future', *Di* 45.1: 74–82.

Kateregga, B. D., and D. W. Shenk (1981), *Islam and Christianity: A Muslim and a Christian Dialogue*, rev. ed., Grand Rapids: Eerdmans.

Keener, C. S. (1996), 'Jesus the Deliverer (1:5–6)', *Revelation*, NIVACNT.

Keener, C. S. (2001a), *Acts*, BBCNT (EIRC).

—— (2001b), *Ephesians*, BBCNT (EIRC).

—— (2001c), *Hebrews*, BBCNT (EIRC).

Kehl, M., and W. Löser (eds.) (1982), *The Hans Urs von Balthasar Reader*, tr. R. J. Daly and F. Lawrence, New York: Crossroad.

Kelly, J. N. D. (1977), *Early Christian Doctrines*, 5th ed., London: A. & C. Black.

Kent, Jr., H. A. (1997), *Philippians*, EBC.

Kerr, H. T. (ed.) (1974), *A Compend of Luther's Theology*, Philadelphia: Westminster.

Kieffer, R. (2000), 'John', OBC.

Knox, D. B. (1959), *Justification by Faith*, London: Church Book Room.

Kugel, J. L. (2007), *How to Read the Bible: A Guide to Scripture, Then and Now*, New York: Free.

Lactantius (2007), *On the Anger of God*, NA.

Lane, A. N. S. (2005), 'Justification by Faith', *DFTIB*, 111–249.

Lane, W. L. (2001), *Hebrews*, BBCNT (EIRC).

—— (2004a), *Hebrews 1–8*, WBC.

—— (2004b), *Hebrews 9–13*, WBC.

Letham, R. (1993), *The Work of Christ*, Leicester: IVP.

—— (2001), *The Lord's Supper: Eternal Word in Broken Bread*, Philipsburg: Presbyterian & Reformed.

Levinson, B. M. (2003), 'Deuteronomy', JSB.

Lewis, A. E. (2001), *Between Cross and Resurrection: A Theology of Holy Saturday*, Grand Rapids: Eerdmans.

Lewis, C. S. (1958), *Mere Christianity*, London: Collins.

—— (1969), *Reflections on the Psalms*, London: Collins.

Lieu, J. (2000), '1 John, 2 John, 3 John', OBC.

Lincoln, A. T. (2002), *The Letter to the Colossians: Introduction, Commentary, and Reflections*, NIBC 11.

—— (2004), *Ephesians*, WBC.

Link, H.-G., and C. Brown (2006), '*Hilaskomai*', *NIDNTT*.

Liu, T., G. Preece and W. S. Li (2005), *Marketplace Ministry*, Lausanne Occasional Paper 40.

Longenecker, R. N. (2004), *Galatians*, WBC.

Macauley, R. (n. d.), 'The Great Commissions', *L'Abri Papers*, Greatham, UK: L'Abri Fellowship, RM03.

McCheyne, R. M. (1961), *Sermons of Robert Murray McCheyne*, London: Banner of Truth Trust.

Maccini, R. G. (2001), 'Testimony/Witness', *NDBT* (EIRC).

McCormack, B. L. (ed.) (2006), *Justification in Perspective: Historical Developments and Contemporary Challenges*, Grand Rapids: Baker Academic.

—— (ed.) (2008), *Engaging the Doctrine of God: Contemporary Protestant Perspectives*, Edinburgh: Rutherford House; Grand Rapids: Baker Academic.

McCrone, M. (1993), *Brush up your Shakespeare!* London: Pavilion.

McCullagh, C. B. (1988), 'Theology of Atonement', *Theology* 91: 392–400.

McCurdy, L. (1999), *Attributes and Atonement: The Holy Love of God in the Theology of P. T. Forsyth*, Carlisle: Paternoster.

MacDonald, M. (2000), '1 Corinthians', OBC.

McGougall, J. A. (2006), 'Sin – No More? A Feminist Re-envisioning of a Christian Theology of Sin', *ATR* 88.2: 215–235.

McGrath, A. E. (2007a), *Christian Theology: An Introduction*, 4th ed., Oxford: Blackwell.

—— (ed.) (2007b), *The Christian Theology Reader*, 3rd ed., Oxford: Blackwell.

McGuckin, J. A. (2004), *The Westminster Handbook to Patristic Theology*, Louisville: Westminster John Knox.

McKnight, S. (2007), *A Community Called Atonement*, Nashville: Abingdon.

Mare, W. H. (1997), *1 Corinthians*, EBC.

Markham, I. S. (2008), *Understanding Christian Doctrine*, Oxford: Blackwell.

Marshall, I. H. (1966), *Christian Beliefs*, London: Inter-Varsity Fellowship.

—— (1990), *Pocket Guide to Christian Belief*, 3rd ed., Leicester: IVP.

—— (2001), 'Redemption', *DLNTD* (EIRC).

Martin, R. P. (2001), 'Center of Paul's Theology', in *DPHL* (EIRC).

—— (2004), *2 Corinthians*, WBC.

Mason, A. (2000), 'Unitarianism', *OCCT*, 730–732.

Meeks, W. A. (ed.) (1993), *The HarperCollins Study Bible: New Revised Standard Version*, New York: HarperCollins.

Michaels, J. R. (2004), *I Peter*, WBC.

Migliore, D. L. (2004), *Faith Seeking Understanding: An Introduction to Christian Theology*, 2nd ed., Grand Rapids: Eerdmans.

Milne, B. (1982), *Know the Truth: A Handbook of Christian Belief*, Leicester: IVP.

Moltmann, J. (1982), *The Crucified God*, tr. R. A. Wilson and J. Bowden, London: SCM.

Montague, G. T. (1976), *The Holy Spirit: Growth of a Biblical Tradition: A Commentary on the Principal Texts of the Old and New Testaments*, New York: Paulist.

Moo, D. J. (2001), *Romans*, NBCRev (EIRC).

Morris, L. (1983), *The Atonement: Its Meaning and Significance*, Leicester: IVP.

—— (1997), *Hebrews*, EBC.

—— (2001a), 'Guilt and Forgiveness', *NDT* (EIRC).

—— (2001b), 'Reconciliation', *NBD* (EIRC).

—— (2001c), 'Redemption', *DPHL* (EIRC).

Motyer, J. A. (2001), 'Judgment', *NDBT* (EIRC).

Mozley, J. K. (1915), *The Doctrine of the Atonement*, London: Duckworth.

Muller, R. A. (1986), *Dictionary of Latin and Greek Theological Terms: Drawn Principally from Protestant Scholastic Theology*, Grand Rapids: Baker.

Murphy-O'Connor, J. (2000), 'Colossians', OBC.

Murray, J. (1961), *Redemption, Accomplished and Applied*, London: Banner of Truth Trust.

—— (1976), *The Atonement*, Nutley, N. J.: Presbyterian & Reformed.

Murray, R. (2000), 'Philippians', OBC.

Muslow, M., and J. Rolls (eds.) (2005), *Socinanism and Arminianism: Antitrinitarianism, Calvinist and Cultural Exchange in Seventeenth-Century Europe*, Leiden: Brill.

Neill, S. (1976), *Jesus Through Many Eyes: An Introduction to the Theology of the New Testament*, Philadelphia: Fortress.

Nevin, J. W. (2000), *The Mystical Presence: A Vindication of the Reformed or Calvinistic Doctrine of the Holy Eucharist*, Eugene: Wipf & Stock.

Newbigin, L. (1969), *The Finality of Christ*, Richmond, Va.: John Knox.

Noll, M. A. (1993), 'Father of Modern Evangelicals?', *Christian History* 38, 12.2: 42–44.

Noll, M. A., and D. F. Wells (eds.) (1988), *Christian Faith and Practice in the Modern World: Theology from an Evangelical Point of View*, Grand Rapids: Eerdmans.

Nolland, J. (2004), *Luke*, WBC.

Oakes, E. T. (2005), *Pattern of Redemption: The Theology of Hans Urs von Balthasar*, New York: Continuum.

O'Brien, P. T. (2004), *Colossians, Philemon*, WBC.

Olson, R. E. (2006), *Arminian Theology: Myths and Realities*, Downers Grove: IVP.

Packer, J. I. (1973), *Knowing God*, London: Hodder & Stoughton.

—— (1993), *Concise Theology: A Guide to Historic Christian Beliefs*, Wheaton: Tyndale.

Packer, J. I., and M. Dever (2007), *In My Place Condemned He Stood: Celebrating the Glory of the Atonement*, Wheaton: Crossway.

Page, S. (2001), 'Ransom Saying', *DJG* (EIRC).

Pannenberg, W. (1982), *The Apostles' Creed*, tr. M. Kohl, London: SCM.

—— (1994), *Systematic Theology*, tr. G. W. Bromiley, vol. 2, Grand Rapids: Pacific Lutheran Theological Seminary / Institute for Theology.

—— (2001), 'Confessions of a Trinitarian Evolutionist', <http://www.3sympatico.ca/ian.ritchie/CTSNewsletter.html>, accessed 7 Oct. 2002.

Pascal, B. (1972), *Pascal s Pensées*, tr. A. J. Krailsheimer, Harmondsworth: Penguin.

Payne, T. (ed.) (2000), *D. Broughton Knox: Selected Works*, vol. 1, Kingsford, Australia: Matthias.

Pelikan, J. (1971), *The Christian Tradition: A History of the*

Development of Doctrine. Vol. 1: *The Emergence of the Catholic Tradition (100–600)*, Chicago: University of Chicago Press.

Perkins, P. (2002), *The Letter to the Ephesians: Introduction, Commentary, and Reflections*, NIBC 11.

Peters, T. (2005), 'Models of Atonement', *Theological Brief for PLTS/ITE*, 1–18.

Peterson, D. (2001a), *Hebrews*, NBCRev (EIRC).

—— (ed.) (2001b), *Where Wrath and Mercy Meet: Proclaiming the Atonement Today*, Carlisle: Paternoster.

Pinnock, C. H. (1996), *Flame of Love: A Theology of the Holy Spirit*, Downers Grove: IVP.

—— (2006), 'Theological Autobiography: Confessions of a Post-Conservative Evangelical Theologian', *Di* 45.4: 382–388.

Piper, J. (1986), *Desiring God: Meditations of a Christian Hedonist*, Portland: Multnomah.

Pitstick, A. L., and E. T. Oakes (2006), 'Balthasar, Hell, and Heresy: An Exchange', *First Things* 168: 25–32.

—— (2007a), 'More on Balthasar, Hell, and Heresy', *First Things* 169: 16–19.

—— (2007b), 'Responses to "Balthasar, Hell, and Heresy"', *First Things* 171: 5–14.

—— (2003), *Essentials of Christian Theology*, Louisville: Westminster John Knox.

Placher, W. C. (2003), *Essentials of Christian Theology*, Louisville: Westminster John Knox Press.

Plantinga, A. (1980), *God, Freedom and Evil*, Grand Rapids: Eerdmans.

Plummer, R. L. (2005), 'The Great Commission in the New Testament', *SBJT* 9: 4–11.

Porter, S. E. (2001a), 'Peace', in *NDBT* (EIRC).

—— (2001b), 'Peace, Reconciliation', *DPHL* (EIRC).

Preece, G. (ed.), (2002), *Rethinking Peter Singer: A Christian Critique*, Downers Grove, Illinois: Intervarsity Press.

Ramm, B. (1967), *The Christian View of Science and Scripture*, Exeter: Paternoster.

Rashdall, H. (1919), *The Idea of Atonement in Christian Theology*, London: Macmillan.

Reid, D. G. (2001), 'Triumph', *DPHL* (EIRC).

Reid, G. (1996), 'The Decay of Evangelists?', *Anvil* 13.1: 45–56.

—— (1980), *The Great Acquittal: Justification by Faith and Current Christian Thought*, London: Fount.

Roach, K. (2000), 'Changing Punishment at the Turn of the Century: Restorative Justice on the Rise', *CJC* 42: 3; reproduced by Questia, <http://www.questia.com/reader/print>, accessed 15 July 2008.

Robinson, D. W. B. (1971), 'The Theology of Evangelism', *Interchange* 3.1: 2–4.

Rosner, B. S. (2001), 'Biblical Theology', *NDBT* (EIRC).

Rowland, C. C. (2002), *The Book of Revelation: Introduction, Commentary, and Reflections*, NIBC 12.

Rowley, H. H. (1954), *The Servant of the Lord and Other Essays on the Old Testament*, London: Lutterworth.

Rudd, K. (2008), 'Full Transcript of PM's Speech', *The Australian*, 13 Feb. 2008, <http://www.theaustralian.news.com.au/story/0,25197,23207256-5013172,00html>, accessed 13 Feb. 2008.

Russell, B., 'A Free Man's Worship', <http://users.drew.edu/~jlenz/fmw.html>, accessed 4 Sept. 2007.

Ryken, L. L. (1980), *The Literature of the Bible*, 6th ed., Grand Rapids: Zondervan.

Ryken, L. L., J. C. Wilhoit and J. C. Longman III (2001a), 'Bible', *DBI* (EIRC).

—— (2001b), 'Glory', *DBI* (EIRC).

—— (2001c), 'Comedy as Plot Motif', *DBI* (EIRC).

Ryle, J. C., 'Warnings to the Churches – the Fallibility of Ministers', <http://www.sermonindex.net/modules/articles/index.php?view=article&aid=2121>, accessed 30 July 2008.

Ryrie, C. C. (1995), *Dispensationalism*, rev. ed., Chicago: Moody.

Sampley, J. P. (2002a), *The First Letter to the Corinthians: Introduction, Commentary, and Reflections*, NIBC 10.

—— (2002b), *The Second Letter to the Corinthians: Introduction, Commentary, and Reflections*, NIBC 11.

Sanders, J. (ed.) (2006), *Atonement and Violence: A Theological Conversation*, Nashville: Abingdon.

Sanner, A. E. (1983), 'Total Depravity', *BDT*, 524–525.

Schmiechen, P. (2005), *Saving Power: Theories of Atonement and Forms of the Church*, Grand Rapids: Eerdmans.

Schwartz, B. J. (2003), 'Leviticus', JSB.

Scobie, C. H. H. (2003), *The Ways of Our God: An Approach to Biblical Theology*, Grand Rapids: Eerdmans.

Scott, J. M. (2001), 'Adoption, Sonship', *DPHL* (EIRC).

Seifrid, M. A. (2001), 'Righteousness, Justice, and Justification', *NDBT* (EIRC).

—— (2007), 'Romans', CNTUOT.

Shuster, M. (2004), *The Fall and Sin: What We Have Become as Sinners*, Grand Rapids: Eerdmans.

Sklar, J. (2005), *Sin, Impurity, Sacrifice, Atonement: The Priestly Conceptions*, Sheffield: Sheffield Phoenix.

Smalley, S. S. (2004), *1 John*, WBC.

Smith, D. L. (1994), *With Willful Intent: A Theology of Sin*, Wheaton: Victor.

Solzhenitsyn, A. I. (1974), *The Gulag Archipelago, 1918–1956: An Experiment in Literary Investigation*, tr. T. P. Whitney, vol. 2, New York: Harper & Row.

Sproul, R. C. (1977), *Knowing Scripture*, Downers Grove: IVP.

Spykman, G. J. (1992), *Reformational Theology: A New Paradigm for Doing Dogmatics*, Grand Rapids: Eerdmans.

Staniforth, M. (ed. and tr.) (1972), *Early Christian Writings: The Apostolic Fathers*, Harmondsworth: Penguin.

Stevenson, J. (ed.) (1970), *A New Eusebius: Documents Illustrative of the History of the Church to A.D. 337*, London: SPCK.

—— (1976), *Creeds, Councils, and Controversies: Documents Illustrative of the History of the Church A.D. 337–461*, London: SPCK.

Stott, J. R. W. (1969), *The Meaning of Evangelism*, London: CPAS.

—— (1979), *Focus on Christ: An Enquiry into the Theology of Prepositions*, Glasgow: Collins.

—— (1996), *The Cross of Christ*, 2nd ed., Leicester: IVP.

Swinburne, R. (1989), *Responsibility and Atonement*, New York: Oxford University Press.

Sykes, S. (1997), *The Story of Atonement*, London: Darton Longman & Todd.

Symonds, R. (2002), 'The South Stoke Festival of Thought', *Philosophy Pathways* 32, <http://www.philosophypathways.com/newsletter/issue32.html>, accessed 14 Oct. 2007.

Tennent, T. C. (2007), *Theology in the Context of World Christianity: How the Global Church Is Influencing the Way We Think About and Discuss Theology*, Grand Rapids: Zondervan.

Thielicke, H. (1969), *Theological Ethics*. Vol. 2: *Politics*, Philadelphia: Fortress.

—— (1977), *The Evangelical Faith*. Vol. 2: *The Doctrine of God and of Christ*, tr. and ed. G. W. Bromiley, Grand Rapids: Eerdmans.

—— (1979), *Theological Ethics: Foundation*, Grand Rapids: Eerdmans.

Thompson, J. A., 'Genesis 1-3: Science? History? Theology?', <http://www.iscast.org.au/papers/?action=detailed&ID=132&back=1>, accessed 16 June 2008.

Thompson, M. (2004), 'From the Trinity to the Cross', *RTR* 63.1: 16–28.

Thompson, M. B. (2005), *The New Perspective on Paul*, Cambridge: Grove.

Tidball, D. J. (2001), 'Evangelism, Theology of', *NDT* (EIRC).

Tidball, D. J., D. Hilborn and J. Thacker (eds.) (2008), *The Atonement Debate: Papers from the London Symposium on the Atonement*, Grand Rapids: Zondervan.

Tierno, J. T. (2006), 'On Defense as Opposed to Theodicy', *IJP* 59: 167–174.

Tobin, T. H. (1993), '4 Maccabees', HSB.

Torrance, T. F. (1992), *The Mediation of Christ*, 2nd ed., Colorado Springs: Helmer & Howard.

Towner, S. W. (2005), 'Clones of God: Genesis 1:26–28 and the Image of God in the Hebrew Bible', *Int* 59: 341–356.

Tozer, A. W. (1965), *The Knowledge of the Holy*, London: James Clarke, 1965.

Travis, S. H. (2001), 'Judgement of God', *NDT* (EIRC).

Trelstad, M. (ed.) (2006), *Cross Examinations: Reading on the Meaning of the Cross Today*, Minneapolis: Augsburg Fortress.

Trites, A. A. (2006), 'Witness, Testimony, 7', *NIDNTT*.

Tucker, K. B. W. (2000), 'Easter', *OCCT*.

Tuckett, C. M. (2000), 'Mark', OBC.

Twelftree, G. H. (2001), 'Spiritual Powers', *NDBT* (EIRC).

Vanhoozer, K. J. (2005), *The Drama of Doctrine: A Canonical Linguistic Approach to Christian Theology*, Louisville: Westminster John Knox.

Volf, M. (1996), *Exclusion and Embrace: A Theological Exploration of Identity, Otherness, and Reconciliation*, Nashville: Abingdon.

Vorländer, H. (2006), 'Forgiveness', *NIDNTT*.

Ward, K. (2004), *What the Bible Really Teaches: A Challenge for Fundamentalists*, London: SPCK.

Ware, B. A. (2005), *Father, Son, and Holy Spirit: Relationships, Roles, and Relevance*, Wheaton: Crossway.

Ware, K. (1981), *The Orthodox Way*, London: Mowbray.

—— (1996), *How Are We Saved? The Understanding of Salvation in the Orthodox Tradition*, Minneapolis: Light and Life.

Warfield, B. B. (1958), *Biblical Foundations*, London: Tyndale.

—— (1968), *Biblical and Theological Studies*, Philadelphia: Presbyterian & Reformed.

—— (1970), *The Person and Work of Christ*, Philadelphia: Presbyterian & Reformed.

Watson, P. S. (1984), *The Message of the Wesleys: A Reader of Instruction and Devotion*, Grand Rapids: Francis Asbury.

Watts, J. D. (2004), *Isaiah*, WBC.

Watts, R. E. (2007), 'Mark 10:45', CNTUOT.

Weaver, J. D. (2001), *The Nonviolent Atonement*, Grand Rapids: Eerdmans.

Webster, J. (2003), *Holiness*, Grand Rapids: Eerdmans.

Webster, J., and G. P. Schner (2000), *Theology after Liberalism: A Reader*, Oxford: Blackwell.

Wenham, G. J. (2004), *Genesis 1–15*, WBC.

Whale, J. S. (1957), *Christian Doctrine*, London: Fontana.

——(1960), *Victor and Victim: The Christian Doctrine of Redemption*, Cambridge: Cambridge University Press.

Whybray, R. N. (2000), 'Genesis', OBC.

Wilkins, M. J. (1996), *Matthew*, NIVACNT.

Williams, J. G. (ed.) (1996), *The Girard Reader*, New York: Crossroad and Herder.

Williams, J. R. (1996), *Renewal Theology: Systematic Theology from a Charismatic Perspective*, Grand Rapids: Zondervan.

Williams, R. (2007), *Tokens of Trust: An Introduction to Christian Beliefs*, Louisville: Westminster John Knox.

Willimon, W. H. (2008), 'An Interview with William H. Willimon', *Modern Reformation* 17.5: 42–44.

Wolters, A. M. (1985), *Creation Regained: Biblical Basics for a Reformational Worldview*, Grand Rapids: Eerdmans.

Wolterstorff, N. (1983), *Until Justice and Peace Embrace*, Grand Rapids: Eerdmans.

—— (2008), *Justice: Rights and Wrongs*, Princeton: Princeton University Press.

Wright, C. (2005), *Haslam's Journey*, Godalming, Surrey: Highland.

Wright, C. J. H. (2006), *The Mission of God: Unlocking the Bible's Grand Narrative*, Downers Grove: IVP.

—— (2008), 'Atonement in the Old Testament', in Tidball, Hilborn and Thacker 2008: 4, 69–82.

Wright, D. F. (2007), 'The Great Commission and the Ministry of the Word: Reflections Historical and Contemporary on Relations and Priorities', *SBET* 25: 132–157.

Wright, N. T. (2001), 'Justification', *NDT* (EIRC).

—— (2002), 'The Letter to the Romans: Introduction, Commentary, and Reflections', *NIBC* 10.

—— (2003), *The Resurrection of the Son of God*, Minneapolis: Fortress.

—— (2004), *Paul for Everyone: Romans Part One Chapters 1–8*, London: SPCK; Louisville: Westminster John Knox.

—— (2005), *The Last Word*, San Francisco: HarperSanFrancisco.

Yarbrough, R. W. (2001a), 'Atonement', *NDBT* (EIRC).

—— (2001b), 'Forgiveness and Reconciliation', *NDBT* (EIRC).

Young, F. (1975), *Sacrifice and the Death of Christ*, London: SPCK.

Young, W. P. (2007), *The Shack*, Los Angeles: Windblown Media.

Zimmerli, W., and J. Jeremias (1979), *The Servant of God*, tr. H. Knight et al., London: SCM.

Index of authors

Index of Scripture references

Index of subjects

Printed and bound by CPI Group (UK) Ltd, Croydon, CR0 4YY

21/08/2024

14544525-0003